JESUS LIVED IN INDIA

Holger Kersten is an author specializing in religious history. He studied theology and pedagogics at Freiburg University, Germany, and has travelled extensively in the Middle East and India. He is the co-author of *The Jesus Conspiracy*

D0731487

JESUS
LIVED IN INDIA

His Unknown Life Before and
After the Crucifixion

Holger Kersten

ELEMENT
Shaftesbury, Dorset ● Rockport, Massachusetts
Brisbane, Queensland

© Holger Kersten 1986, 1994

First published in Great Britain in 1994 by
Element Books Limited
Shaftesbury, Dorset SP7 8BP

Published in the USA in 1994 by
Element Books, Inc.
PO Box 830, Rockport, MA 01966

Published in Australia in 1994 by
Element Books Limited for
Jacaranda Wiley Limited
33 Park Road, Milton, Brisbane 4064

Reprinted February and April 1995
Reprinted 1996

Cover illustration by Magnum Photos Limited
Cover design by Max Fairbrother
Design by Roger Lightfoot
Typeset by Linda Reed and Joss Nizan
Printed and bound in Great Britain by
Hartnolls Limited, Bodmin, Cornwall

British Library Cataloguing in Publication
data available

Library of Congress Cataloging in Publication data
Kersten, Holger
Jesus lived in India : his unknown life before and after the crucifixion
Translated from the German
Includes bibliographical references and indexes.
1. Jesus Christ–Biography. 2. Jesus Christ–Rationalistic interpretations.
3. India–History–Religious aspects–Christianity
I. Title
BT303.K47 1994 94-33959
232.9'01–dc20 CIP

ISBN 1–85230–550–9

CONTENTS

ACKNOWLEDGEMENTS

Over the ten years that have passed since the first edition of this book came out, hundreds of readers from all over the world have written letters to me, most of them in very positive terms. I wish to extend my thanks to all those who have given me access to important references, interesting additional information, and valuable material. And I also thank those who by their constructive criticism have contributed to the correction of mistakes.

I would like to give particular thanks to my colleague Thomas Gotterbarm for making it possible for me to benefit from his profound knowledge of the languages and mythology of ancient India. And a very special thank you goes too to my co-author on *The Jesus Conspiracy*, Dr Elmar R. Gruber, and to the editor Ria Schulte.

Picture Credits

Cover photo and No. 24: Ars Mundi
Front and Rear endpaper: Eberhard Mörck
No. 2, 3, 5–9, 14–16, 19, 20, 32–34, 39, 41, 42: Holger Kersten
No. 4, 17–21, 35–38: Prof. F. M. Hassnain
No. 13 sculpture of Michelangelo: S. Pietro in Vincoli, Rome
No. 12, 16, 18, 22, 43–46: Eberhard Mörck
No. 10 and 11: Archives of the Museum of Egypt, Cairo
No. 23: Musée Borély, Marseilles
No. 26 multiform painting by Friedrich Hechelmann from *Euch ist heute der Heiland geboren*: Deutsche Bibelgesellschaft, Stuttgart 1992
No. 25: drawing by A. D. Thomas, 1947
No. 29, 30: Giuseppe Enrie, 1934
No. 31 marble sculpture (third century): Vatican Museums, Rome

FOREWORD

It was in 1973, and purely by lucky coincidence, that I first ran across the theory that Jesus had lived in India, and had eventually died there too. Sceptical though noncommittal about the matter, I decided to try to retrace the entire course of Jesus' life. I soon encountered the first obstacle: no contemporary sources could stand up to present-day scholarly scrutiny enough to give the necessary fine detail about the historical Jesus. Who *was* the man? Where was he from? Where did he go? Why was it that he appeared so strange and mysterious to his contemporaries? What was he really after?

Following up my investigations I finally arrived in India, where I became acquainted with several people who had spent considerable time and effort researching into the whole subject of Jesus in India. From them I received a wealth of astonishing information, along with great encouragement and valuable support.

After this book was published for the first time, in Germany in 1983, I received hundreds of letters from enthusiastic readers who not only expressed their delight and wonderment, but also made a large number of valuable comments and important suggestions. But I am particularly grateful in addition to the more discerning critics who took the time thoroughly to examine the claims I made, and so enabled me now to correct a few inaccuracies originally present. In this way, over the course of ten years, an improved work has evolved that has the capacity to allude to even the very smallest, most specialist reference concerning the Indian origins of Jesus' teachings.

Also within these ten years, the book has been translated into no fewer than fifteen different languages (including Croat, Polish, Korean and Chinese – there have been ten editions in Brazil alone). The story of the survival of Jesus and his life in India has deservedly come to gain worldwide attention.

Some of the assertions I make may seem audacious, some even improbable, but I have tried to provide solid evidence for all the claims I have put forward, and to support them with reference to genuinely trustworthy sources. There remains considerable scope for future research in the various individual disciplines.

It has never been part of my purpose to undermine anyone's outlook on Christianity, much less to leave any reader glumly surrounded by shards of shattered faith. It is simply a matter of the greatest importance today to find a way back again to the origins – to the universal and central truth of Christ's message, which has been distorted almost beyond recognition by the profane ambitions of more or less secular institutions that have arrogated to themselves a religious authority ever since the early centuries of the so-called Christian Era.

This book is no proclamation of a new faith, therefore: it is merely an attempt to open a way to a new future, firmly grounded in true spiritual and religious authorities of the past.

> Do not think I am spinning yarns:
> Get up and prove things otherwise!
> All ecclesiastical history
> Is a mishmash of error and coercion.
>
> Johann Wolfgang von Goethe

Holger Kersten,
Freiburg im Breisgau,
March 1993

INTRODUCTION

The ascendancy of science and technology over the past three centuries has been accompanied by a rapid secularization of our (Western) world and a consequent simultaneous recession in religious faith. The glorification of materialist rationalism and the endeavour to explain away every facet of human existence has inexorably led to successive serious depletions in spiritual, religious and emotional life, and finally even to a loss of faith in humanity. Not the least significant among the causes of the widening gulf between religion and science – between belief and knowledge – has been the behaviour of the long-established Churches. For fear of losing their eminence in secular spheres, they asserted authority where they had absolutely none: in the field of empirical knowledge. This merely emphasized a need for greater differentiation between authorities.

The resultant schism between scientific thinking and religious belief has presented every thinking person with an apparently unresolvable dilemma. Spiritual sentiments have become increasingly restricted as the ranks of those who publicly doubt the veracity of Christ's message have grown in number, and as Christian doctrine has turned more and more into a matter of debate. Even core tenets anchored in ecclesiastical tradition – such as the nature of God, of Christ, of the Church and of divine revelation – have become mere topics for enthusiastic discussion among theologians and laymen alike.

When the most central and fundamental teachings of a Christian Church are no longer accepted as the absolute truth, even among that Church's own hierarchy and administrators, the demise of that Church is undeniably at hand. The message of the empty pews is quite clear. According to a statistical survey carried out in Germany in 1992, only one in four citizens then subscribed to the teachings of the older Churches about Jesus, whereas no fewer than 77 per cent of those asked whether it was possible to be a Christian without belonging to a Church answered in the affirmative. And in not a single sector of the population (as categorized by the survey) did a majority believe the received Christian dogma that Jesus was sent by God. By their own shrill insistence that the traditional, dogmatically fixed creed has general (liberal) applications, the Churches themselves have further hastened the rejection of Christian orthodoxy.

Yet what is today called Christianity is in any case not so much the Word of Christ but something else: Paulinism – for the doctrine as we now know it rests in all its main points not on the message of Jesus, but on the totally different teaching of Paul. Modern Christianity only developed when Paulinism was promulgated as the state religion.

Manfred Mezger cites the Swiss Protestant theologian Emil Brunner on the subject:

> Emil Brunner has called the Church a misunderstanding. From a call, a doctrine was constructed; from free communion, a legal corporation; from a free association, a hierarchical machine. You might say that it became, in all of its elements and in its overall disposition, the exact opposite of what was intended.

A person appears in a time of darkness, bringing a message full of hope, a message of love and goodness – and what do people do with it? They turn it into documentation, discussion, contention and commercialism! Would Jesus really have wished for everything that later happened in his name? Hardly. During his life in Palestine Jesus actually made his disaffection with (Jewish) Church officialdom quite evident, distancing himself from the Church's laws and scriptural authorities, its insistence on preserving verbal niceties with conflicting interpretations as required, its convoluted hierarchy, and the associated cultic worship and idolatry.

Jesus sought to create an immediate link between God and humankind, not to set up bureaucratic channels to go through.

But Jesus' voice no longer reaches us in so naturally direct a fashion. Access to his teachings is gained only through the mediumship of a privileged hierarchy. Jesus has been managed, monopolized, codified. Wherever the true and living faith has disappeared, to be replaced by narrowminded and rigidly dogmatic beliefs, the love of one's neighbour and the tolerance which Jesus taught have been replaced by self-righteous fanaticism. Strife over exactly what is defined as the 'right' faith has left a wide swathe of misery, contention and bloodshed across the time-lines of the Christian Churches. The controversy has raged from the days of the apostles right up until our own times, and continues still to constitute the most problematical obstacle to reconciliation between the various Christian denominations.

The Protestant theologian Heinz Zahrnt wrote:

> I have suffered a profound trauma in my career as a theologian. I feel defiled, humiliated, insulted and put to shame – but not by atheists, those who deny God, mockers or doubters who, although godless, are often very humane – no, by the dogmatists: by those who live by the letter of the teachings, thinking that that gives them the only true view of God. I have been wounded at my very heart, in the one thing that has kept me alive despite my grief: my belief in God . . .

Inasmuch as religious feeling is part of the process of growing up in modern society, it is most often relegated to the category of the irrational, and can then be regarded as unprovable, and so, unreal. Logical thought and action appear alone to determine reality. The transcendental gradually diminishes in importance because it is never personally experienced. And the main reason for this is a fundamental misunderstanding of the nature of God. The Divinity is not remote from us at some mystically infinite distance, but inside each one of us. It should inspire us to lead our lives in harmony with the Infinite – to recognize our short existence on Earth as a part of the eternal Whole.

For centuries, Western thought has viewed the individual falsely as a being separate from God. In the 'enlightened' twentieth century, modern Western thought seems less certain than ever about possible answers to the most ancient human questions about God and the meaning of life. All over the world, new spiritual centres have sprung up, attempting to give answers to these questions – questions which the rigidly held precepts of Church officialdom cannot answer. A kind of ecumenical world religion of the future is in ascendance. It is moving towards self-realization, towards a search for Enlightenment, towards a mystical and consummate vision of the cosmic context of one's individual existence, and all this by means of contemplation, self-knowledge and meditation.

The most forceful impetus for promoting such an internalization of religion has always come, and continues to come, from the East, primarily from India. Western Man must now *reorient* himself in the most literal sense of the word – turn towards the eastern dawn. The Orient is the origin and source of our experience of the inner realm.

We should not expect belief in God to be finally eradicated, nor should we fear spiritual and moral decay. Indeed, we can hope for a germination of the seed of the Spirit, a flowering of the inner life. No gradual but complete elimination of religious faith awaits us. On the contrary, a blossoming of spiritual consciousness is at hand, and this not just for the chosen few but for all in the all-embracing ecumenism of world religions. Moreover, the goal is not in the transient world of superficial appearances, but represents a grand spiritual awakening, a turning to transcendental values, the true way of 'deliverance from evil'.

> Through Knowledge (of Truth)
> All evils are washed away.
> The true Enlightened One stands firm,
> Scattering the clouds of delusion
> Like the sun shining in a cloudless sky.
>
> Buddha

Chapter One

THE UNKNOWN LIFE
OF JESUS

Nicolai Notovitch's Discovery

Towards the end of 1887, the Russian historian and itinerant scholar Nicolai Notovitch reached the Himalayan state of Kashmir, in northern India, on one of his many journeys to the Orient. He planned to go on an expedition from Srinagar, capital of Kashmir, to the Ladakh region across the Great Himalaya. With him he had enough funds to equip himself adequately, and to hire an interpreter and ten bearers to accompany him and his servant. After a somewhat adventurous trek, having successfully braved many trials and difficulties, the caravan finally reached the 3500-metre-high Zoji-la pass on the natural border between the 'Happy Valley' of Kashmir and the arid 'lunar' landscape of Ladakh.

The Zoji-la, negotiable only for a few months in the year, was at that time the only route of access from Kashmir to that strange and remote country.[1] Notovitch wrote in his diary, 'What a great contrast I experienced, leaving the cheerful, open countryside and the handsome people of Kashmir to travel into the forbidding, barren mountains of Ladakh and its beardless, sturdy inhabitants!' The strong-featured Ladakhis soon nonetheless proved to be a friendly lot and 'extremely open'.

Notovitch eventually arrived at a Buddhist monastery where, as a European, he was afforded a reception that was much more cordial than any Asiatic Muslim might have expected. He asked a lama why he should be favoured in this way, and the following conversation took place:

'The Muslims have little in common with our religion. Indeed, not long ago they waged an all-too-successful campaign to forcibly convert a number of our Buddhists to Islam. It has caused us immense difficulty to reconvert these ex-Buddhist Muslims back to the way of the true God. Now the Europeans are altogether different. Not only do they profess the essential principles of monotheism, they have almost as much title to be considered worshippers of Buddha as the lamas of Tibet themselves. The only difference between the Christians and ourselves is that, after having adopted the great doctrines of Buddha, the Christians have parted from him completely by creating for themselves a different Dalai Lama. Our Dalai Lama alone retained the divine gift of seeing the majesty of Buddha, and the power to act as an intermediary between Earth and Heaven.'

'Who is this Christian Dalai Lama you are talking about?' asked Notovitch. 'We have a Son of God, to whom we direct our fervent prayers, and whom in time of need we beseech to intercede for us with our one and indivisible God . . .'

'It is not of him I speak, Sahib! We too respect the one you recognize as Son of the one God – not that we see in him an only Son, rather a Being perfect among all the elect. The spirit of Buddha was indeed incarnate in the sacred person of Issa, who, without aid from fire or sword, has spread knowledge of our great and true religion throughout the world. I speak instead of your earthly Dalai Lama, him to whom you have given the title "Father of the Church". This is a great sin; may the flocks be forgiven who have gone astray because of it.'

And so saying, the lama hastened to turn his prayer wheel.

Understanding the lama to be alluding to the Pope, Notovitch probed further.

'You tell me that a son of Buddha, Issa, spread your religion over the Earth. Who is he, then?'

At this question the lama opened his eyes wide and looked at his visitor in astonishment. After uttering a few words the interpreter did not catch, he explained:

'Issa is a great prophet, one of the first after the twenty-two Buddhas. He is greater than any one of the Dalai Lamas, for he constitutes part of the spiritual essence of our Lord. It is he who has enlightened you, who has brought back within the fold of religion the souls of the erring, and who allows every human being to distinguish between good and evil. His name and his deeds are recorded in our sacred writings.'

By this time Notovitch was feeling quite stunned at the lama's words, for the prophet Issa, his teaching, his martyrdom, and the reference to a Christian Dalai Lama were increasingly reminiscent of Jesus Christ.

He ordered his interpreter not to leave out a single word that the lama spoke.

'Where are these writings now to be found? And by whom were they originally written down?' he finally asked the monk.

'The principal scriptures, written over the centuries in India and Nepal according to various historal sources, are to be found at Lhasa to the number of several thousand. There are copies in some of the chief monastic foundations, made by the lamas during their sojourns at Lhasa at different times, and presented by them afterwards to their own monasteries in remembrance of their pilgrimage to the home of their great master, our Dalai Lama.'

'But you yourselves – have you no copies relating to the prophet Issa?'

'We have none. Our monastery is not an important one, and since its founding, the succession of our lamas has only had a few hundred manuscripts given into its keeping. The great monasteries own thousands of them. But these are sacred objects, and not for you to see anywhere.'

Notovitch resolved to try to examine these scriptures in the further course of his travels. Later he arrived in Leh, the capital of Ladakh, from where he went on to Hemis (Tibetan *Byang-cchub-bsam-gling* 'Isle of contemplation for the perfect'), 'one of the most distinguished monasteries in the country'.

There he witnessed one of the traditional religious festivals that take place several times each year, and as the head lama's guest of honour he had an opportunity to find out a great deal about the customs and daily life of the lamaist monks. He finally succeeded in turning the conversation round to his chief interest, and to his pleasure learned that in the monastery there were indeed scriptures about the mysterious prophet Issa, whose life seemed to bear such astounding similarities to the stories of Jesus the Nazarene.

But for the time being the guest was obliged to defer the pursuit of his enquiries, for simply to find those books among the many thousands would itself have taken a considerable time.

Returning to Leh, Notovitch sent the head of the Hemis monastery some valuable gifts in the hope of being allowed to return in the near future, and so perhaps catch a glimpse at last of the precious manuscripts. It so chanced that, a little time later while out riding near Hemis, he fell from his horse, landed awkwardly enough to break a leg, and was perforce compelled to entrust himself into the care of the monks. Recovering in bed, he sent out a heartfelt plea, and two large bound volumes of loose leaves yellowed with age were finally brought to him. The reverend abbot himself proceeded to read aloud from the extraordinary document, which was written mostly in single verses that did not follow on from each other. Notovitch took careful notes of his interpreter's renditions in his travel diary. Later, some time after his expedition had come to an end, he arranged the verses in chronological order and succeeded in rounding off the many separate texts so as to give a continuous narrative.[2]

Its contents may be succinctly outlined (using the French translation as a basis):

A short introductory section precedes a brief description of the early history of the people of Israel and the life of Moses. An account then follows of how the eternal Spirit resolves to take on human form 'so that he might demonstrate by his own example how moral purity may be attained, and by freeing the soul from its rude mortality, achieve the degree of perfection required to enter into the kingdom of Heaven, which is unchanging and ruled by eternal happiness'. And so a divine infant is born in far-away Israel, and is given the name Issa.[3] Sometime during the fourteenth year of his life, the lad arrives in the region of the Sind (the Indus) in the company of merchants, 'and he settled among the Aryans, in the land beloved of God, with the intention of perfecting himself and of learning from the laws of the great Buddha'. The young Issa travels through the land of five rivers (the Punjab),[4] stays briefly with the 'erring Jains',[5] and then proceeds to Jagannath, 'where the white priests of Brahma honoured him with a joyous reception'. At Jagannath Issa/Jesus learns to read and understand the Veda. But by then instructing the Sudras of the lowest castes, he incurs the displeasure of the Brahmans, who feel their position and power threatened. After spending six years in Jagganath, Rajagriha, Benares and other holy cities, he is compelled to flee the Brahmans who are outraged at his continuing to teach that it is not the will of God that the worth of human beings should be judged by their caste.

There is an extraordinary correlation between the accounts in the texts found by Notovitch and those of the Gospels, a correlation that can shed more light on Jesus' own personality – especially in what he said. Notovitch's Issa opposes the abuses of the caste system, which rob the lower castes of their basic human rights, saying, 'God our Father makes no difference between any of his children, all of whom he loves equally.' And later on his travels he takes issue with a rigid and inhumane adherence to the letter of the law, declaring that 'The law was made for Man, to show him the way.' He consoles the weak: 'The eternal Judge, the eternal Spirit, who forms the sole and indivisible World-soul . . . will proceed sternly against those who arrogate His rights to themselves.' When the priests challenge Issa to produce miracles, to prove the omnipotence of his God, he retorts, 'The miracles of our God have been performed ever since the first day when the universe was created; they take place every day and at every moment. Those who cannot perceive them are robbed of one of the most beautiful gifts of life.' Challenging the authority of the priests, he makes his position quite clear: 'So long as the people had no priests, they were ruled by natural law and they preserved the flawlessness of their souls. Their souls were in the presence of God, and to commune with the Father they had no need to resort to the mediation of an idol or a beast, nor to fire, as is practised here. You say that the sun must be worshipped, as must the spirits of good and the spirits of evil. Well, I tell you your doctrine is an utterly false one, for the sun has no power of its own, but solely through the will of the invisible Creator, who gave it birth, and who has willed it to be the star to light the day, and to warm the labour and the seed-time of Man.'

Notovitch's text goes on to describe how Issa goes further into the Himalayan ranges, to Nepal, where he remains for six years and dedicates himself to the study of Buddhist scriptures. The doctrines that he teaches widely there are simple and clear, and are particularly aimed at uplifting the oppressed and the weak, whose eyes he opens to the falsity of the priests. Finally, he moves on towards the West, passing through various countries as an itinerant preacher, preceded well in advance by a celebrated reputation. He also stands up to the priests of Persia, who expel him one night in the hope that he would quickly fall prey to wild animals. But Providence allows the holy Issa to reach Palestine safely, where the wise men inquire of him 'Who are you, and from what country do you come? We have never heard of you and do not even know your name.'

'I am an Israelite,' Issa replies, 'and on the day of my birth I saw the walls of Jerusalem and heard the sobs of my brothers in their slavery and the wails of my sisters condemned to live among the heathen. And my soul grieved sorely when I heard that my brothers had forgotten the true God. As a child, I left my parents' home to live among other peoples. But after hearing of the great sorrows that my brothers were suffering, I returned to the land where my parents lived, in order to bring my brothers back to the faith of our ancestors, a faith which enjoins us to be patient on Earth so that we might achieve the consummate and highest happiness in the Beyond.'

It is remarkable how this latter text agrees in all its main points with information given in the biblical Gospels.

The two manuscripts from which the lama at the monastery of Hemis read aloud to Notovitch, selecting all the passages dealing with Jesus, were collections of various Tibetan writings. The originals had been compiled in the old Indian language Pali[6] during the first two centuries AD, and kept in a monastery near Lhasa which was directly affiliated to the Potala Palace of the Dalai Lama.

Back in Europe, Notovitch tried to get in touch with several Church dignitaries of high official standing in order to tell them of his astounding discovery. The Metropolitan of Kiev advised him in the strongest terms not to publicize what he had found, but refused to give any reason. In Paris, Cardinal Rotelli explained that publication of the texts would only provide fuel for those who hated, despised or misunderstood the Gospel teachings, and would be premature at that time. At the Vatican, a close colleague of the Pope put it this way: 'What good will printing it do? No one will see it as of any great significance, and you will make a lot of enemies. But you are still very young. If it is a question of money, I could arrange for a payment to be made in exchange for your notes, to remunerate you for the work you have done and the time it has taken . . .' Notovitch rejected the offer.

Only the critic, religious historian and celebrated Orientalist Ernest Renan showed a lively interest in the notes. But even then, it soon became clear to Notovitch that Renan was interested solely in using the material for his own purposes, as a member of the Académie Française, and so he did not follow up his proposals.

At long last he managed to get the manuscript published, but it did not cause much of a stir. The power and influence of the Christian Churches are so great that doubts about the authenticity of canonical teachings are simply not permitted any credence. Critics and sceptics are condemned as godless heretics, and muzzled or ostracized. At the time Notovitch himself was in no position to gather enough scientific support for his documentary evidence to ensure that it would be given serious and scholarly consideration.

Who Was Notovitch?

Nicolai Alexandrovitch Notovitch[7] was born on 25 August 1858 in Kerch', in the Crimea, the second son of a rabbi. Little is known of his childhood, but he evidently received a school education good enough later as a young man to go to the university of St Petersburg, where his main subject was history. But before that, following the introduction of compulsory military service in Russia in the year 1874, Nicolai Notovitch underwent his military training at the age of about seventeen, and then fought in the Serbian campaign against the Turks in 1876. Soon after this he took part in the Russo-Turkish war (1877–8). It would seem that Notovitch also served in the military during his student days, because in a short notice in the *Daily News* of 23 June 1894 we read that he had been an 'officer with the Cossacks'.

During the 1880s he wrote and produced a play, *Mariage idéal*, that received some small public acclaim. He was later to write another, called *Gallia*, for which he also composed incidental music.

Notovitch's historical studies had evidently engendered a lively enthusiasm for pan-Slavic ideas. Whereas his brother Osip, who had gained a doctorate as a jurist in St Petersburg, turned to philosophical and literary pursuits, Nicolai was more interested in the influence of Russian politics on world events. Both brothers nonetheless worked as journalists after their studies. In 1873 Osip Notovitch secured a post as arts editor on a daily newspaper in St Petersburg. Later (in 1883), Nicolai was also to work for this daily as correspondent for the Orient.The Notovitch brothers were among those who felt constrained by the acutely anti-Semitic policy of Tsar Alexander III, and this moved Osip to join the Russian Orthodox Church when still a young man. Nicolai must have taken the same step, because he publicly acknowledged his adherence to the Russian Orthodox religion in the French journal *La Paix*.

The year 1887 saw the appearance of Notovitch's first publication, a translation in French of the work of a Russian general, which documented his support for the idea of a Franco-Russian alliance.[8] His second work, published in French in 1890, also dealt with the *Question de l'Alliance Franco-Russe*. In the years 1883 to 1887, as correspondent of the newspaper *Novaya Vremiya*, Notovitch undertook a number of journeys through the Balkans, the Caucasus, Central Asia and Persia. This led to a meeting with

Aloysius Rotelli (1833–91), who was papal legate in Istanbul from January 1883 until May 1887, and who was later to advise Notovitch as Cardinal in Paris.

In 1887 Notovitch set out on his important journey to India. The dates for his stay in Kashmir and Ladakh can be fixed at between 14 October and about 26 November.

His activities thereafter focused mainly on the literary sphere. He stayed for a considerable time in Paris, where from 1889 onwards he published numerous articles in the press – for example in *Le Figaro, Le Journal* and *La Science Française*. And it was because Notovitch fully expected publication of the Buddhist story of the life of Jesus to be blocked by the censors in his native land, owing to the restrictive nature of official policy on religious matters there, that he handed his manuscript to a publisher in Paris. Nevertheless, the first Russian extracts from his book, translated from the German, appeared in 1895 in the journal *Vera i Razum* (No.22, pp. 575–614), having successfully got past the censor.

Shortly after the appearance of his work *La Vie Inconnue de Jésus Christ*, towards the end of 1895, Notovitch was arrested while on a visit to St Petersburg, and imprisoned in the Fortress of Peter and Paul. Accused of literary activity 'dangerous to the state and to society', he was exiled without trial to Siberia by the head of a ministry department. His banishment ended in 1897, but even while he was in Siberia Notovitch wrote several articles about his 'extraordinary adventure', which appeared anonymously in the journal *La Science Française*.[9] And in his novel *Une Française en Sibérie* his main theme was once more the memoirs of a Russian revolutionary.

On his return from an extended journey to Egypt in mid-1898, Notovitch set up a publishing house in Paris to produce the fortnightly journal *La Russie*, which concerned itself primarily with political and economic affairs. In the journal he continued to publish his own essays and reports.

On 2 June 1899, Notovitch was accepted into the celebrated Société d'Histoire Diplomatique, the membership of which was made up of high-ranking diplomats and noted historians, and included constituents of the Rothschild family. From 1903 to 1906 Notovitch appears to have stayed in a flat in London, at least intermittently. He then probably returned to Russia. Dating from 1906 there is also an extensive contract drawn up between him and the Shah of Persia detailing the building of roads and pipelines in Iran.[10] In 1910 another Russian edition of the Buddhist story of

Jesus' life, *The Life of Saint Issa*, appeared. Up to the year 1916, Nicolai Alexandrovitch Notovitch is named in a Russian catalogue of journals as the editor and publisher of various periodicals in St Petersburg.[11] But after that, not a single trace of Notovitch is to be found anywhere. Perhaps he was keeping a low profile, sheltering from the many attacks mounted by his opponents. It is even conceivable that the militant agitator was once and for all removed from circulation.

Criticism and the Critics

Following the appearance of the first editions of Notovitch's book in 1894, an article was published in the English journal *The Nineteenth Century* in October of the same year by the renowned German expert on India Max Müller, in which he set out to expose Notovitch's discovery as a fraud. In his piece, Oxford professor Müller – who had never been to India himself – published a letter dated 29 June 1894, in which a British colonial officer, whom Müller had contacted, confirmed that the presence of a certain Notovitch in Ladakh was 'not documented'. Müller's motives can best be discerned from a letter he wrote in 1856 to a friend: 'India is much riper for Christianity than Rome or Greece were at the time of St Paul.'[12] He adds that he would not like to go to India as a missionary himself because that would make him dependent on the authorities, and goes on:

> I should like to live for ten years quite quietly and learn the language, try to make friends, and then see whether I was fit to take part in doing something that might help to overthrow the ancient evil of Indian priestcraft, and to create an opening for simple Christian education.

This shows clearly enough what Müller really had in mind, and at the same time demonstrates the motivations of the opponents who were repeatedly attacking Notovitch.

Shortly after this article, in May–June 1895, J. Archibald Douglas, a teacher at the Government College in Agra, made his way to Ladakh, from where he attempted to expose Notovitch as a fraud. His report came out in April 1896 in the *Orientalischen Bibliografie*[13] under the lurid heading 'Documents Prove Notovitch Swindle!'

Initially Douglas had found no trace of Notovitch in Ladakh, but he was soon obliged to acknowledge confirmation by the doctor, Karl Marx. Finally he allegedly paid a visit to the Hemis monastery. In his later report Douglas said that the abbot of Hemis had never met Notovitch. The April 1896 issue of *The Nineteenth Century* (pp. 667–78) contains a statement by Douglas to the effect that the lama, on being confronted with Notovitch's text, spontaneously cried out, '*Sun, sun, sun, manna mi dug!*', which Douglas and his interpreter took to mean 'Lies, lies, lies, nothing but lies'. The remarkable thing here is that the words quoted make no sense at all in Tibetan, or in any Tibetan dialect, or for that matter in any other Asiatic language.

However Douglas elicited these statements, he was concerned at any rate to turn these claims into official documents by adding his seal and signature. In an afterword to the article by Douglas, Professor Max Müller appends a fulsome apology to the monks of Hemis for ever having at first considered that Notovitch could have been misled by the monks. He speaks of the 'annihilation of Mr Notovitch' by Archibald Douglas.

So we have two testimonies: that of the Russian journalist Notovitch, and that of the British professor Douglas. The fact that Douglas said he did not see the writings discovered by Notovitch certainly does not prove that the writings never existed.

In fact, there were other witnesses, both before and after Notovitch, who did see the contested writings in Hemis with their own eyes.

Forty years before Notovitch's visit to the Hemis lamasery, a certain Mrs Harvey described the Tibetan texts that mention Jesus in her book *The Adventures of a Lady in Tartary, Thibet, China and Kashmir*, which appeared in 1853.

After Notovitch there were several eyewitnesses who saw the relevant documents before they finally disappeared. One of them was the Indian monk Swami Abhedananda, whose given name was Kaliprasad Chandra (born 1866), who studied at the Oriental Seminary in Calcutta, and who later visited England, where he met Max Müller. In 1922 Abhedananda went on a pilgrimage to Tibet, and from the diary notes he made on the journey he subsequently compiled a book entitled *Kashmir and Tibet*. On the way to Tibet he visited the Hemis monastery where, because he had heard about Notovitch's discovery, he asked the monks of the monastery whether the Russian's story was true. 'They told me that the report was completely true' (p. 230). The abbot then led the visitor through the rooms of the monastery until he came to a shelf, from where he lifted out a manuscript and showed it to him. This manuscript was said to be a copy of the original kept in the Marbour monastery near Lhasa, the lama explained. At Abhedananda's request the abbot helped him to make a translation of the text. Until then Abhedananda had been sceptical about Notovitch's publications – but when he saw the manuscript for himself, he no longer doubted that the controversial discovery was authentic.

Not long after Abhedananda, in 1925, the Russian archaeologist and painter Nicolas Roerich, who spent the greater part of his life in India, made further references in print to Tibetan writings which reported that Jesus had returned from the Himalaya to Palestine at the age of twenty-nine.[14] In the course of following up his investigations, Roerich made enquiries about the documents among the people of Ladakh, and learned 'the legend of Issa in various forms. The locals know nothing of any published book [that is, Notovitch], but they know the legend and speak with worshipful reverence of Issa.'[15]

After that, Lady Henrietta Merrick confirmed the existence of the writings in her book *In the World's Attick*, published in 1931. She writes: 'In Leh is the legend of Christ who is called "Issa", and it is said that the monastery at Hemis holds precious documents fifteen hundred years old which tell of the days that he passed in Leh, where he was joyously received and where he preached.'[16]

In 1939 a Swiss matron named Madame Elisabeth Caspari visited the Hemis monastery while on a pilgrimage to Mount Kailasa. She was one of a small group in the company of Mrs Clarence Gasque, the president of an organization called the World Association of Faith. The librarian of the monastery showed her the old manuscripts and said, 'These books tell of your Jesus' stay here.' And Mme Caspari briefly took one of the three books shown to her in her hands. None of the ladies present had ever heard of the discoveries of Nicolai Notovitch, and so they did not pay too much attention to the writings.

The texts were evidently removed from the monastery sometime afterwards.

Notovitch's Journey to Ladakh

Immediately after the publication of Notovitch's book, critical voices were heard right across Europe, raised by people who thought it their duty to try to silence Notovitch, and even questioning whether his journey to Ladakh had ever taken place. But the journey is well attested to not only by Notovitch's own account but by a number of independent authorities – there are other sources which make it perfectly possible to reconstruct his journey and to reach an objective view of the events.

In the autumn of 1887, Notovitch set off for India as a correspondent for the Russian journal *Novaya Vremiya*, and visited Kashmir and Ladakh in the period from 14 October to around the end of November. In Notovitch's paper *La Russie* dated 1 March 1900 there is a brief description of the itinerary: '. . . I visited Baluchistan, Afghanistan and the North of India, as well as the provinces lying between the Indus and the border of Afghanistan.'[17] The geographical and chronological data are confirmed by the *Frankfurter Zeitung*, which contains an announcement that Notovitch had stayed in the town of Simla, situated at a height of 2180 metres at the edge of the Himalayan mountains, and then left from there for the north-west regions of India, going first of all to Quetta (now in Pakistan, near the border with Afghanistan).

On returning from Afghanistan to India, Notovitch followed the Indus upstream to Rawalpindi. From there he turned to the south-east and travelled to Amritsar in the Punjab, where he visited the Golden Temple, the main shrine of the Sikhs. Leaving Amritsar he went to visit the tomb of Maharajah Ranjit Singh (1780–1839) at Lahore, and from there on 14 October 1887 took the train back to Rawalpindi. There he assembled his baggage with the help of his French-speaking servant (who hailed from the French colony of Pondicherry in southern India), and started for Kashmir over the Himalayan foothills in a horse-drawn carriage. On the evening of 19 October they reached the Kashmir capital Srinagar.

Notovitch described his first impressions graphically: 'On arriving at the town itself, one sees a whole row of boats and floating houses in which entire families live together.' He stayed at the well-known Nedou's Hotel, open all the year round (which still exists today, and from which the Swedish explorer Sven Hedin left for his Trans-Himalaya expedition in the early 1900s). During his stay in the town, Notovitch made the acquaintance of a Frenchman called Peychaud, who looked after the vineyards of the Maharajah Pratap Singh. Peychaud lent Notovitch a dog which had accompanied an expedition in the Pamir mountains two and a half months before. A week later, on 27 October, Notovitch departed from Srinagar to continue on his journey to Ladakh, and just two days afterwards he met Sir Francis Younghusband (1863–1942, later to be appointed High Commissioner of Kashmir) in Mateyan, where he happened to be making a stopover during his adventurous overland journey from Peking to Rawalpindi.

During the next part of his journey to Ladakh, Notovitch collected several *mani* stones on which were engraved the sacred formula of the Tibetans *Om mani padme hum*, which he later bequeathed to the museum of the Trocadero Palace in Paris.[18] To this day there is a piece of Kashmiri fabric in the Musée de l'Homme registered under his name. In gratitude for the donation of his collection, he was later made a member of the French Légion d'Honneur.[19]

Notovitch spent the night of 3–4 November in the Hemis monastery, where he awoke with severe toothache. He sent a messenger to the local governor, who replied advising him to visit Dr Marx of the Ladane Charitable Dispensary. Karl Rudolph Marx (also Marx-Weiz), a missionary belonging to the Moravian Brothers[20], had studied medicine in Edinburgh, and since December 1866 had been the director of the hospital in Leh. The diaries of Dr Marx confirm that he did indeed treat Notovitch (Plate 4).

Notovitch, having planned to travel back to Kashmir, suffered such an awkward fall from his horse that he broke his right leg below the knee. The accident happened near the monastery of 'Piatek' (presumably Spitok Gompa, *dPe-thub* in Tibetan). The notice in the *Frankfurter Zeitung* mentioned earlier confirms this event. Notovitch then allowed himself to be carried back to the Hemis monastery, where in due course the precious texts were read out to him.

Most of the information concerning the life and work of Nicolai Notovitch comes from the research work of Dr Norbert Klatt, published in *Orientierungen* Nr 13/1986 by Evangelische Zentralstelle für Weltanschauungensfragen.

A Mysterious Order

The mystical order of the Nath Yogis (also called Gorakhath or
Navnath), found in many parts of India, has preserved an old
Hindu Sutra known as the *Natha Namavali*, which tells of the great
saint Isha Nath, who is said to have come to India at the age of
fourteen years. After he returned to his home country and started
to spread the teaching there, he fell victim to a conspiracy and was
crucified. By means of the yogic powers he had attained in India
he was able to survive execution, and finally – with the help of the
supernatural powers of his Indian teacher Chetan Nath, a Nath
Guru – he came once more to India, where he is said to have
founded an Ashram monastery among the outlying foothills of the
Himalayan mountains.

The Shaivite (Shiva-centred) Nath Yogis, easily recognized by
their large earrings, represent one of the oldest Hindu orders of
monks, whose origins are lost in the twilight of history, at a time
well before the birth of Jesus and the beginning of our era, a time
perhaps coincidental with Mahayana Buddhism. In contrast to
many other Hindu orders and sects, the Nath Yogis do not recognize the caste system and the primacy of the Brahmans. They look
on all people as brothers and sisters, and accept all seekers into
their ranks regardless of their background and status. The parallels
with the attitude of Jesus towards the Jerusalem temple priests and
towards non-Jews, Samaritans and sinners would be hard to miss.

As modern research into the life of Jesus stands, it is really not
possible to *disprove* Jesus' stay in India. There is no historically reliable source, nor any indication in the Gospels, to give us any more
information than the woefully scant details we already have about
the most likely sections of his life (somewhere between his twelfth
and thirtieth years). It is almost as if the life of Jesus actually began
in his thirtieth year, when he was baptised by John. In Luke alone
we find one suggestive sentence: 'And Jesus increased in wisdom
and stature, and in favour with God and man' (Luke 2:52).

Chapter Two

WHO WAS JESUS?

The Secular Sources

The human personality of Jesus of Nazareth is the single subject that has had by far the greatest impact on the minds and attentions of the peoples of the world, while also representing the focus of countless books and of passionate debate. Yet Jesus' personality has remained stubbornly veiled from scholarly scrutiny. For fifteen hundred years the only accounts were those which showed Jesus as Saviour along the lines of the official ecclesiastical theology, and which had been written with the specific aim of supporting the faith of contemporary Christians, or of converting other people to Christianity. It was during the Renaissance in Europe that the first critical thinkers emerged, and in the Age of Enlightenment, in the seventeenth and eighteenth centuries, that for the first time studies were published which asked whether Jesus of Nazareth had actually ever lived. From the nineteenth century, scientific methods of historical research began to be applied to the books of the New Testament, and it is for this institution of systematic investigation into the life of Jesus that German Protestant theology may take full credit, having been responsible for the most significant advances in historical and critical research.

The best-known of these seekers of truth, the doctor and theologian Albert Schweitzer, regarded his investigation into the life of Christ as the most important and heady development in personal religious understanding. Today it is difficult for us to grasp what restrictive mental barriers had to be overcome to arrive at a historical view of the life of Jesus. According to Schweitzer it was actually dissatisfaction, and even focused antipathy, that fostered the most scientific approach. 'Finding out as much as possible about the life of Jesus is tantamount to bringing the Church up short by its basic truths, a quest for knowledge that involves a struggle more painful and more concerted than any previously.'

Well over 100,000 monographs have since been written on the subject of Jesus, yet the results of all this research into the historical Jesus can only be described as disappointing. Who *was* Jesus Christ? When was he born? What did he look like? When was he crucified? When, how, and where did he die? The books that were written in the first two centuries of our era contain too few indications to give us any real information about the person Jesus Christ. Later ancient sources are, almost exclusively, tendentious confessions of faith that take for granted a belief in Jesus as the Messiah and Son of God. It is practically impossible to find any really objective testimonies even in the secular literature.

The result is that modern science is still unable to give the exact year of Jesus' birth. Possible years range from the seventh to the fourth year before the change from BC to AD. Christ was certainly born during the reign of Herod, who died four years before our 'Christian era' (that is, in 4 BC!). Jesus' childhood and adolescence are almost entirely ignored in the biblical Gospels although the early years of life are crucial to the forming of a person's character. Even in the nebulous accounts of the short period in which he carried out his public work we find only scanty information about his life. Contemporary historians seem never even to have heard of Jesus, or if they had, to regard him as unworthy of mention. How could proper historians make no reference at all to the many amazing miracles and extraordinary events described in the Gospels?

Tacitus (about AD 55–120) in his *Annals*[1] mentions the 'superstitious sect' of the Christians, who derive their name from a certain Christus reported to have been executed at the time of the Emperor Tiberius under the governor Pontius. This short account was written by the great Roman historian in around AD 108 – some eighty years after the Crucifixion – and was based on stories circulating at that time. Pliny the Younger[2] (about AD 61–114) and Suetonius[3] (about AD 65–135) also mention the Christian sect, but do not have a single word to say about the person Jesus Christ.

The historian Suetonius was treasurer to the Roman Emperor Hadrian, and so had access to state documents in the imperial archives. Drawing on these documents, he made notes of all the historically significant events that had taken place during the reigns of previous emperors. They included an event that occurred in the time of the emperor Claudius, who reigned from AD 41 to 54. Claudius had expelled the Jews from Rome because they were under the influence of a certain 'Chrestos', and had caused civil unrest. This shows that there were already followers of the Christian religion in Rome in about AD 50.

The Jewish historian Joseph ben Matthias (AD 37–about 100), who became a Roman citizen and took the name Flavius Josephus, published an imposing work entitled *The Antiquities of the Jews* in about the year 93. It represents a kind of history of the world from the time of Creation up to the beginning of the reign of the Emperor Nero, and was intended specially to acquaint non-Jewish readers with the history of the Jews. He gives a very detailed account of politics and society at the time of Jesus, and refers also to John the Baptist, Herod, and Pontius Pilate, but there is only one solitary mention of the name Jesus Christus, and that is in reference to the stoning of a man named James (Jacob) 'who was a brother of Jesus, who they call Christus'. Not until the third century was a work produced at the hands of a Christian – a forgery entitled *Testimonium Flavianum*, in which the Jewish Josephus is apparently converted to Christianity and attests to the miracles and the Resurrection of Christ.[4] But the Church writers Justin Martyr, Tertullian and Cyprian are evidently unaware of any such Christian change of heart, and Origen[5] (about 185–254) makes a point of saying more than once that Josephus did not believe in Christ.

The writer Justus of Tiberias, also Jewish, was a contemporary of Josephus and lived in Tiberias, near Capernaum where Jesus was said often to have often stayed. He wrote an extensive history that began with Moses and went up to his own times, but never once did he mention Jesus. The great Jewish scholar Philo of Alexandria was a contemporary of Jesus; some fifty of his writings have come down to us. He proves to be something of a specialist on biblical writings and on Jewish sects, but he too has not a single word to say about Jesus.[6] It is only from the embittered anti-Christian Celsus that a few historical facts can be gleaned – although he is hardly flattering to whom he calls the 'idealized' Jesus. Celsus' belligerent writings contain some information that is examined in greater detail later in this book.

The one real source for historical research would thus seem to be the collection of scriptures that is the New Testament.

The Gospels

The Greek term for 'gospel' is *eu-angelion*, which simply means 'good tidings'. It existed as a compound word long before Christianity applied it to the message of Jesus. One of the titles given to the Emperor Augustus, for example, was Saviour of the World, and his birthday was accordingly referred to as 'the day of the *eu-angelion*'.

The New Testament contains four Gospels named after Matthew, Mark, Luke and John. They represent a selection from a much larger number of Gospels that were in use among the various communities and sects of early Christianity before the New Testament was formally put together. Texts that were later taken out are called apocryphal (from the Greek *apo-kryphos* 'hidden', therefore 'more obscure'). Many were destroyed, but some of those that have survived shed a very ambiguous and intriguing light on the person of Jesus of Nazareth.

The sheer number and diversity of religious groupings threatened to split early Christian communities into countless factions and to cause internecine strife within Christendom. The Roman author Ammianus Marcellinus commented: 'Not even wild animals thirsty for blood rage against each other in the way that many Christians rage against their brothers in faith.'[7] Even the early Church authority Clement of Alexandria perceived such dissension over the various tenets of faith as the greatest obstacle in spreading the faith.[8] And Celsus, the overt critic of Christianity in the second century, wrote that the single element that the various groups held in common was the adjective 'Christian'.[9] In the face of such a plethora of fundamentally differing writings on Christ's life, acts and sayings, the leaders of the early Church saw only one way out of a chaotic situation that was inexorably leading towards the complete destruction of the conflicting communities: a unification, a closing of the ranks, by formally authenticating a group of selected Gospels that had been made to agree.

Papias of Hierapolis, who is counted among the Apostolic Fathers, made an attempt to do this in about AD 110, but failed because of the resistance of individual communities. It was not until the end of the second century that Irenaeus – who even then had to rely on the threat of holy sanctions – managed once and for all to institute the four Gospels in the canon that is still considered valid today. The criterion for the inclusion of each of them was that they could all be directly traced back to a disciple of Jesus, although that too was not straightforward, of course. It remains impossible to determine exactly when and how these Gospels came into being because there is no original text of any of them extant – moreover, there is no clue as to where an original might ever have been located. To date them is similarly impossible, even in approximate terms. The most probable dates, according to the most recent research, are for Mark shortly before AD 70, for Matthew shortly after AD 70, for Luke somewhere between AD 75 and 80 (some authorities would prefer a date closer to AD 100), and it would seem that the Gospel of John was not written until as late as the first decades of the second century. So if Jesus was crucified in around AD 30, the first written records of his existence evidently did not originate until after two or three generations had passed (for the moment leaving aside the epistles of Paul, which call for special treatment).

The first three of the Gospels – Matthew, Mark and Luke – are very similar to each other. Indeed, Matthew and Luke seem to derive much of their textual content from Mark. The Gospel According to Mark must therefore have existed before the Gospels of Matthew and Luke. The canonical Mark text contains descriptions of a few events that are not included in either Matthew or Luke, however, and for which they substitute stories that have no parallel in Mark or are expressed very differently from them. This rather suggests that the two later Gospels used a kind of 'proto-Mark' as a source, which was formed into the canonical text only subsequently.

Much has been written by theologians in support of the existence of this hypothetical proto-text, but the theologian Gunther Bornkamm believes that 'the attempt to reconstruct proto-Mark remains a futile undertaking'.[10]

In the Mark text there is an evident desire to keep the messianic status of Jesus as secret as possible. Jesus does not permit any proclamation that he is the Messiah, and indeed he expressly forbids his disciples to declare any such thing (Mark 8:30).

In Matthew, Jesus is portrayed as the consummation of the Mosaic religion, and as the Messiah announced by the prophets. It has long been accepted by theologians that the Gospel concentrates on depicting Jesus as the Word Made Flesh. In addition, the writer of Matthew was evidently no historian, and never intended to write either a chronological account or a biography of Jesus.

The writer of Luke's Gospel includes a number of distinct historical events in his account of Jesus' life. And yet despite this, no coherent life story emerges. Again, then, there is a lack of any genuinely chronological, historical foundation – there must simply have been no more biographical material available because even these early Christian communities no longer possessed such data. Even at this early stage, the historical figure of Jesus had already been pushed far into the background in favour of his religious image. The text of Luke contains little of Judaism and, written in Hellenist style, is aimed mainly at the Greeks and Romans. Here Jesus is no longer a national Messiah but the Saviour of the world.

On one point, Luke's Gospel even directly contradicts the Gospels of Mark and Matthew: their version of Jesus' final words sends the apostles out into the world preaching to all nations, whereas in the 24th chapter of Luke the exact opposite is stated: they are told to 'tarry . . . in the city of Jerusalem, until ye be endued with power from on high' (Luke 24:49).

In the Acts of the Apostles (attributed to the author of Luke's Gospel), the presence of the disciples in Jerusalem is referred to more than once, and with special emphasis. The writer is endeavouring to prove that Jerusalem was Christianity's focal point of origin, although it is a historical fact that Christian communities by then already existed elsewhere. Luke makes a point of dwelling on the miracle of Pentecost in order to show how the existence of Christian sects beyond Palestine can be accounted for as radiating from that centre. By a 'divine' miracle the disciples suddenly receive the gift of speaking in 'foreign tongues', so providing a simple solution to the potential problem of language barriers.

The Gospel ascribed to John is without doubt the latest of all the canonical accounts of the life of Jesus. Early Christian writings first mention the existence of the Gospel in the mid-second century. A few lines of a papyrus record written in Greek, discovered by the English historian Grenfell, indicate that the Gospel cannot be older than the early second century. It is more a philosophical work constructed on the basis of, and complementary to, the first three Gospels. Irenaeus claims that the author John was the man called John who was the favourite of Jesus, but this idea can definitively be ruled out because the simple fisherman from Galilee could hardly have been educated extensively enough in theology and in philosophy, or have been so literate in Greek, as the author of this Gospel evidently was.

In the Gospel of John there are authentic details of Jesus' life, but they are thoroughly embedded in a matrix of religious philosophy centred on Jesus. Added to this, there is the time-lapse of at least eighty years between the Crucifixion and the writing of the Gospel, so although the contents of the book correspond closely to the ideas of Jesus, the book represents only a very fragile medium for research into Jesus' life.

In a considerable number of Protestant theological writings, the so-called *Collection of Jesus' Sayings* (also known as Q or *Logia*) has recently been accorded immense importance. Rudolf Bultmann holds that the Sayings were compiled in the very first Palestinian communities; they belong to the oldest traditions of these communities. But Bultmann adds, 'There is no certainty that the words of this oldest stratum of oral tradition were actually spoken by Jesus. Perhaps this stratum itself has its own more complex historical background.' He continues, 'The tradition collects the Lord's sayings, remoulds them, and adds to them. Furthermore, other kinds of sayings are also collected, so that some of the words included in the *Collection of Sayings* will have been put into Jesus' mouth by others.'

Historians today are able to present practically complete life stories of Pontius Pilate and of Herod – characters whose main interest is simply their connection with Jesus. Equally complete biographies of other contemporaries, and of prominent figures of even earlier periods, are similarly available. Yet a few meagre lines containing little descriptive detail are all there is to show for the life of Jesus until his thirtieth year, and even these are too scanty to serve as documentary evidence. A New Testament scholar in Tübingen, Ernst Käsemann, sums up the results to date of research into the life of Jesus.

> It is shattering to find just how little [of what the New Testament says about Jesus] can be described as authentic . . . All that can be attributed with some degree of confidence to the historical Jesus himself is a few words of the Sermon on the Mount, some parables, the confrontation with the Pharisees, and a few other odd phrases here and there.[11]

Biblical experts still disagree among themselves about which 'quotes' can genuinely be ascribed to Jesus. In his book *The Unknown Words of Jesus* (*Unbekännte Jesus-Worte*[12]), the religious historian Joachim Jeremias narrows the selection down to a mere twenty-one quotations that definitely issued from the mouth of Jesus. And the theological critic Bultmann maintains that 'the personality of Jesus, the clear picture of himself and his life, have vanished beyond recall.'[13]

The Witness Paul

The earliest documents concerning Jesus are the writings of Paul. Paul came from a strict Jewish family, and had acquired Roman citizenship through his father, who had paid a high price for it. This permitted him to change his original Jewish name, Saul, to Paul (Paulus). Belonging to the patrician class, he was brought up in the strict Pharisaic tradition. He received an extensive and thorough education, gained an excellent knowledge of the Greek language, and was also widely read in Greek poetry and philosophy. At the age of about eighteen or twenty (after Jesus' Crucifixion), he went to Jerusalem and devoted himself to intensive theological studies as a student of Gamaliel I. He then became a fanatical zealot, narrow-minded, straightlaced, a strict adherent of the law, and a most vehement opponent of the early Christian sects whom he saw as an obstacle to his professional progress. Paul even went so far as to apply to the high priest for special permission to persecute the followers of Christ beyond the city limits of Jerusalem, hoping that the great zeal he intended to display in carrying out this task would also make an impression upon the religious hierarchy. Then, near Damascus, he was suddenly overwhelmed by the powerful aura of Jesus and his teachings, struck too by the realization of the undreamed-of potential afforded by his position. He became intoxicated by the idea that he might take up the role of spiritual leader over a gigantic movement of the future.

As with Jesus and the apostles, there is hardly a single historical text about Paul himself. Everything we know about him comes almost exclusively from the letters (epistles) attributed to him and the Acts of the Apostles, and these tend to have a decidedly tendentious slant, are forgeries in part or in full, or are patched together from a few genuine text fragments. The letters to Timothy and Titus, and the letter to the Hebrews are thought to be entirely spurious. The authenticity of the letters to the Ephesians and the Colossians, and the second letter to the Thessalonians, is hotly contested.

What is called Christianity today is largely a teaching of precepts artificially created by Paul, and should more correctly be called Paulinism. The religious historian Wilhelm Nestle makes the point by saying, '"Christianity" is the religion founded by Paul; it replaced Christ's Gospel with a Gospel about Christ.'[14]

In this sense, Paulinism corresponds to the misinterpretation and falsification of Christ's actual teachings in a manner initiated and organized by Paul. It has long been accepted by theological research that the Christianity of the organized Church, with its central tenet of salvation through the vicariously sacrificial death of Jesus, is based on a misinterpretation. 'All the beautiful aspects of Christianity can be traced to Jesus, all the not-so-beautiful to Paul', said the theologian Overbeck.[15] By grounding the hope of salvation firmly on the expiatory death of God's first-born, Paul was actually taking a retrograde step back to the primitive Semitic religion of prehistoric times, when every father was obliged to give up his first-born in bloody sacrifice.

Paul also paved the way for the later ecclesiastical doctrines of original sin and the divine Trinity. As long ago as the early eighteenth century, the English statesman and philosopher Lord Bolingbroke (1678–1751) could distinguish two completely different religious faiths in the New Testament: that of Jesus and that of Paul.[16] So too Kant, Lessing, Fichte and Schelling also sharply differentiate between the teaching of Jesus and what the 'apostles' made out of it. Many highly reputable modern theologians have since come to support and defend these observations.

Paul, the impatient zealot, markedly different from the original apostles, the 'epitome of intolerance' (as the theologian A. Deissmann describes him[17]), opened up deep rifts between 'true believers' and 'non-believers'. Paul placed little emphasis on the actual words and teachings of Jesus, but was preoccupied with his own teachings. He put Jesus on a pedestal and made him into the Christ figure that Jesus never intended to be. Today a profound new understanding of Christianity is possible by rejecting all that is obviously bogus, and by turning to the true, undiluted teachings of Jesus and the real essence of religious faiths. That we still can come to such a new understanding perhaps makes it easier to forgive Paul his distortions, for it may be that without Paul and his fellow fanatic zealots, no knowledge of Jesus would have been handed down at all.

The theologian Grimm put it in a nutshell: 'However deeply these teachings may have become ingrained in Christian thought, they still have nothing to do with the real Jesus.'[18]

Conclusions

The known sources evidently cannot provide any detailed or fundamental information abiout the historical person who was Jesus. Such sources as the documentation discovered by Nicolai Notovitch in Ladakh may, therefore, fill an extremely important gap in what is known about the life of Christ, for which there are otherwise no historical records. Nevertheless, such an astounding discovery – which instantly sheds light on some of the deepest shadows of the 'Christian' religion – would seem to have no relevance at all unless it is viewed in the context of the latest results provided by the most objective and extensive historical research, freed of all institutional dogmatism. Scientific research and scientific freedom are both required if a picture of the human Jesus is to gradually come together, true to life.

Perhaps it is only possible today to learn who Jesus was and what he really wanted, by studying the tradition he inspired, the results of his teachings, his lofty morals, and his profound ethical and spiritual nature.

What Albert Schweitzer said in 1913 is more valid today than ever: 'Modern Christianity must always be prepared to face the possibility that the historicity of Jesus could be revealed at any time.'[19] And Rudolf Bultmann said, 'It would not surprise me in the least if they were now to find Jesus' bones!'[20]

My Travels in the Himalayan Mountains

In 1973, a short report appeared in a major German weekly[21] outlining how an Indian professor was claiming in all seriousness to have found the tomb of Jesus Christ in India. The article was even accompanied by photographs showing the alleged tomb. The professor bluntly declared that Jesus not only spent his youth in India, but survived the Crucifixion by means of a technique, before returning to India. There he lived as an itinerant teacher until he died at a ripe old age, and his body was interred in the Kashmiri capital, Srinagar.

This was a truly amazing claim – and the journal that dared to publish it was duly swamped with thousands of letters full of invective and virulent protests. Some letters, however, contained interested enquiries from more open-minded people who had always suspected there was something of the pious fairytale in the old versions of the virgin birth, resurrection and ascension of Jesus.

It seems most surprising that none of the sceptics ever followed up the question of where Jesus could in fact have been buried – because although the various miracles Jesus is supposed to have performed can be explained away one way or another, it is quite impossible for the body of Jesus simply to have risen up into the air, being 'carried up into heaven' as Luke (24:51) puts it. Moreover, there is no room for physical matter in the spiritual domain.

After years of study during which my university professors could come up with nothing but unsatisfactory, not to say evasive, answers to my queries on the historical figure of Jesus, I decided that once I had finished my course as a religious teacher I would myself go to India to carry out my own research. Accordingly, I flew via Egypt to India early in 1979, and landed in Bombay. From there I went on by train and bus to the Himalayan foothills at Dharamsala, where the Dalai Lama had resided since his flight from Tibet in 1959. My intention was to ask him respectfully for a letter of introduction to the abbot at the Hemis monastery, a letter that would also grant me permission to look at the manuscripts about which Notovitch had written almost one hundred years previously. After having had to wait four days for an audience, I finally received the precious document, complete with the signature of His Holiness the fourteenth Dalai Lama. I continued my journey by road to Kashmir, where I heard that the famous mystery plays that Notovitch had also described were to be performed a few days later. The festival, known to the Tibetans as *Cham* or *Setchu*, honours the Buddhist saint and prophet Padmasambhava, and takes place from the ninth to the eleventh day of the fifth month in the Tibetan calendar.

Today it is possible to reach Leh, the capital of Ladakh, in relative comfort by taking a two-day bus trip over the outlying ranges west of the Great Himalaya. When I eventually arrived at Hemis, the festival was already in full swing. There was a huge crowd in which, although the country had been opened to foreigners only five years before, a large number of Western tourists were evident. I had no wish to make my presence or purpose known while that hubbub was going on, so I went back to Leh, where I let three weeks pass before I returned once again to Hemis.

Hemis is the largest, richest, and most important abbey in

Ladakh. Its name is derived from the Dardic[22] word *hem* or *hen* (Sanskrit *hima* 'snow'), which tends to suggest that there was a settlement here prior to the present Tibetan culture.

Patience and perseverance are important virtues that foreigners must prove themselves to possess, so I received little attention to begin with. I joined the monks in the kitchen, which looked rather like a medieval alchemist's laboratory, where I drank the salted butter tea and waited. As evening approached, a monk, gesturing silently, showed me a small room in which I could sleep. During the following days, I was left mostly to my own devices, and I spent the time roaming through the dim passageways of the monastery, going for long walks in the countryside, and only rejoining my friends in the kitchen when I felt the pangs of hunger. On the morning of the fourth day of my stay in the monastery, a young monk appeared in my cell and motioned me to follow him. I was led through dark corridors and up steep wooden steps, into the upper regions of the monastery that I had not visited up till then. At last we came to the roof of the grand temple building. On a large terrace under the shelter of a projecting gable over the doorway to the topmost room of the complex, an assembly of monks was sitting around an imposing table. A dignified middle-aged monk seated at the far side of the table then addressed me in almost impeccable English. It was Nawang-Tsering, the secretary and interpreter of the abbot, who explained that His Holiness, the Dungsey Rinpoche, had heard of my interest and wished to speak with me.

While waiting for my audience, I learned from Nawang-Tsering that the former abbot of Hemis, who was also the head of the Duk pa Kagyu pa sect of Tibetan Buddhism, had been missing since the invasion of Tibet by Communist Chinese troops. The abbot, who at the time had been engaged in higher studies in his native Tibet, refused to leave his homeland without his parents, unwilling to abandon them to an uncertain fate, and was then himself not allowed to leave. After a while, the Communist government prohibited all correspondence with him, and the last anyone had heard of the High Lama was that he was a prisoner in a labour camp.

After fifteen years during which no further news of him had been heard, the abbot was declared dead, and a replacement sought in the form of a young reincarnation. Six years after the presumed time of death, the lamas lighted on a two-year-old boy who lived near the mountain town of Dalhousie (Darjeeling) in north-eastern India, and who was duly consecrated as Drug pa Rinpoche in 1975 at the age of twelve. The boy's mentor was the old Dungsey Rinpoche, and the years between his discovery and his consecration were spent in intensive studies and instruction.

Among the monks I could not help noticing a tall man of about thirty years of age, who was clearly not of Tibetan origin since he had the facial features of a Westerner. It turned out that the young man was an Australian, had already been living at the Hemis monastery for several years, and spoke fluent Tibetan. He showed some interest in my research. When I was finally summoned to the audience, the Australian accompanied me to serve as my interpreter for the Holy One, who spoke only Tibetan. We entered a magnificently decorated low-roofed room, in which a venerable old man was sitting in the pose of a Buddha on a small throne. In front of him was an ornate silver teacup upon a little stand. After bowing to him with folded hands, I was permitted to sit before him on the carpet. My gaze was met by a pair of alert and flashing eyes that radiated goodness and wisdom, set in a smiling face adorned with sculptured wrinkles and a thin white beard. I showed him my letter of introduction, and attempted to convey to him how important these texts could be for the whole of Christendom.

With an understanding smile, the wise lama instructed me first to find the Truth for myself, before attempting to convert the whole world. The Australian translated only a fraction of what the lama told me. Finally, the old man informed me that the scriptures in question had already been looked for, but nothing could be found.

This piece of news struck me like a bolt from the blue, and in some shock and disappointment I took my leave. The lama's words might mean that the monastery would keep its precious secret for many years yet. But later I managed to discover that an old diary dating from the nineteenth century was located in the Moravian Church Mission in Leh, in which the missionary and Tibetan scholar Dr Karl Marx had mentioned Notovitch's stay at the monastery in Hemis.

On my return to Leh I immediately searched out the Moravian Mission, founded by the German order of lay brothers back in 1885.

Zealous Christian missionaries had come to Tibet long before then, though. Capuchin monks repeatedly visited Lhasa from as early as the fourteenth century, in the hope of converting Tibetans

to Christianity – an endeavour that was not to be blessed with success. When the Christian missionaries told the Tibetans that Christ
had sacrificed himself on the Cross for the redemption of humanity, and finally rose again to life, the Tibetans accepted the entire
story as something they already knew all about and exclaimed
enthusiastically, 'It was he!' The pious Buddhists were completely
convinced that Christ was an incarnation of Padmasambhava. The
missionaries came to the conclusion that they had better stop trying to convert the population, not because they encountered too
much resistance but, on the contrary, because their teachings were
interpreted as confirmation of the teachings that had been proclaimed by Sakyamuni, Padsambhava, and other Buddhist saints.[23]
Today there are fewer than 200 Christians in the entire population
of Ladakh.

Father Razu, the director of the Christian Mission, a Tibetan by
birth, received me cordially and, over tea and fresh pastries, told
me the history of the Mission. But he could not show me the precious diary that was the real reason for my visit, because it had
mysteriously disappeared three or four years earlier. A delegation
of the Moravian Church from Zurich had been staying in Leh at
the time, and the grandson of the celebrated Dr Francke, Dr Marx's
partner, had also spent some time in the house. The friendly priest
had no explanation for the book's disappearance, but he recalled
that a certain Professor Hassnain from Srinagar had taken some
photographs of the relevant pages many years before. Hassnain
was the professor who had supplied the reporter of *Stern* maga-
zine with information for the report that appeared in 1973.

After making further efforts to trace the missing diary at the
municipal library and the library of the nearby village for Tibetan
refugees, Chaglamsar, I resolved to end my stay in the 'lunar landscape' of Ladakh and to travel back over to the idyllic 'Happy
Valley' of Kashmir. Near the village of Mulbek there is a bas-relief
sculpture of Maitreya, the Saviour of the Buddhists whose future
coming was promised by Sakyamuni, chiselled into a vertical wall
of rock, a full twelve metres high (Plate 5). The name *Maitreya* is
related to the Aramaic *meshia* – the *Messiah* that the Jews continue
to hope for as their Saviour.

Kashmir is sometimes called the Switzerland of India because
of its fertile valleys and their large, smooth lakes and clear rivers,
surrounded by green wooded mountains, lying at the foot of the
'roof of the world'. This paradise has attracted people from far-off
regions ever since ancient times, and especially during the Golden

The Province of Jammu and Kashmir in Northern India.

Age of Kashmir, when pilgrims came to the green valleys from all over the world in order to study the teachings of Gautama Buddha at the feet of the celebrated scholars of Kashmir. Kashmir was regarded as the centre of Mahayana Buddhism, the seat of a school of the noblest spiritual values and cultural endeavours. The region's conversion to Islam has left only fragments of the once extensive monasteries, temples and teachings of the ascetics.

Despite its idyllic location, Srinagar is a noisy and turbulent city, humming with commercial activity. The city is spread between and over several lakes, on the left bank of the large Lake Dal, and is thus interlaced by a number of waterways that have given Srinagar the atmosphere of a Venice of the East. A considerable proportion of the population live in the houseboats that lie in great numbers on the canals of the old town, or moored to the banks of the lakes and beside the 'floating gardens'. The houseboats vary greatly in design and construction, from simple *dongas* to artistically carved and luxurious floating palaces that have every conceivable comfort and convenience – depending, of course, on the wealth of the owners.

A short distance out of town, on a small lake, I found bed and

board on an old but quaint little boat, which was to serve as my
home for the whole season. From this boat it was possible to be
paddled to any point in the city in small, covered taxi-boats,
shikaras. A vast flotilla of boats run by the traders transported and
delivered all the necessities of life. Even a small waterborne post
office made daily rounds. Needless to say, it was very pleasant to
stay in such an idyllic setting, and many Europeans and
Americans were drawn to spend even longer periods of time in
these houseboats, perhaps while learning Sanskrit, perhaps simply
enjoying the feel of the place – at least until the outbreak of disturbances in 1989.

From my boat I could reach the modern University of Kashmir
on foot in ten minutes, and I was to spend a great deal of time
there, for this was where Professor Hassnain taught. He was the
man I wanted to contact in Srinagar, and about whom I had heard
so much.

Professor Hassnain is a scholar of international reknown, the
author of several books, a visiting professor in Japan and the
United States, the Director of the Kashmir Research Centre for
Buddhist Studies, and a member of the International Conference
for Anthropological Research in Chicago. In addition, until his
retirement in 1985 he was executive director of all the museums,
collections and archives in Kashmir, working from his office at the
Ministry of Culture.

Once I had told him of my hopes and plans, he began with great
enthusiasm to tell me about his own research, putting off all his
other appointments until the next day. After several hours of lively
conversation, he closed up his office and invited me to visit him at
his home. Despite his important position, Professor Hassnain
remains a modest man, friendly and congenial.

Over the course of our meetings, I subsequently learned all that
he had managed during the past twenty-five years to discover
about Jesus' stay in India. But all his evidence – facts, implications,
associations, apparent connections – could be taken as no more
than contributing to a dubious, if not absurd, hypothesis unless it
is also seen in the light of the most up-to-date research into the life
of Jesus. The professor's discoveries have first to be placed on a
firm scientific footing, and the true origins and evidence of the
teachings of Jesus revealed. Only then can the three most important questions be addressed:

Could Jesus really have travelled to India in his youth?

Could he have survived the Crucifixion (not fairly soon afterwards ascending to 'heaven')?

Could he actually have returned to India, to die in old age in Srinagar?

Without such preliminary investigation, anyone brought up in the Christian tradition might be pardoned for dismissing the story of Jesus' life in India with a pitying smile. It is hard indeed to kick against the current of almost two thousand years of deeply-rooted convention. All the same, just because a story has been told for two thousand years does not mean that it is true.

Chapter Three

MOSES AND THE CHILDREN OF GOD

The Origins of the Hebrews

Modern research is of the opinion that Abraham, the patriarch of the Hebrews, was in fact a historical person, and was born in the eighteenth century BC. According to the Old Testament Yahweh commanded him, 'Get thee out of thy country, and from thy kindred, and from thy father's house, unto a land that I will shew thee' (Genesis 12:1). But where was the original home of Abraham's forefathers?

Genesis 29 tells how Abraham's grandson Jacob journeyed to his maternal uncle Laban's establishment in the land of the 'sons of the east'. Even more pointedly, in the book of Joshua the patriarchs of the people of Israel are said originally to have come from the east:

> Thus saith the Lord God of Israel, Your fathers dwelt on the other side of the flood in old time, even Terah, the father of Abraham, and the father of Nachor; and they served other gods.
>
> And I took your father Abraham from the other side of the flood, and led him throughout all the land of Canaan, and multiplied his seed, and gave him Isaac.
>
> (Joshua 24:2–3)

Several passages in Genesis indicate that Abraham's first home was in the region of Haran. According to Genesis 12:4, it was while Abraham was living in Haran that he was commanded by God to depart from his homeland. Later, Abraham sent his eldest servant back to Haran 'unto my country, and to my kindred', in order to find a wife for his son, Isaac (Genesis 24:4). Haran is generally assumed to have been the place in the Mesopotamian lowlands now called Harran or Eski-Charran (in modern Turkey).

There is, however, a small town in northern India called Haran, a few kilometres north of Srinagar (the capital of Kashmir), in which the remains of ancient walls have been excavated and dated by archaeologists back to long before the Christian era (Plates 7 and 8). Although it is no longer possible to reconstruct the wanderings of the nomadic Hebrew tribes in detail, there is some evidence to suggest that in around 1730 BC they began to make their way towards Egypt under the leadership of Jacob.

The Egyptian priest and historian Manetho reported that 'people of a peasant culture appeared unexpectedly from the east, boldly entered our country, and forcibly took possession of it, without encountering any serious resistance.' Murals in Egyptian burial chambers clearly depict these conquerors as having a light skin coloration and black hair.

The speech delivered by Stephen in his own defence, as quoted in Acts of the Apostles, provides a brief account of how Abraham, the patriarch of the Jews, was compelled to go to the land that the God of Glory wished to show him. He departed from 'the land of the Chaldaeans, and dwelt in Charran' (Acts 7:4), travelling via Mesopotamia. It is not inconceivable that the nomadic families led by Abraham named the place in north-west Mesopotamia, where they settled temporarily, after their own home town.

From Haran the group finally advanced to Canaan, where Abraham sired his son Isaac, who in turn fathered Jacob and Esau. Twelve sons were born to Jacob, who were to become the patriarchs of the Jewish tribes. Joseph, second youngest of Jacob's twelve sons, was sold by his jealous brothers into bondage in Egypt, where the Hyksos were in power at the time. In Egypt, Joseph rose to a position of great power as the second-in-command to Pharaoh himself. Soon after, when Canaan was afflicted by a famine, the eleven brothers of Joseph heard that 'there was corn in Egypt', and set off for that land. Joseph disclosed himself to his brothers, and had his father Jacob and the entire clan join him in Egypt, where they first settled in the province of Goshen – a Semitic settlement dating from this time and located on the north-eastern Nile delta has been fully documented. The Hebrews soon came to people the whole land, gaining wealth, influence and power.

The description 'Hebrew' was thus originally applied not to a national or ethnic group, but to any persons of no fixed abode and with few rights, whose fate was to serve the Egyptians as a form of cheap labour and later even as cheap forced labour, as is evident in sources dating from the fourteenth and thirteenth centuries BC. The detailed account given in Exodus 1:11 – in which the ancestors of the Israelites are conscripted for the construction of the towns Pithom and Raamses – would strongly suggest that Ramses II (1290–24 BC) was the oppressive pharaoh responsible. It was at that time, or very shortly afterwards, that some of the Semitic tribes left Egypt under the leadership of Moses, in search of the land of their fathers, the land of milk and honey that had been promised by Yahweh.

Who Was Moses?

The name of the man who laid down the social and religious laws in ancient India was Manu.

The lawgiver of the Egyptians was called Manes.

The Cretan who codified the laws of the ancient Greeks – laws that he had learned in Egypt – was called Minos.

The leader of the Hebrew tribes and the promulgator of the Ten Commandments was called Moses.

Manu, Manes, Minos and Moses, foremost contributors to the world's humanity, all belonged to the same archetypal pattern. All four stood by the cradle of important civilizations of the ancient world. All four laid down laws and instituted a theocratic priestly society.

In Sanskrit, *manu* signifies a man of excellence, a lawgiver. When a civilization begins to develop, there are always certain people who are called to greatness; they are beloved by the populace and are extraordinarily efficient in everything they do. Instead of mere force of arms, which served as the highest law to primitive peoples, the power of these cultural and spiritual leaders is drawn from the one supreme Being, or God. Such men are endowed with an aura of mystery, and their human origins become transfigured. They are deemed to be prophets or messengers of God, for they alone can shed light on why and how things happen in the prehistoric past. In their skilled hands, every physical phenomenon is transformed to become a manifestation of a heavenly power, which they can summon or suppress at will. Conjurors ('magicians') in both Israel and India, for instance, certainly knew how to put a snake into a catatonic trance so that they could display it stiff as a rod or staff, before transforming it back to its original condition – a feat still performed by Indian fakirs.

And yet there is always a certain ambivalence in the role of such spiritual leaders. Literal adherents of the verses of Manu joined with the Brahmans (the most influential caste, the priests) to topple the social structure of the Veda, which finally led to society's hardening into a rigid caste system locked in a suffocating framework of laws and taboos. Moses was made to act out a similar despotic role in relation to the people of Israel, the 'children of God'.

The etymology of the name Moses is a matter of debate. In Egyptian, *mos* simply means 'child' (or literally 'is born', as in Thut-moses, 'Thoth is born'). According to the biblical derivation, based on Hebrew elements, the name derives from *mo* 'water' and *use* 'save', in reference to the legend of the baby Moses' being found in a floating basket of reeds (Exodus 2:10).

It is not possible to form a consistent picture of the historical person of Moses, for the tradition has left a number of unanswered questions. Historical research into the Old Testament has shown that Moses was clearly not the author of 'the five books of Moses' attributed to him. In fact the Pentateuch, in the form in which we have it today, was compiled from centuries of oral and written tradition. The lack of uniformity in overall vocabulary, the contradictions and repetitions, and the differences in basic theological tenets all constitute firm evidence that a variety of sources was used.

But even if much has been obscured by the passing of intervening millennia, it has at least been established that Moses was a genuinely historical figure. We can assume that he grew up in the royal court, was brought up by the priests, and attained such a high level of education that he became influential as an administrator in all departments of the state. Moses made use of a peculiar mixture of pure doctrine and curious magical practices – a mix apparently suffused with Vedic incantations as well as elements of Egyptian religious ritual. His intention was after all to proclaim the existence of the One God, the God of Israel, beside whom no other gods were to be worshipped. And he was obliged to resort to 'wonders' to lend weight to God's – as it coincided with his own – will. The official stance of the Church has been to reject Greek and Roman mythology as the religious roots of Christian belief, but the accounts of Moses have been accepted *in toto*, however difficult it may be to accept that the vengeful God described as a devouring fire is the same God of the New Testament.

Whoever opposed Moses in his quest for power was destroyed. Fire was the method used for such eliminations, and was frequently used also to demonstrate power – for Moses seems often to have resorted to illustrating his point in a rather incendiary manner. He evidently had a great variety of magic tricks at his disposal. Following his appearance before the wise men and sorcerers of Egypt (Exodus 7:8–13), Moses was accredited a great magician even among the ancient Greeks. In the early Christian era, apocryphal writings of magical content were composed to complement the Pentateuch, associating themselves with the authority of Moses. Editions of the 'Sixth' and 'Seventh Books of Moses', which came to light fairly recently, returned to the Egyptian tradition, offering a mix of spells, sorcery, magical incantations and texts containing esoteric doctrines of various backgrounds.

In his book *The Biblical Moses*[1], which appeared in 1928, Jens Juergens showed that Egyptian priests were able to make gunpowder and use it in fireworks or primitive flares as early as six thousand years ago. Research undertaken by the English archaeologist Professor Flinders Petrie[2] also proved that Moses wielded authority not only over the Egyptian temples, but also over the royal mines in the Sinai region – including therefore the sulphur mine at Gnefru, which had been under excavation since the fifth millennium BC. So Moses knew about the production of gunpowder through his priestly training, and the composition (sulphur, saltpetre and charcoal) was simple enough technically. When his subjects refused to attend to his words (and he did preach at some length, 'from morning unto even', Exodus 18:14), he could have called forth a 'devouring fire' that was guaranteed to have the desired effect.[3]

As the representative of his fiery God, Moses could give orders for anything he wanted, and if anyone proved reluctant to come up with the sometimes weighty contributions he demanded, a suitably impressive demonstration of his power was all that was needed to restore the peace – as happened on Mount Sinai (Exodus 19:1–25). When Korah and his clan rose in rebellion against Moses, 250 men were 'consumed by fire' (Numbers 16:1–35), and shortly afterwards no fewer than a thousand more perished in flames when they too revolted against Moses. On another occasion, two of Aaron's sons were experimenting in the tabernacle with a 'strange fire before the Lord, which he commanded them not', and were burned to death (Leviticus 10:1–7). It seems that even Moses may have suffered such severe burns in an explosion that he was obliged to wear a head-bandage (Exodus 34:29–35).

Moses is still very much regarded as the great lawgiver, but the

Ten Commandments in fact represent no more than a codified summary of laws that had been in force among the peoples of the Near East and India long before Moses' time. The same precepts are even to be found among the famous laws promulgated by the Amorite King Hammurabi of Babylon (1728–1686 BC) five hundred years earlier. All these laws were probably based on the millennia-old Indian Rig Veda.

Nor is Moses the originator of monotheism. The notion of a single invisible and almighty God, the Creator of the Universe, a Father of love and goodness, of compassion, sensibility and trust, had long already been in evidence in the Vedas and in the tradition that became the Nordic *Edda*. Zarathustra, founder of Zoroastrianism, also expressly proclaimed his God to be the One and Only.

In the papyrus of Prisse (dating from about one thousand years before Moses) God says of himself: 'I am the unseen One who created the heavens and all things. I am the Supreme God, made manifest by Myself, and without equal. I am yesterday, and I know the morrow. To every creature and being that exists I am the law.'

This One God without equal was referred to in Egypt as 'the nameless', 'the One Whose name cannot be spoken', long before Moses: *Nuk pu Nuk* 'I am who I am'. (Compare this with the account in Exodus 3:14, where God declares: 'I am that I am.')

There can no longer be any doubt that Moses actually existed. His 'miracles' are nonetheless for the most part based on much older traditions – for instance, on the legend of the ancient (originally Arab) god Bacchus, who was rescued from the water like Moses, who crossed the Red Sea on foot, who inscribed laws on stone tablets, whose armies were led by columns of fire, and from whose forehead shone rays of light.

The Indian epic called the Ramayana tells of the hero Rama, who led his people on a journey through the heart of Asia finally to reach India more than five thousand years ago. Rama, too, was a great lawgiver and a hero of extraordinary powers. He caused springs to gush forth in the deserts through which he led his people (cf Exodus 17:6), provided them with a kind of manna to eat (cf Exodus 16:3–35), and suppressed a virulent plague with the sacred drink *soma*, India's 'water of life'. Finally he conquered the 'promised land', Sri Lanka, after invoking a hail of fire to fall on its king. In order to reach Sri Lanka, he crossed the sea via a land bridge apparently exposed by the low tide at a place still known as the Bridge of Rama. Like Moses, Rama is also depicted with rays of light streaming from his head (the flames of the enlightened one, Plate 13).

Zarathustra, like Moses, also possessed a sacred fire that he could put to use in various ways. According to the Greek writers Eudoxus, Aristotle and Hermodoros of Syracuse, Zoroaster (that is, Zarathustra) lived about five thousand years before Moses, and like him, was of royal blood, was taken from his mother, and was left exposed to the wild. In his thirtieth year he became the prophet of a new religion. Heralded by peals of thunder, God appeared to him robed in light, seated on a throne of fire on the holy mountain Albordj, encircled by flames. There, God bestowed on him His sacred law. Finally, Zoroaster likewise wandered with his followers to a remote 'promised land', and came to the shores of a sea where, with God's help, the waters parted so that His chosen people might cross the sea on foot.

Perhaps the most familiar episode in Jewish history begins with the emigration of the tribes of Israel from Egypt under the leadership of Moses, to search for another land in which to settle as a newly independent nation. The land of Goshen, in which the Israelites lived beforehand, has not yet been located beyond all doubt but must have been somewhere in the eastern part of the Nile delta. Passages in the Bible mention a change of pharaohs at the time, which would coincide with the expulsion of the Hyksos at the beginning of the 18th dynasty under Amasis I. The direct route from the Red Sea (Sea of Reeds) to Palestine was due northeast, but the Philistines were blocking the way there. Why Moses did not then take the route via Beersheba – the place where Jacob had set up a sanctuary, and rich in other patriarchal traditions – remains a complete mystery. Be that as it may, he took them all south instead. By the third month of the Exodus, the people had arrived at the Sinai massif. It was probably on the mountain now known as Jebel Musa ('Moses' mountain') that the fiery God Yahweh's impressive demonstration took place. According to biblical tradition, the Israelites remained there for eight months before endeavouring to move on towards the Promised Land. Their first attempt failed, however, and the people of Israel had then to wander in the wilderness for a further forty years, or so the Bible says (forty was a mystical figure simply representing 'a large number').

Reaching the valley of the River Jordan, Moses sensed that he was not long for this world (Deuteronomy 31:2). Realizing that it would not be given him to see his people to the end of their long journey, he reiterated the laws that were to be regarded as sacred in the Promised Land, gave his final instructions, appointed men to offices to be taken up once the Jordan had been crossed, delivered a farewell speech, and at last climbed Mount Nebo to see 'the land of milk and honey' before he died. There he met his end (Deuteronomy 34:5) – but his place of burial remained a mystery, for '. . . no man knoweth of his sepulchre unto this day'. It is all the more surprising that Moses' grave should not be found for the Bible gives a very detailed description of the site, complete with place-names:

> And Moses went up from the plains of Moab unto the mountain of Nebo, to the top of Pisgah, that is over against Jericho . . . over against Beth-peor . . .
>
> (Deuteronomy 34:1, 6)

It seems equally improbable that the people of Israel would not have arranged for a place of burial worthy of their great saviour and leader: some fragmentary vestiges should still be visible somewhere. Some remains do indeed exist – but not in Palestine. They are in northern India.

The Tomb of Moses in Kashmir

The Bible names five landmarks in relation to Moses' burial site (Deuteronomy 34:1–7): the Plains of Moab, Mount Nebo (in the Abarim mountains), the peak of (Mount) Pisgah, Beth-peor, and Heshbon. The Promised Land beyond the Jordan had been expressly reserved for the children of Israel, and not for all Hebrews (Numbers 27:12). If it is possible to find the places mentioned in the texts, the true location of the Promised Land should also become clear.

The literal meaning of *Beth-peor* is 'place that opens out', as might refer to a valley that opens on to a plain. The River Jhelum in the north of Kashmir is called Behat in Farsi (Persian), and the small town of Bandipur at the point where the valley of the Jhelum opens out on to the broad plain of Lake Wular used to be called Behat-poor. Beth-peor, then, would seem to have become first Behat-poor and latterly Bandipur in the Sopore district 70 kilometres north of Srinagar, the capital of Kashmir.

Some 20 kilometres north-east of Bandipur lies the small village of Hasba or Hasbal. This is the biblical Heshbon (Deuteronomy

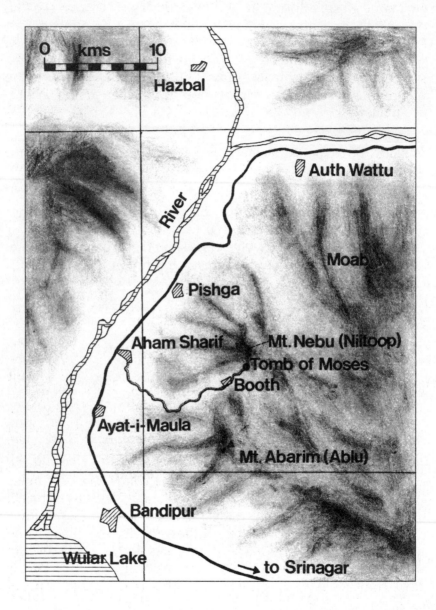

Sketch-map showing the area around the 'Tomb of Moses': Mount Nebo, the peak of Mount Pisgah, the mountains of Abarim (Ablu/Abul), Beth-peor (Bandipur), Heshbon (Hazbal), and the Plains of Moab.

4:46), which is mentioned in connection with Beth-peor and Pisgah. On the slopes of Pisgah (now Pishnag), to the north of Bandipur, just 1.5 kilometres north-east of the village of Aham-Sharif, a natural spring yields water with curative properties. The valley and the plains of Mowu correspond to the Plains of Moab, ideal alpine pasture some 5 kilometres north-west of Mount Nebo. Mount Nebo is a single mountain in the Abarim range, and is always mentioned in connection with Beth-peor.[5] Mount Nebo, also called Baal Nebu or Niltoop, offers a splendid view of Bandipur and the entire highlands of Kashmir.

> And the Lord said unto him, This is the land which I sware unto Abraham, unto Isaac, and unto Jacob, saying, I will give it unto thy seed. I have caused thee to see it with thine eyes, but thou shalt not go over thither.
>
> So Moses the servant of the Lord died there in the land of Moab, according to the word of the Lord.
>
> And he buried him in a valley in the land of Moab, over against Beth-peor: but no man knoweth of his sepulchre unto this day.
>
> (Deuteronomy 34:4–6)

All the five named landmarks are thus to be found in one well-defined location.

It is possible to go as far as the village of Aham-Sharif about 12 kilometres from Bandipur – by car. From here, walking is the only way to reach the little village of Buth at the foot of Mount Nebo, climbing westwards for about an hour along a barely trace-able path. The mountain's shape and its luxuriant vegetation are strongly reminiscent of hills in Europe. The path crosses several fields before finally reaching the small hamlet of Buth directly beneath Mount Nebo. The *wali rishi* is the official guardian of the tomb. He leads visitors to an area above the village that resembles an unfenced garden, and that contains a small cabin-like shrine. This modest hut serves as the tomb of an Islamic saint, Sang Bibi, a female recluse, and of two of her followers. To one side, in the shadow of the little wooden building, lies an unprepossessing stone column that rises about a metre from the ground and is almost completely covered by grass: this is the tombstone of Moses.

The *wali rishi* explains that the *rishis* have been reverently tending the grave for more than 2700 years. Everything fits the tradition: the grave is near the Plains of Moab, near the peak of Pisgah, on the mountain of Nebo, across from Beth-peor, and the site commands a splendid view of a fresh and blossoming 'land of milk and honey', forever green, a true paradise. In the same vicinity, as in other parts of Kashmir, there are quite a few places with biblical names, in addition to one or two sites named Muqam-i-Musa, 'the place of Moses'. North of Pisgah lies the small village of Heshbon (Deuteronomy 4:44–49), which is today called Hasbal. And in Bijbihara, south of Srinagar, a place on the riverbank is still referred to as 'Moses' bath-place', where there is a magic stone called Ka-Ka-Bal or Sang-i-Musa ('Stone of Moses'). According to legend, the stone – about 70 kilograms in weight – is supposed to rise by itself and remain suspended at about one metre off the ground if eleven people touch it with one finger while chanting the magic spell 'Ka-ka, ka-ka'. The number eleven represents the tribes of Israel.

Another place named after Moses is near Auth Wattu ('Eight paths') in the Handwara district. The rocks at the confluence of the rivers Jhelum and Sind (this is not the Indus), near Shadipur north of Srinagar, are called Kohna-i-Musa, 'Cornerstone of Moses'. Moses is believed to have reclined on the rocks there. He is also said to have rested at Ayat-i-Maula (or Aitmul, 'Sign of God'), 3 kilometres north of Bandipur.

From Conquest to Exile

Following Moses' death, the twelve tribes of Israel gradually assumed control of Canaan under the leadership of Joshua, dividing the territory up between themselves by drawing lots in the thirteenth century BC. The whole process of gaining possession of the land and putting it to their own uses altogether took about 150 years. In the song of Deborah (Judges 5:8), the population is estimated at 40,000 people, governed by strict rulers and leaders – the 'Judges' – in accordance with the laws of Moses. But even the power of the Judges was not sufficient over the long term to transform volatile nomads into a united people. The Israelites needed a king to rule them with a firm hand, and Samuel, the last of the Judges, finally anointed Saul King of Israel at the end of the eleventh century BC. Not until the reign of King David (around the middle of the tenth century), however, did Israel finally become a single, united nation. And the nation's capital was Jerusalem, where the famous Temple was constructed during the reign of David's son, Solomon.

Solomon is renowned worldwide for his wisdom. But the biblical texts attributed to him were certainly written well after his time, and who the teachers were that imparted their wisdom to him is nowhere recorded.

In his book about the natural history of the region of Travancore in southern India (now the state of Kerala), Dr Mateer writes:

> There is a curious fact connected with the name of this bird which casts some light upon scriptural history. King Solomon sent his navy to Tarshish (1 Kings 10:22), from where it returned after three years bringing 'gold and silver, ivory, and apes, and peacocks'. Now the word used in the Hebrew Bible for peacock is *tukki*, and because the Israelites naturally had no name for these fine birds until they were first imported into Judea by King Solomon, there is no doubt that *tukki* is simply the old Tamil word *tokei*, the name of the peacock . . . Also, the ape or monkey in Hebrew is *koph*, the Indian word for which is *kapi*. Ivory . . . is abundant in southern India, and gold is widely distributed in the rivers of the Western coast. So the 'Tarshish' referred to was undoubtedly the Western coast of India, and Solomon's ships were the first East Indiamen.[6]

To this, with grateful acknowledgement, can be added the fact that apart from 'gold and silver, ivory, and apes, and peacocks', King Solomon and his friend King Hiram (he of masonic connotations) brought something else home with them from India: their 'magic' and their 'wisdom'. Other historians, including the famous expert on India Max Müller,[7] also trace the Hebrew name of the peacock and the monkey back to Indian origins.

According to the First Book of Kings (9:13), Solomon presented Hiram, the King of Tyre, with twenty towns, among them a place named Kabul (Cabul). But Kabul is the name of the capital of Afghanistan, formerly part of India.

Kashmir is still known among the local Muslim population as Bagh-i-Suleiman, the 'Garden of Solomon', and on a mountain that overlooks the city of Srinagar there stands a small temple called Takht-i-Suleiman, the 'Throne of Solomon'. According to an inscription, the 'new temple' was restored in AD 78 by King Gopadatta (also called Gopananda) on the foundations of an older, ruined building. Tradition has it that Solomon once visited the region, and that it was he who divided the mountain Barehmooleh in order to create a channel for the water that still flows into the large Lake Dal. Tradition likewise accredits him with the construction of the small temple building that retains his name[8] (Plate 9). The hill on which the Takht-i-Suleiman stands is sacred also to the

Hindus, and today its peak is crowned with a Hindu temple. Meanwhile the Buddhists of Ladakh believe the Throne of Solomon to have been the abode of the saint Padmasambhava, who brought Mahayana Buddhism to Tibet in the eighth century.

The Takht-i-Suleiman of Srinagar is not the only mountain throne of the biblical king in the huge expanse of land that stretches from Palestine to India. In north-western Iran, south of the town of Tabriz, set in an extraordinarily beautiful landscape comparable with the 'Happy Valley', there is another mountain which bears the same name. It is known particularly for its extensive ruins, the oldest sections of which date back to the early first millennium BC. In later times an important Zoroastrian temple of fire was erected here, and in the heyday of the Sassanians – the last pre-Islamic dynasty to rule Persia, from the fourth to the sixth centuries AD – the enormous palace of the Khosraus was built on the mountain. Oriental legend in general affords this mountain an important role. One of the three Wise Men (Magi) from the Orient was said to have died here after his return from Bethlehem, for example.

On Solomon's death in around 930 BC, his son Rehoboam succeeded him. But he had scarcely mounted the throne before a revolt broke out against the royal house, led by an exiled Ephraimite, Jeroboam, on the pretext of exorbitant taxation. The rebellion caused a secession: the kingdom was split into two parts. The ten tribes of the north formed an independent state under the name Israel, and made Jeroboam their leader. The two tribes of the south renamed their territory Judah, and continued to be ruled by the House of David. The two opposing brother states existed alongside one another for more than 250 years, as the total population grew to about 300,000.

The partitioned country, during what is often called the Age of the Two Kingdoms, suffered both internal strife and a number of invasions by more powerful neighbouring states. Eventually Israel, under the rule of Jehu and his descendants (845–747 BC), was first occupied for three years by the Assyrians, led by Sargon II, and finally overrun when its capital, Samaria, was captured in 722 BC. Judah held out for another hundred years as a vassal state paying tribute, until the Babylonian king Nebuchadnezzar finally took Jerusalem and destroyed it in 587 BC, so putting an end also to the state of Judah. The conquerors forcibly expelled the population. The deportation of the two tribes that made up the southern kingdom, Judah and Benjamin, was initially deferred for a time, but in due course Nebuchadnezzar had them hauled off into exile in

Babylon. After more than fifty years there, about half of all the deportees were permitted to return to their native land by Cyrus II, King of the Medes and Persians, in 535 BC.

The ten tribes that the Assyrians had deported some 130 years earlier from the northern state of Israel, who constituted very much the greater part of the Hebrew people, were overtaken by a very different fate. Most of them left for the East, and were never heard of in Palestine again. 'So was Israel carried away out of their own land . . . unto this day' (2 Kings 17:23). Numbering many thousands, they entered history as 'the ten lost tribes of Israel', and are even now often described as having altogether vanished without trace. But there are many clear indications that most of these 'lost tribes of Israel', after centuries of homeless wandering and administrative turmoil, finally arrived at their Promised Land, the 'land of the fathers' – northern India, where they have enjoyed peace and tranquillity to the present day.

The Flood in Kashmir

According to the chronology of the Bible, Abraham was a direct descendant of Noah, the man chosen by God to be the only person to survive the Flood with his family. The biblical account makes no reference to the origins of Abraham's father, simply listing a genealogy right back to Noah and the time when the great Flood occurred. A layer of clay two to three metres in breadth was actually discovered by archaeologists excavating in the area around Ur in Mesopotamia, and there were pottery fragments both above and below the clay. But the layer proves no more than that there once was a serious outbreak of flooding in the district around Ur.

A document in cuneiform from Nineveh describes the end of this catastrophe: 'All mankind had turned to clay. The land had become as flat as a roof.'

This layer of clay has been seen as evidence of the great Flood of the Bible, and it would fit very neatly into history as presented by the Bible were it not for the fact that archaeologists estimate the date of this flood at about 4000 BC. But the nomadic Semitic tribes and their flocks had certainly not reached the land of the two rivers by that time.[9] So they could not have survived this flood later to give their eyewitness testimony to it. The Flood of the biblical account must have been a different one.

The Flood actually represents something of a universal tradition, recounted in the mythology of almost every race. There have been many Ice Ages on the Earth, and no doubt catastrophic inundations arising from various causes have been equally numerous.

The Sumerian *Epic of Gilgamesh* was discovered around the beginning of the twentieth century in the ruins of the ancient library of Nineveh, written in cuneiform on tablets of baked clay. One of its heroes, Utnapishtim, the Sumerian Noah, is described as surviving a great flood caused by an arbitrary act of the gods. As in the Bible, a man builds a ship following a divine warning, and in this way survives a flood, which then destroys all life around him.

Alexander von Humboldt mentions the same legend among the Peruvians, and in one account of the Flood in Polynesia, the hero is even called Noa. More than 250 versions of the legend of the Flood have been recorded worldwide. But which is the Flood of the biblical account?

Because the Vedas of India are without doubt the oldest traditions in the history of humanity, it would seem logical to assume that the Vedic account of the Flood represents the very first Flood narrative to be passed down. The texts give a complex description of the event:

> The gods had decided to cleanse the world with an enormous flood, but Manu, the great seer and sage, was to be exempted in order to preserve the human race. The god Vishnu thereupon took on an Earthly incarnation for the first time as an avatar, in the form of the fish Matsya, and revealed himself to Manu on the bank of a river. The fish warned Manu that the Earth was soon to be submerged, and that everyone living on it would perish. He ordered the sage to build a ship to carry himself and his family, as well as the seven great *Rishis* (seers), the seeds of every plant, and one pair of each kind of animal. And he was also to take the Vedas, to ensure that the sacred texts were preserved. Just as the construction of the ship was completed, the great rains began, the rivers burst their banks, and Vishnu as the fish positioned himself at the prow of the boat, his horn above the water. Manu fastened a rope to the horn, and the fish pulled the ship safely through the raging elements until they found shelter on the peaks of the Himalayan mountains (cf Genesis 6–8).

The Vedic Flood lasted 40 days – a duration that coincides exactly with that described in the account of the Flood in Genesis.

The German word for the Flood is *Sintflut*, the first element of which has an obscure etymology. Most authorities generally derive it from Old High German *sint*, meaning 'total', so Sintflut corresponds to 'total flood'. (Modern German has the alternative form *Sündflut*, a later corruption with the apparent, but not altogether irrelevant, meaning 'flood of sin'.)

But there is another possible etymology. *Sindhu* is the old name of the powerful river to which the subcontinent of India owes its name: the Indus.[10] In ancient times, 'India' referred to the lands beyond the Indus, including what are now Tibet and Mongolia. Later, the land on the southern and western side of the river as far as modern Iran were also included in the term 'India'.

Seen from the West, the Sindhu/Indus is the largest and most powerful river to be crossed on the way to India. It flows from north to south through what is now Pakistan, and out via a colossal delta into the Arabian Sea. 'The other side of the river', where Abraham came from,[11] might perhaps have been the land beyond the Indus, which serves as a natural barrier between India and the West.

The river also gave its name to the area called Sind, now the most southerly province of Pakistan, its capital at Karachi. The province is 140,000 square kilometres in area, and extremely fertile due to constant flooding, and is accordingly very well populated.

There is yet another river with the name Sindh in the province of Kashmir in northern India. This other Sindh is not as big as its better-known twin, but is certainly perhaps as important to a derivation for the German word Sintflut. This Sindh flows in the north of the Kashmir valley through the very area visible from Mount Nebo, from which Moses is said to have glimpsed the Promised Land before dying (Plate 15).

The source of this Sindh is not far from the Cave of Amarnath, which is especially sacred to the Hindus, and which attracts thousands of pilgrims for the night of the August full moon each year. Legend has it that the god Shiva initiated his consort Parvati in the mysteries of Creation (!) at this spot.

Three days of walking following the course of the river downstream brings a visitor to the village of Sonamarg, the 'Golden meadow', still a good 2,600 metres up. Notovitch passed through here before crossing over the 3500-metres-high Zoji-la Pass to the plateauland of Ladakh. The path from Sonamarg follows the river all the way down to Srinagar, 84 kilometres on, leading over ancient wooden bridges, past small villages set among lush green meadows and fruit trees bearing apricots, pears and apples. Artistically carved windowframes and decorated wooden roofs bear witness to the prosperity of the region. The farther towards Srinagar, the more luxuriant and fertile the valley seems, vast terraces of rice and corn fields appearing on both sides. Finally, the valley opens right out at a place called Kangan.

All in all, Kashmir is like one enormous Garden of Eden – and its enormous marshy areas and large, shallow lakes are evidence of a gigantic flood in times long ago.

Kashmir, the 'Promised Land'

According to the Bible, Paradise – the place where humankind was created, lay to the East. 'And the Lord God planted a garden eastward in Eden; and there he put the man whom he had formed' (Genesis 2:8). The next few verses specify the geographical location of the Garden of Eden further by mentioning four rivers: 'And a river went out of Eden to water the garden; and from thence it was parted, and became into four heads' (Genesis 2:10). In Mesopotamia, the land 'between the rivers', usually considered to be the Garden of Eden, there are only two rivers (as the region's name implies).

In contrast, northern India can boast five great rivers, all tributaries of the Indus (Sindh) that spread over a vast area, giving the region its name – the land of five rivers, the Punjab. Since the partition of India in 1947, the province has been divided between the two countries India (Bharat) and Pakistan. The five tributaries of the Indus to the west of the river are the Jhelum, the Chenab, the Ravi, the Beas and the Sutlej. One of the earliest attested civilizations in India was based in the Punjab region – the Indus culture, dating from around 3000 BC – and in Kashmir archaeologists have even found traces of a civilization going back 50,000 years.

The name Kashmir (Sanskrit *Kashmira*; Kashmiri *Kashir*) has been etymologically derived in at least three different ways.

Cush (Kush) was a grandson of Noah, whose descendants were to populate the Earth, giving their names to the countries in which they settled. The descendants of Cush have traditionally, and for more than two thousand years, been associated with Ethiopia, but Genesis also says of the waters flowing out of Eden, 'And the name of the second river is Gihon: the same is it that compasseth the whole land of Ethiopia' (Genesis 2:13). Virtually every single name in the Bible has been subject to considerable phonetic and orthographic modification through the influence of other languages. So the 'Kush' of the Bible could easily have become 'Kash'. In Farsi (Persian), *mir* means something of value, a jewel; in Russian, *mir* is a region occupied by a community; and in Turkish, *Mir* is a title of respect.

Another interpretation centres on the Hebrew word *kasher* (also *kashir* or, as generally in English, *kosher*), which means 'approvable', especially in relation to food. According to Jewish law[12] only animals that have been ritually slaughtered and bled can be used for food. The Jews have always distinguished themselves from others by their dietary regulations, and so were called Kasher, as was the land that they came to inhabit. Later, Kasher turned into Kashmir. The Kashmiris of today stil call their country Kashir, and its inhabitants Kashur.

Yet another etymological possibility turns on the name of a Vedic seer, Kashyapa, who is said to have lived in the region in ancient times. Kashyapa means 'turtle' in Sanskrit. According to the cosmology of the day, the slightly rounded surface of the Earth bordered by the oceans was the back of a turtle swimming in water. In some Vedic texts the name Kashyap was also given to God the Creator, and 'Kashyap-Mar' – which became Kashmir, according to this derivation – would then mean 'the land of God'.

The Ten Lost Tribes of Israel

It was in the nineteenth century – as enthusiastic colonization spread apace – that the West began to take a more serious interest in the countries of the Far East, and reports began to filter in from several Western explorers describing their astonishment at encountering tribes all over the north-west of India who were clearly of Jewish descent.

The missionary doctor Joseph Wolff, for example, reported in his two-volume work *Narrative of a Mission to Bokhara in the Years 1843–1845:*[13]

All the Jews of Turkistan assert that the Turkomauns are the descendants of Togarmah, one of the sons of Gomer, mentioned in Genesis 10:3 . . . The Jews in Bokhara are 10,000 in number. The Chief Rabbi assured me that Bokhara is the Habor, and Balkh the Halah, of 2 Kings 17:6, but that in the reign of Genghis Khan they lost all their written accounts.

The tradition is an old one at Bokhara, that some of the Ten Tribes are in China . . . Some Affghauns claim a descent from Israel. According to them, Affghaun was the nephew of Asaph, the son of Berachia, who built the Temple of Solomon. The descendants of this Affghaun, being Jews, were carried into Babylon by Nebuchadnezzar, from whence they were removed to the mountain of Ghoree, in Affghaunistan, but in the time of Mohammed turned Mohammedans. They exhibit a book, *Majmooa Alansab*, or 'Collection of Genealogies' written in Persian . . . Captain Riley, I was surprised to find, looked upon the Affgauns as of Jewish descent.

And finally Wolff writes: 'I spent six days with the children of Rechab [Bani Arhab] . . . With them were children of Israel of the tribe of Dan, who reside near Terim in Hatramawt.'[14]

G. T. Vigne, a French travelling scholar and member of the Royal Geographical Society, in *A Personal Account of a Voyage to Chuzin, Kabul, in Afghanistan* wrote:[15]

The father of Ermiah was the father of the Afghans. He was a contemporary of Nebuchadnezzar, called himself Beni Israel and had forty sons. But a descendant in the thirty-fourth generation was called Kys, and he was a contemporary of the prophet Mohammed.

Dr James Bryce and Dr Keith Johnson note in their *Comprehensive Description of Geography*,[16] under the heading Afghanistan, that the Afghanis 'trace their lineage back to King Saul of Israel and call themselves "Ben-i-Israel".'

According to A. Burnes, the Afghan legend of Nebuchadnezzar confirms that the Israelites were transplanted from the Holy Land to Ghore, in north-western Kabul province. They remained Jewish until AD 682, when the Arab sheikh Khaled-ibn-Abdalla converted them to Islam.

To the works quoted above could be added a great deal more literary evidence that focuses on the settlement by the Israelites in the region of Afghanistan and surrounding territories. One of the most important contributions is *The Lost Tribes* by Dr George Moore,[17] who found many Hebrew inscriptions on archaelogical sites in India. Quite close to Taxila, now in Sirkap, Pakistan, a stone was dug up that bears an inscription in Aramaic, the language that Jesus spoke (Plate 17).

Latest research in the Pakistani part of Kashmir has brought to light thousands of rock inscriptions and pictures dating from the prehistoric, early Buddhist, and post-Christian periods. The discovery site is in the valley of the upper Indus, where the famous

1 Nicolai Notovitch

2 The Hemis Monastery is located at an altitude of nearly 4000 metres amid the Himalayan mountains, some 34 kilometres away from the capital of Ladakh, Leh.

3 The books in the monastery library are made up of loose pages bound together with bands of coloured silk and protected by a pair of wooden covers.

4 Two pages from Dr Marx's diary, on which it is recorded that Notovitch was treated by him for toothache.

5 *The Buddha Maitreya (the One who is to come) at Mulbek, where Islamic Kashmir meets Buddhist Ladakh.*

6 *The view from the 'Throne of Solomon' over Srinagar showing the houseboats and the 'floating gardens' along the banks of Lake Dal.*

7 and 8 The excavations at Haran, 12 kilometres north of Srinagar.

9 The author with Professor Hassnain in his garden in Srinagar, the Kashmiri capital.

10 and 11 Frescoes in an Egyptian tomb. Above: An Egyptian official receives Semitic nomads. The Semitic tribespeople are distinguishable from the Egyptians by their lighter skin colour and different profile. Joseph came to Egypt with a group like this.

12 *The tombstone of Moses. Its custodian, the wali rishi, crouching beside it, claims to be of Jewish descent.*

13 Moses radiating beams of light (rather like horns), much as Bacchus is said to have done. Sculpture by Michelangelo.

14 *The plain as it widens outside the town of Bandipur (formerly Behatpoor and Beth-peor), with the marshy Lake Wular.*

15 *The smaller River Sindh, and the flooded Kashmir valley in the background.*

caravan trail known as the Silk Route once passed. Among these inscriptions were some in Hebrew, dated by the researchers to the ninth century AD – the time when Islam was just beginning to penetrate through into India.[18]

The eleventh-century Arab historian Biruni wrote that at that time no foreigners were being allowed into Kashmir, other than Hebrews.

As early as in the nineteenth century, a society was founded in England that had as its aim the rediscovery of the ten lost tribes of Israel. It was called The Identification Society of London, and most works on the subject by British authors have been issued by the society. There is no need here to list the more than 30 authors and their works which prove that the Kashmiri population is of Israelite descent.

Of more immediate interest is the fact that well over 300 of the names of geographical features, of towns, regions and estates, and of tribes, clans, families and individuals in the Old Testament can be matched with linguistically related or phonetically similar names in Kashmir and its environs.

Name in Kashmir	Name in the Bible	Bible Reference
Amal	Amal	1 Chronicles 7:35
Asheria	Asher	Genesis 30:13
Attai	Attai	1 Chronicles 12:11
Bal	Baal	1 Chronicles 5:5
Bula	Balah	Joshua 19:3
Bera	Beerah	1 Chronicles 5:6
Gabba	Gaba	Joshua 18:24
Gaddi	Gaddi	Numbers 13:11
Gani	Guni	1 Chronicles 7:13
Gomer	Gomer	Genesis 10:2

and so on

Place in Kashmir	(Province)	Biblical Name	Bible Reference
Agurn	(Kulgam)	Agur	Proverbs 30:1
Ajas	(Srinagar)	Ajah	Genesis 36:24
Amariah	(Srinagar)	Amariah	1 Chronicles 23:19
Amonu	(Anantnag)	Amon1	Kings 22:26
Aror	(Awantipur)	Aroer	Joshua 12:2
Balpura	(Awantipur)	Baal-peor	Numbers 25:3
Behatpoor	(Handwara)	Beth-peor	Deuteronomy 34:6
Birsu	(Awantipur)	Birsha	Genesis 14:2
Harwan	(Srinagar)	Haran	2 Kings 19:12

and so on

The inhabitants of Kashmir are different from the other peoples of India in every respect. Their way of life, their behaviour, their morals, their character, their clothing, their language, customs and habits are all of a type that might be described as typically Israelite. Like present-day Israelis, the Kashmiris do not use fat for frying and baking: they only use oil. Most Kashmiris like boiled fish, called *fari*, eaten in remembrance of the time before their Exodus from Egypt – 'We remember the fish, which we did eat in Egypt freely' (Numbers 11:5).

Butchers' knives in Kashmir are made in the half-moon shape typical of the Israelites, and even the rudders of the boat people (Hanjis) are of the similarly typical heart shape.

The men wear distinctive caps on their heads. The clothing of the old women of Kashmir (Pandtanis) is very similar to that of Jewish women, and like them they also wear headscarves and laces. Like young Jewish girls, the girls of Kashmir dance in two facing columns with linked arms, moving together forwards and backwards to the rhythm. They call their songs *rof*.

After bearing a child, a woman of Kashmir observes forty days' seclusion for purification; this, too, is a Jewish custom. Many of the older graves in Kashmir are aligned in an east-west orientation, whereas Islamic graves normally point north-south. A great number of such graves are to be found in Haran, Rajpura, Syed Bladur Sahib, Kukar Nagh and Awantipura. In the cemetery at Bijbihara, the place where the bath and stone of Moses are located, there is also an old grave that has an inscription in Hebrew.

Sixty-five kilometres to the south of Srinagar, and just a few kilometres from the 'Bathplace of Moses', is the Temple of Martand. This impressive building's outside walls, which date from the eighth century, feature carvings of a number of Hindu deities. But together with these parts of the structure that derive from more recent times, considerably older walls and ruins have been discovered, which have yet to be dated accurately, but which are clearly many centuries older than the Hindu temple built over them (Plates 21 and 22).

Could this perhaps be the temple that a man 'whose appearance was like the appearance of brass' showed to the prophet Ezekiel during the time of the Babylonian Exile (586–538 BC)? In fact the Temple of Martand does stand on a 'very high mountain' unknown to Ezekiel: a Himalayan peak. And at its side 'a spring' gushes forth, to flow into the Jhelum farther downstream (Ezekiel 40–43).

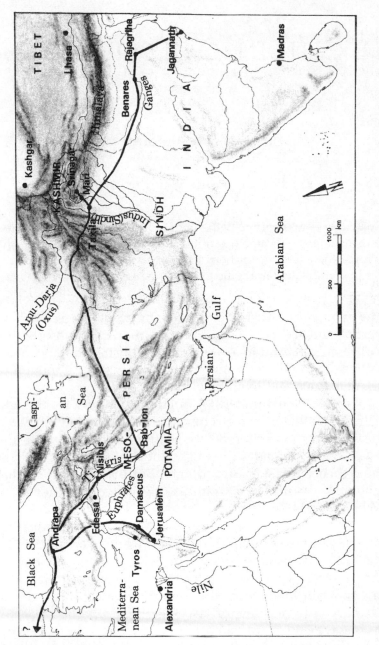

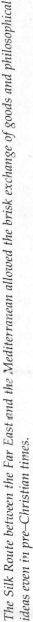

The Silk Route between the Far East and the Mediterranean allowed the brisk exchange of goods and philosophical ideas even in pre–Christian times.

Chapter Four

THE CHILDHOOD OF JESUS

The Wise Men's Star

In the Gospel According to Matthew, in the second chapter, we read:

> Now when Jesus was born in Bethlehem of Judea in the days of Herod the king, behold, there came wise men from the East to Jerusalem,
>
> Saying, Where is he that is born King of the Jews? for we have seen his star in the East, and are come to worship him.
>
> (Matthew 2:1–2).

Had some extraordinary astronomical event really taken place that night there would also have been some mention of it in contemporary secular records. And in any case, any unusual conjunction of planets in the night sky, whenever reported, is simple enough to check up on mathematically today.

Even Johannes Kepler undertook such calculations. He thought that the star of Bethlehem might have been a nova that appeared as the result of a conjunction between Jupiter and Saturn in the year 7 BC. His idea of a nova (literally a 'new' star) was rejected as a workable theory by later astronomers. But the conjunction that Kepler thought was the cause of it has itself come to be generally accepted by many as the Bethlehem event. In the course of the year 7 BC, the conjunction of Saturn and Jupiter in the constellation Pisces occurred no fewer than three times. (Coincidentally, Pisces corresponds to 'Fish', and it was a fish that became a symbol for Christ and was a secret sign of recognition among the early Christian communities.) Such an encounter in this sign of the Zodiac occurs only once every 794 years: everybody who saw them must have been captivated for months by the impressive sight of the two planets in such close proximity as to appear in the night sky as a double star of great brilliance.[1]

In 1925 the Orientalist Paul Schnabel succeeded in deciphering a cuneiform slate almost 2000 years old that had been found at the observatory at Sippar, on the Euphrates. It contained a careful description of the astronomical event of the year 7 BC – the great conjunction between the planets Jupiter and Saturn in the constellation Pisces.[2]

Towards the end of 8 BC, Jupiter and Saturn were visible only after twilight in the western sky, some 16° or so apart, Jupiter moving out of the constellation Aquarius and Saturn already in Pisces. In February of 7 BC, both planets disappeared in the rays of the sun and remained occluded for several weeks. The astrologers of the Middle East impatiently awaited the reappearance of Jupiter, expecting it to be an outstandingly spectacular occasion at dawn on the thirteenth of Adaru in the year 304 of the Seleucid era – or 16 March 7 BC. Thereafter they watched Jupiter move ever nearer to Saturn, until the two planets finally 'touched' at the end of the month of Airu (29 May 7 BC). This conjunction, at which both Jupiter and Saturn had an altitude of 21° in Pisces, separated by only 1° in declination and with precisely the same azimuth, was to recur twice more in the same year in much the same way, on 3 October and 5 December.

Both planets were visible from dusk until dawn, reaching their maximum altitude at around midnight. As the sun sank in the west, the planets rose in the east, and as they in turn vanished below the western horizon, the dawning sun reappeared in the east. At the beginning of the year, therefore, the pair of planets emerged from occlusion by the light of the sun (a heliacal rising), and at the end of the year they once more disappeared into the sun's rays (a heliacal setting). Every night of the year Jupiter and Saturn were visible, never leaving each other's company by more than 3°. Such a sight was not to be seen again in the Zodiacal sign of Pisces for another eight hundred years.

In the Gospel According to Matthew, the star is mentioned three times. The wise men first say, ' . . . for we have seen his star in the East . . .' The original Greek text, for 'East', uses the word *anatole*. Historical linguists have discovered that *anatole*, used in the singular, had a meaning of particular astronomical significance. It referred to the appearance of the Morning Star, a star (or planet) that preceded the sun at dawn, rising in the east shortly before sunrise. Used in the plural, the same word had a geographical connotation, and referred instead to the land of the East, the Orient. So three wise men could indeed have followed the celestial phenomenon from the east to the west.

The second reference to the astronomical event in Matthew's Gospel also bears a special meaning in Greek: 'Then Herod, when he had privily called the wise men, inquired of them diligently what time the star appeared' (Matthew 2:7). The Greek verb meaning 'appeared' was also an astronomical technical term relating to the first appearance of a Morning Star in the east. Contemporary popular belief held that each person's 'own star' rose at the moment of his or her birth. What Herod's question implies is that the birth must have occurred a good while before. According to the Babylonian calendar, Jupiter had appeared to rise during the last month of year 304 of the Seleucid era. The year 305 (6 BC) began with the spring month of Nisannu, which also marked the beginning of the Jewish New Year. When the wise men arrived in Jerusalem, the conjunction between Jupiter and Saturn would have been well into its second year, and Jesus – probably born in 7 BC – would then have been almost two years old. It was presumably for this reason that Herod massacred all the children of certain communities up to the age of two.

What impelled these mysterious sages of the East (the Greek word *anatole* is in the plural here) to undergo the rigours of a journey that lasted many months, perhaps even two years on the outward leg alone, and that entailed such great sacrifice? Where did they come from, and why did they go on searching so persistently for a small boy? Traditional theology provides no solution to the question of who these 'three wise men' actually were.

Who Were the Three Wise Men?

In the ancient Greek text, the wise men are called *magoi* (from Old Persian *magus*). The Magi of the Bible story were first elevated to kingship in the sixth century by Caesarius of Arles. In the ninth century, these 'kings' were given the spuriously coined names Caspar, Melchior and Balthasar. The earliest sources do not actually specify how many Magi there were, but their number has been fixed at three ever since the days of Origen,[3] perhaps because there were three gifts given.

What is certain is that the Magi came on a long journey from the East, and that they were well versed in 'magical' practices, were expert astronomers, and were by no means poor.

This means that the story of the star's coming to a standstill immediately over the stable of a rustic inn, in which a newborn infant was lying only a few hours old, is just religious myth. It is much more likely that the child, by then almost two years of age, was sought out and visited at the home of people who were aware of the divine stature of the boy. The circle evidently did not enjoy the favour of Herod, however, because when the king heard what the three were seeking, he was extremely shocked, and 'all Jerusalem with him'. Whether the child could perhaps have been seen as the messianic Saviour whose coming was awaited by the secret sects of Qumran, the Nazarenes and the Essenes, is a theme that is taken up later in this book. Nonetheless, it is now known that the monastery of Qumran, close to the Dead Sea, was deserted for ten years during the rule of Herod the Great – that is, that the mysterious and esoteric sect was proscribed for those years. Such an enforced ban could account for the king's wrath, and for his attempt to ensure that the child was killed.

Could the members of the forbidden sect perhaps have retained links with their brethren in India, with the lost tribes of the House of Israel?

The apocryphal *Gospel of the Nazarenes*[4] contains the following passage:

> When Joseph raised his eyes and looked out, he saw a group of travellers approaching, coming directly towards the cave; and he said, 'I will get up and go to receive them.' Immediately after going out, Joseph said to Simon, 'The people approaching would seem to be astrologers, for look how they are constantly peering up into the sky and talking among themselves. But they seem also to be foreign, for their appearance is different from our own; their clothing is very rich and their skin quite dark, and they are wearing caps on their heads, and their gowns look soft to me, and their legs are covered too.'

At this distance in time it is well-nigh impossible to prove that the Magi came either from Persia or from India. Yet it is absolutely amazing how much the story of the three wise men corresponds with accounts of the methods by which reincarnations[5] of great Buddhist dignitaries are located in Tibet after their demise, even to this day. The way in which such a search is carried out, following ancient and traditional ritual, is described in the present Dalai Lama's own accounts of his 'discovery' as a little boy,[6] and in the book by the Austrian Heinrich Harrer, who spent seven years at the court of the god-king in Lhasa.[7]

Just How Do You Locate a Reincarnation?

Shortly before his death in 1933, the thirteenth Dalai Lama trans-
mitted some indications of the place and time of his next reincarnation. Every day his body was positioned in the Potala Palace,
facing southward in the traditional seated posture. But one morning his face was seen to be turned to the east. And on a wooden
pedestal a short distance north-east of the shrine on which his
body was seated, a star-shaped fungal plant appeared in a sudden
and mysterious manner. On receiving these signs, the head lamas
performed a magic ritual during which they interrogated a monk
who had been put into a trance, and whose charge it was to act as
an oracle. The monk cast a white ceremonial scarf in an easterly
direction, and strange cloud formations appeared to the north-east
over Lhasa. But after this the lama magicians received no further
signs for another two years. Finally, the acting head lama (the
'regent lama') was inspired to make a pilgrimage to the holy lake
of Lhamoi Latso, near Ch' Khor Gyal, 144 kilometres away.
Tibetans believe that the future is mirrored in the clear waters of
this mountain lake. After days of preparatory meditation, the
regent lama had a vision of a three-storey monastery with gilded
roofs, alongside which was a small Chinese farmhouse with beau-
tifully decorated gables and green roofing-tiles. Superimposed
over this scene were the three Tibetan letters Ah, Ka and Ma. A
detailed description of the vision was committed to paper and
kept strictly secret. Full of gratitude for the divine instructions, and
with complete confidence, the regent lama returned to Lhasa, and
preparations were made in the palace for the forthcoming search.

Most important to these preparations were the pronouncements
of the astrologers, without whose calculations no significant moves
could be made at all. At last, in 1937, various expeditions were
despatched from Lhasa to seek out the holy child according to the
heavenly omens, in the direction indicated. Each group included
wise and worthy lamas of highly distinguished status in the theoc-
racy. In addition to their servants, each group took costly gifts with
them, some of them from among the possessions of the deceased.
The gifts were meant as tokens of worship for the new Dalai Lama,
but also constituted a test by which the identity of the new reincarnation might be verified.

The dead Dalai Lama could theoretically be reborn many thousands of kilometres from his previous dwelling-place – and that,
indeed, turned out to be the case with the fourteenth Dalai Lama.

The search led well beyond the borders of central Tibet into the district of Amdo in the region of Dokham, which was under Chinese administration. The birthplace of the reformer of Lamaism, Tsong Kapa, there were a number of monasteries in the area.

The expedition found several potential candidates, but none of them precisely matched the details of the vision or the astrological pronouncements. Finally, during the winter, near the village of Taktser, the team arrived at the three-storey monastery of Kumbum, ornate in its gilded roofs and adjacent to a charming little farmhouse with a turquoise roof and carved gables. It all tallied exactly with the regent lama's vision.

Two lamas of high rank disguised themselves as servants, and a young monk of their party played the role of their master. The disguise was meant to conceal the actual purpose of their visit for the time being, to avoid unnecessary commotion and allow the delegation to inspect the place in a tranquil atmosphere. The monks entered the house with two officials from the local monastery. The two high clerics – one of whom was Lama Kewtsang Rinpoche from the monastery of Sera in Lhasa – were led into the kitchen in their assumed role of servants, while the other monk was shown into the main room. In the farmhouse kitchen, the children of the family were playing, and as soon as the disguised Lama Rinpoche took his seat in the room a little two-year-old boy rushed forward and plumped himself down on the lama's lap. The revered monk was wearing a string of prayer-beads that had belonged to the deceased Dalai Lama, and the boy seemed to recognize it and tugged at it as though he wanted to have it. The lama promised to give the boy the beads if he could guess who his visitor was – whereupon the boy immediately gave the answer '*Sera-aga*', 'The Lama of Sera' in the local dialect! The boy's ability to recognize a lama disguised as a servant was surprising enough, but that he somehow knew that the lama came from Sera astonished even these monks, who were accustomed to miraculous events. The lama then asked the boy what their alleged 'master' was called, and he replied 'Lobsang'. The servant's name was indeed Lobsang Tsewang.

The high-ranking lamas spent the entire day observing the child, restraining themselves as best they could from according him the profound reverence that they were convinced was his due, for they were quite sure that they had at last found the reincarnation. But they left the next day, to return with all the other members of the expedition a few days later. It was only when the child's parents espied the procession of high dignitaries in full costume approaching their humble home that they realized that their son must be a reincarnation. In the neighbouring monastery of Kumbum a particularly holy lama had recently died, and the farmers believed that their darling boy might be his reincarnation. One of the farming couple's elder sons had in fact already undergone a test to investigate whether it was he who was the reincarnation.

It is not unusual for such reincarnated children to remember objects and people known to them from their previous life. Some are even able to recite scriptures that they have not been taught. In the isolated tranquillity of Tibet there has always been an abundance of evidence that former lives may overlap into the present. In the West, however, such accounts rarely surface because Westerners tend to belittle the very idea that a dead person may be reborn in a new body.

The four chief *Bonpos* of the delegation from Lhasa then proceeded to carry out the prescribed tests. First they offered the child two almost identical strings of black prayer-beads, one of which had belonged to the thirteenth Dalai Lama. Without hesitation, the child chose the correct one, hung it around his neck, and danced gaily around the room with it. The test was repeated with several more strings of precious prayer-beads. Then the delegation offered the boy two different ritual drums – one large and ornate, decorated with gold, and a much plainer drum that had once belonged to the deceased Dalai Lama. The boy took the plainer of the drums, and went on to play upon it, beating out a rhythm in precisely the way these drums are used in religious ceremonies. Finally, two walking sticks were presented to the child, and the boy first touched the wrong stick, paused, considered both sticks for a short while, and finally chose the stick that had belonged to the god-king. The spectators, who had been surprised at the boy's apparent hesitancy, were at once told by the Rinpoche how the second stick had also been used for a time by the thirteenth Dalai Lama before he gave it to Lama Kewtsang.

(There is a clear parallel here between such a presentation of the deceased king's precious possessions and the costly gifts brought by the Magi from the East to the boy Jesus. It is also obvious that a child must have attained an age of at least around two years before being ready for such a test.)

To these proofs was added an interpretation of the three letters that the regent lama had seen in his vision. It was surmised that the first letter, Ah, stood for Amdo, the district in which the boy was found. The two letters Ka and Ma were taken to refer to a small lamasery on the mountain above the village of Taktser, Ka(r)ma Rolpai Dorje – where the thirteenth Dalai Lama had stayed some years before when travelling back from China. At the time, the thirteenth Dalai Lama's visit had created something of a sensation over the whole region, and among the people blessed by their god-king was the father of the new reincarnation, then just nine years old. Moreover, the former Dalai Lama was said to have gazed at the farmhouse where his reincarnation was later discovered, and to have remarked somewhat wistfully how beautiful and serene the place was. It is also reported that the Dalai Lama had left behind a pair of boots in the small lamasery – an action that might, in the event, be said to hold a certain foresighted symbolism.

The delegates were totally satisfied with every confirmatory detail: the reincarnation had been found. Announcing the discovery and appending the evidence, they sent a coded telegram to Lhasa via China and India, and by return received instructions that everything must henceforward be organized with the utmost secrecy in order not to jeopardize matters by getting on the wrong side of the Chinese authorities. In particular, because the search had taken place on Chinese soil it was essential to pull the wool over the eyes of the Chinese officials to get the young king out of their charge. The governor of the province, Ma Pufang, was told that the boy was to be taken to Lhasa because he was one of many possible successors to the deceased Dalai Lama. Ma Pufang first demanded 100,000 Chinese dollars for releasing the child, and when he found this sum readily forthcoming demanded a further payment of 300,000 dollars. The worst the delegation feared was that if they were to admit having found the true god-king, China might insist on sending some troops with him to Lhasa 'for his protection'.

Again the parallels with the similar situation in Jerusalem two thousand years ago are striking: there the divine child had to be smuggled out of the country in order to avoid the Roman governor of the province, Herod. 'Then Herod, when he saw that he was mocked of the wise men, was exceeding wroth' (Matthew 2:16).

For security reasons, all correspondence between Amdo and Lhasa was conveyed by couriers, which always took several months. So it was a further two years before the caravan with the delegation, the child and his family, were finally able to set out for

Lhasa. The trek to the border of central Tibet lasted many months, but when they arrived it was to find a cabinet minister and his entourage there to welcome them, and to find the choice of the Dalai Lama confirmed in a letter from the acting regent lama. It was not until that moment that the parents of the boy realized that their son was no less a figure than the new ruler of all Tibet.

Very comparable with this well-attested story of how the Dalai Lama was located is another case that happened quite recently.

Tibetan scroll pictures, gilded statues of Buddha and fresh flowers adorn the bedroom of the little Spanish boy Osel. He sits on velvet cushions embroidered with brocades and wears a splendid little jacket. Tibetan Buddhists around the world are convinced that the two-year-old Osel Hita Torres is actually the reincarnation of the Lama Thubten Yeshe, who died in 1984 after a heart attack. During his lifetime he founded thirty-one Buddhist centres in the Western world, including one in Spain, the country in which he had most enjoyed staying.

Near the city of Granada is the Buddhist centre called Osel Ling ('Town of the little light'), which is run by Paco and Maria Hita, a bricklayer and a postage-stamp dealer, who are the parents of little Osel. The boy was barely seven months old when Lama Zopa, a disciple of Thubten Yeshe, recognized him as the reincarnation of his departed mentor. Lama Zopa had been given the task of searching for the departed soul by the Dalai Lama, after Thubten Yeshe had appeared to his disciple as a child in a dream. The Dalai Lama himself expressed a wish to see the boy, so Paco and Maria travelled with Osel to India, where he was set the prescribed tests. In one of them he was shown a number of strings of prayer-beads, some very precious, and confidently chose the one that had previously belonged to Lama Thubten Yeshe.

On 19 March 1987, the Spanish boy – then two years old – was ceremonially enthroned as a reborn lama.

Since then, Osel has attended a monastic school in Nepal. His education will take forty years altogether, and only then can he assume the role of abbot of the Nepalese monastery of Kopan as successor to Yeshe. Osel is the first reincarnation of recent times to be found outside the usual areas of Buddhist culture.

The Flight to Egypt

After the wise men of the East had located the child Jesus near Jerusalem, his father Joseph received an instruction from God: 'Arise, and take the young child and his mother, and flee into Egypt, and be thou there until I bring thee word: for Herod will seek the young child to destroy him' (Matthew 2:13). The route of the flight would probably have taken them via Hebron to Beersheba, and from there across the desert to the Mediterranean. Only here, on the border of Egypt, were they safe. At the time, some one million Jews were living in Egypt – two hundred thousand in Alexandria alone. By custom the country had for some time been a haven for Jews, who lived in what were virtually colonies complete with synagogues, schools and everything else to make an expatriate feel at home.

The massacre of the innocents perpetrated by Herod and referred to in the Gospels is confirmed by a report written during Jesus' lifetime by members of the sect of Essenes. The sect was apparently the object of Herod's oppression, and was obliged to operate in secret in their own country. 'The next king was an upstart not of the priestly class, an audacious and godless person. He killed both old and young, and the entire land was filled with a terrible dread of him' (Ass. Mos. 6:22).

Professor Hassnain once told me that Buddhist missionary schools – *viharas* – existed in Alexandria even before the Christian era. My Chinese Buddhist handbook defines a *vihara* as a place 'which is either an academy, a school or a temple, and serves in the study or practice of Buddhism. Such buildings were ideally constructed with red sandalwood (chandana), consisted of thirty-two rooms, each of which were eight "tala-trees" high; with a garden, a park, a bathing pool and tea kitchen, amply furnished and adorned with wall-hangings, and well stocked with provisions, beds, mattresses, and all the necessary comforts.'[9] It is thus quite conceivable that Jesus was introduced to the wisdom of Eastern philosophy from early childhood by Buddhist scholars in Alexandria. Thorough academic instruction of this kind could go quite a way towards explaining, after all, how Jesus was able to astonish the priests in the Temple of Jerusalem with his wisdom as a mere twelve-year-old boy. 'And all that heard him were astonished at his understanding and answers' (Luke 2:47).

In those days, about twelve was the age at which it was customary for a boy to get married. Jesus succeeded in avoiding this fate too. He was now old enough to continue his studies in the place that might well have been the home of his real spiritual fathers – in India.

Not until ten full years had passed since the death of the hated usurper Herod (which occurred shortly before Passover in the year 4 BC) was Jesus able to return to the land of his birth without danger:

> But when Herod was dead, behold, an angel of the Lord appeareth in a dream to Joseph in Egypt,
>
> Saying, Arise, and take the young child and his mother, and go into the land of Israel: for they are dead which sought the young child's life.
>
> And he arose, and took the young child and his mother, and came into the land of Israel.
>
> But when he heard that Archelaus did reign in Judea in the room of his father Herod, he was afraid to go thither [Archelaus was Ethnarch (local governor) of Judea and Samaria from 4 BC to AD 6 – that is, until the time Jesus was twelve or thirteen years old]: notwithstanding, being warned of God in a dream, he turned aside into the parts of Galilee:
>
> And he came and dwelt in a city called Nazareth: that it might be fulfilled which was spoken by the prophets, He shall be called a Nazarene.

(Matthew 2:19–23)

Chapter Five

EASTERN WISDOM IN THE WEST

The Expansion of Buddhism

The worldwide spread of Buddhism, even before the pre-Christian era, can be fundamentally attributed to the initiative of one of the greatest rulers not only in the history of India but in the history of the world: the Emperor Ashoka, who lived from about 273 to 232 BC. Ashoka was one of the most influential figures, politically, ethically and culturally, of all time. During his reign, the first of the wars between Rome and Carthage spilled over into Europe. Having experienced for himself the obscenities of war while he was a young man, the Emperor determinedly renounced violence, devoting himself instead to the peaceable teachings of Buddhism.

Many of his beneficent laws and decrees have come down to us today preserved in the form of individual inscriptions on the walls of buildings and temples. In one decree, the Emperor give orders that every living being is to be protected: 'All people are my chil dren. Just as I would wish my children to enjoy every blessing and joy that are to be found in heaven and on earth, so I do wish the same for all people.'

Ashoka built no fewer than 84,000 Buddhist monasteries in India, and constructed hospitals for both human and animal patients throughout his enormous empire. He arranged for the convening of the second Buddhist World Council in Pataliputra (corresponding to modern Patna), the capital of his empire, in which thousands of monks took part. And in accordance with the ordinances of Buddha, Ashoka set up the intricate organization by which Buddhist teachings were spread abroad, incidentally sending something of the spirit of India to remote countries at the same time. A supreme patron of proselytism, he despatched Buddhist missionaries not only to all the towns of India and Sri Lanka, but also to Syria, Egypt and Greece via the Silk Route.

The spreading of the teachings of Buddha was one of the obligations that Sakyamuni (the 'sage of the Sakyas', Buddha) himself had imposed on his following:

> Go, O monks, and travel afar, for the benefit and welfare of many, out of compassion for the world, to the advantage and welfare of gods and of mortals. And let not two of you take the same path. Preach the teaching that leads to good . . . Preach it in spirit and in letter. Show in your perfect sinlessness how the religious life should be lived.

The monks lived as beggars, totally reliant on the alms of the ordinary people. They owned nothing more than the clothes on their backs. Their life was one of renunciation, but there was no need for ascetic austerity. The principal occupational requirement was to meditate on the Teachings, and gradually to free themselves from mortal passions and worldly desires. To join the order, a person had only to 'go out into the open', *pravrayja* – both to quit his or her house (and with it the trappings of lay life) and to take up the life of wandering without any personal possessions.

The initiate would then don the yellow robe, have his head shaved, and utter a threefold incantation. The minimum age was seven – the age of Rahula, the Son of the Enlightened One, when he joined the community.

At his initiation, the novice is informed of the four basic rules of monastic life:
- to feed oneself by alms alone;
- to dress oneself in clothes taken up from the dust;
- to stop a while at the foot of trees;
- to heal one's wounds with natural remedies.

Monks led a completely nomadic existence. Scriptural records tell how Buddha and his companions wandered the entire length of the mid-Ganges basin, meditating and preaching the Buddhist teachings, sometimes singly but more often in groups, from town to town and from village to village.

A remarkable parallel may be drawn between this and the sending out of Jesus' disciples, who likewise went out preaching 'unto the nations', in their case in one last final attempt to convince Israel of his message:

> And he called unto him the twelve, and began to send them forth by two and two; and gave them power over unclean spirits;
>
> And commanded them that they should take nothing for their journey, save a staff only; no scrip, no bread, no money in their purse:

But be shod with sandals; and not put on two coats.

And he said unto them, In what place soever ye enter into an house, there abide till ye depart from that place.

And whosoever shall not receive you, nor hear you, when ye depart thence, shake off the dust under your feet for a testimony against them. Verily I say unto you, It shall be more tolerable for Sodom and Gomorrha in the day of judgement, than for that city.

And they went out, and preached that men should repent.

And they cast out many devils, and anointed with oil many that were sick, and healed them.

(Mark 6:7–13)

In this form of Christianity, as in Buddhism, there is no question of conversion by force. The preaching was instead for the salvation of many – the many whom Isaiah (53:11) had foretold would be 'justified' by the knowledge of God's 'righteous servant'.

Documents in Sinhalese relate that shortly after the Council of Haran (now Harwan near Srinagar), which occurred during the time of King Kanishka (the AD mid–100s), missionaries were once more despatched to Kashmir, Gandhara, and Mahisamandala, to Vanavasi, to Yonarattha (the 'Land of the Greeks'), and to Sri Lanka.

In the Musée Borély, in Marseilles, are the remains of two figurines in sitting posture, presumably votive idols, which were found in nearby Roquepertuse, in small recesses carved out of the smooth rock wall. Although the statuettes are missing their heads, and the authorities believe they represent Celto-Iberian deities, they look for all the world like early statues of Bodhisattvas and have all the attributes of such Buddhist 'enlightenment beings' – they are seated in the classic posture of Buddha, and wear the Brahman's cord over the shoulder and decorative rings around their necks and upper arms, signifying their holy status. The arms are very carefully positioned so that the gestures of the hands and fingers (*mudra*) take on symbolic meaning (Plate 23). One hand forms the standard gesture of touching the Earth (*Bhumi-sparsha mudra*), representing the summoning of the Earth to be a witness to the truth of the Buddha's words; the other hand is held before the chest in a reassuring pose (*Abhaya mudra*).

Putting a date to these finds seems to present no particular problem: they derive from the second century BC. The small recesses in the sloping rock would have served merely as temporary protection for the statuettes – after all, the original monastic rule for Buddhist monks required them not to live in fixed dwellings but in temporary dwellings such as simple huts and caves. The arrangement of the Roquepertuse shrines is very similar, moreover, to the layout of some of the well-known rock shrines of the East, such as those in Bamiyan (Afghanistan) or at Ajanta and Ellora (India).

Buddhism, which was much more flexible and apolitical than the rigid structure of Brahmanism, would seem also to have been quite capable of accommodating the various invasions by differing peoples who swarmed into the Indus basin, the upper Ganges basin and the Deccan. Such invaders included the Hellenic Bactrians of the second century BC, and the Scythians and Parthians in the first century BC. In the *Milindapanha*, the great conqueror Menander enters into peaceful discussions with the Buddhist monk Nagasena. The Scythian rulers of the Kushan dynasty themselves encouraged the spread of Buddhism after their own conversion. The most famous of them, Kanishka, was as keen an adherent of Buddhism as Ashoka.

The Council of Haran epitomises this period. Several sources describe its taking place under the rule of Kanishka, during the second half of the first century, in Kashmir. The Council seems to have involved only the Buddhist monastic communities of northwestern India, and in particular the Sarvastivadins who were numerous there – theirs was a school of Hinayana Buddhism that had originated in the third century BC, and was eventually to merge with Mahayana Buddhism after the Council of Haran. The Sarvastivadins of Kashmir probably thought it best to submit their understanding of the Tripitaka (the 'Three Baskets' of the Buddhist canon) to an authoritative inspection in order that the diverging, reformist tendencies that had sprung up in their own community could be discussed. At this Council the entire canon of Mahayana Buddhism, as it had developed over the last two centuries BC, was finally codified – an event that marks the emergence of the Mahayana as a religious faith in its own right.

The early Christians of the East evidently displayed little or no opposition to Mahayana Buddhism, as is manifest, for example, in the fourth-century manuscripts found at Turfan in east Turkestan (today the Chinese province of Sinkiang). Christians, Buddhists and Manicheans all lived there in harmony at the same time together, even using the same places of worship.[1] Representations of Buddha as the Good Shepherd Jesus,[2] and a Buddhist *Jesus-Messiah Sutra* have also been discovered in the area.

Therapeuts, Essenes and Nazarenes

On the complete rout and final scattering of the Jews by the Roman Emperor Titus in AD 70, the mysterious community of Essenes then resident in Palestine hid their library of parchment manuscripts and papyrus scrolls in large clay vases in caves within the Qaratania mountains that overlook the Dead Sea. There they remained, forgotten, until in 1947 they were rediscovered and deciphered. Christian theologians were amazed to learn that most of the Beatitudes in the Sermon on the Mount attributed to Jesus somehow featured in the text of the Dead Sea Scrolls, parts of which had been compiled generations before Jesus' time![3]

Was there any link at all between the early Christian movement and the Essenes? Could the Christian religion have begun as an offshoot of Essene modes of worship? Otherwise, where had the Essenes got the selfsame Beatitudes from? Is it possible that Buddhist ideas had permeated through to pre-Christian Judea and Galilee?

Multiple and complex lines of communication between the East and the West have existed since very early times in human history, and there are accordingly a great many parallels between ancient India and ancient Egypt – both civilizations that originated and expanded on the banks of great rivers in the third millennium BC. The sacred plant of India is the lotus, which, growing from the navel of the god Vishnu, brings forth the god Brahma, and on which the contemplative Buddha is enthroned. The lotus is also the sacred flower of Osiris, for long the supreme deity of the Egyptian pantheon and simultaneously god of the dead. In Indian mythology the god Shiva dances in a great fury, holding the lifeless body of his consort over his shoulder, so scattering parts of her body throughout the land. According to the ancient Egyptian version of the same myth, Set, Osiris' malign brother, scatters the fourteen parts of Osiris' body like seeds all over the Earth.

Whereas all the old cultures of the Near East believe in a single and unique universe, which progresses in linear fashion from the Creation to the Last Day, in Egypt as in India the belief is that the world moves in an endless cycle of formation and dissolution. In the Egyptian *Book of the Dead*, Osiris says, 'I am yesterday, today and tomorrow, and I have the power to be born a second time.'

Clay tablets have been found in the valley of the Euphrates originating from the Indus valley culture, which flourished in the second millenium BC. Spices, peacocks, monkeys and sandalwood were exported from India to the West throughout the ancient period. By means so far unknown, the alphabet used to write down the Semitic languages spoken in ancient Ethiopia were borrowed from India. Indian philosophers probably travelled as far as Athens, Sparta and Corinth, and taught the Greek world the wisdom of the *Upanishads*. According to Aristoxenus, who was writing during the time of Alexander the Great, the philosopher Socrates (469–399 BC) met an Indian in Athens. It is likely that the theory of the transmigration of souls implicit in the philosophical works of Pythagoras, Plato and the Stoics was inspired by the teachings of such Indian scholars.

In the year 325 BC, Alexander the Great crossed the Khyber Pass and invaded north-western India. The young Macedonian was not just a great military leader but was also a student of the celebrated Aristotle and deeply fond of philosophy. It was important to him to bring back with him to Macedonia the art and literature of the conquered territories, and as much as possible of their knowledge and ideas. Alexander probably brought a number of Buddhist monks and Hindu yogis to his new cultural and spiritual centre at the mouth of the Nile, the city of Alexandria, where the cornerstone for a world university was laid down. It was thus through wise men from the East that ideas of asceticism and a vegetarian dietary regime – ideas generally foreign to the Mediterranean area before then – came to Egypt.

Two centuries before Christ, a remarkable mystical movement arose among the Jews of Alexandria and Palestine. In Egypt these mystics were known as Therapeuts; their spiritual brethren in Palestine called themselves Essenes and Nazarenes. In this religious movement we find the answers to the questions posed above. The Jewish historian Flavius Josephus, who was present at the destruction of Jerusalem in AD 70, has left us a graphic eyewitness account of the rites of the Essenes. Philo of Alexandria also mentions a short visit to a settlement of Therapeuts on the shores of the Marcotis Sea, where they practised rites that were remarkably similar to those of the Buddhists. Like the Buddhists, the Therapeuts and Essenes renounced meat, wine and sexual excess.

The community of the Essenes lived in caves that had been excavated in the rock walls of the Qaratania mountains beside the Dead Sea, opposite the ancient town of Jericho. At exactly the same time, Buddhist monks were living in caves cut into the rocky cliffs of the mountains and heights along India's west coast, and centring on a temple cave (Chaitya).

Like the Buddhist monks, the Essenes and Therapeuts lived in celibate monastic communities – a way of life that was itself a novelty in the Mediterranean area, for no religious observance like it had been seen there before. They devoted their lives to a search for knowledge of God, and strove to attain it by means of protracted fasts and periods of silence.

Philo mentions that the Essenes stayed away from the bloody rituals performed in the Temple at Jerusalem because they were strongly opposed to animal sacrifice. The Essene religion may well in fact have been instituted as a protest against such gory elements of Jewish orthodoxy and against the rigid severity of the Mosaic Law. A similar development had taken place several centuries earlier in India, after all, when the Buddha protested against Brahmin rules and rituals which had lost their meaning.

The Essene community was made up of monks and lay persons, like the Buddhist Sangha. The monastic community led a communally organized ascetic life in their all but inaccessible caves in the mountains around Jericho, where it was possible for them to live well away from the Orthodox Jewish groups. John the Baptist was one of these Essene recluses. The lay members of the Essenes lived in villages and towns, where they married and brought up children, and strove to lead a pious, pure, spiritual life. As is still the practice in many Buddhist countries, the lay families often gave up their firstborn son to be a monk in the cave monastery. Perhaps John the Baptist was taken into the Essene fold as a child in this way.

The word *Therapeut* means 'one who ministers', and therefore 'healer', and the Therapeut community on the outskirts of Alexandria was no doubt influenced by the presence of Buddhist monks. The Buddhists monks were also called healers or physicians. The Therapeuts (*Therapeutae*) used to sit on reed mats, as was the tradition of Buddhist monks in India, and their custom of baptizing novices at their initiation into monkhood was also taken from Buddhism. They consumed neither meat nor wine, lived in voluntary poverty, fasted at set times, communally recited and sang religious texts and hymns, and clothed themselves in white robes.

Much of a Therapeut's life was passed in silent meditation and the rituals of worship. The Essenes – both the monks up in the mountains and the lay members down in the towns – tended to occupy themselves with agriculture and manual crafts. The Qumran Scrolls relate how both communities expectantly awaited an imminent end of life on Earth, striving to prepare themselves for a future life with God by evincing brotherly love for one another and for humanity in general, and by doing good deeds. The Essenes discerned eight stages of spiritual growth, rather like the Eightfold Path of the Buddhists, and the aim of these (again as in Buddhism) was to reach a higher plane of existence and to attain Enlightenment.

The Synoptic Gospels tell how Jesus instructed his disciples to travel about on foot, staff in hand (like some Hindu monks), and to minister to the people. During his travels through Judea and Galilee, Jesus may well have stayed overnight at the houses of Essenes resident in the various places he visited.

The Essenes baptized their novices at their initiation. On their induction into monkhood, Buddhist novices underwent a similar baptismal rite probably adopted from the Brahmans. The abbot of the Buddhist monastery sprinkled the head of the novice with milk and water once he had confessed his sins. A lamp burning throughout this ritual symbolized new birth. Interestingly, documents of the very early Christian Church record that after baptism a new Christian was described as *illuminatus* (enlightened).

According to Epiphanius of Constantia (Salamis), the Essenes were also called Nazarenes – *Nazarenos* or *Nazoraios*. In ancient Israel, certain seers were described as Nazarites. These Nazarites condemned the gory sacrifices involved in the worship at the Temple, and were consequently loathed by the orthodox Temple priests. The Jewish faithful were thrice daily encouraged to bring down the wrath of God upon them: 'Send thy curse, O God, upon the Nazarites!'

John's Gospel says that Pilate had a sign fixed to Jesus' Cross that, according to the English translation, read 'Jesus of Nazareth, the King of the Jews'. But in most other languages this is translated slightly differently: as 'Jesus the Nazarene, . . .'[4] Research has shown that the epithet *Nazarene* does not refer to the town of Nazareth, which probably did not even exist at the time. One element in the charges against Jesus, then, was evidently that he was a member of the Nazarenes! If, in addition, the words of the inscription have been altered by tradition or by a need to present a different truth – if, for example, the original version read 'Jesus, Leader of the Nazarenes' – it would go a long way towards explaining why Jesus was so detested by the Sanhedrin, the Jewish High Council. He was the leader of a community they abhorred: the Nazarenes.

Jesus the Nazarene

In nearly all the Greek manuscripts, Jesus is given the title 'The Nazarene', virtually always in English translated – wrongly – as 'Jesus of Nazareth'. So in most translations of the Bible, Paul hears a voice on the road to Damascus that says, 'I am Jesus of Nazareth, whom thou persecutest.' In fact the Greek manuscripts contain no such statement, and the version given in the *Jerusalem Bible* is the correct translation: 'I am Jesus the Nazarene, and you are persecuting me' (Acts 22:8).

Was there perhaps some deliberate design behind this inaccurate translation? If the intention was merely to relate Jesus to his place of origin, he should surely have been described as 'Jesus of Bethlehem', for nothing is said to support the claim that Jesus ever lived in Nazareth. In fact, according to Mark's Gospel, his followers lived by the Sea of Galilee, probably in Capernaum, for it is of thereabouts that it is said 'And he . . . came into his own country' (Mark 6:1). At any rate it is from here that 'There came then his brethren . . .' (Mark 3:31) to get him to stay at home. If 'his brethren' had come from Nazareth, they would have had to travel a distance of more than 40 kilometres.

In the Acts of the Apostles, the first Christians are called Nazarenes, while Jesus is himself called 'the Nazarene' six times.

In John's Gospel (1:46), Nathanael asks the apostle Philip, 'Can there [be] any good thing come out of Nazareth?' Implicit in the question is the man's astonishment that anyone coming from such a tiny, insignificant place could be possessed of such profound knowledge, let alone benefit from an education thorough enough to suggest that he had attended some celebrated establishment of learning. (Nathanael had obviously never heard of anything happening there.)

The *Greek-German Dictionary of the Writings of the New Testament and other Early Christian Literature* (1963) openly declares that 'it is very difficult' to find any linguistic connection between the expressions *Nazarene* and *Nazareth*.

The adjectives *Nazarenos*, *Nazorenos* and *Nazoraios* were all variously used to describe Jesus – proving that they are synonyms – and have generally been taken to indicate that Jesus came from the settlement of Nazareth, resulting in his being described as 'Jesus of Nazareth'. As long ago as in 1920, M. Lidzbarski in his work *Mandaean Liturgies* demonstrated that *Nazarene* could not be derived from *Nazareth* by any standard etymological process.

There is no mention of Nazareth in literature older than Jesus' time, and even at that time the place could not have been more than a tiny hamlet – if it existed at all. In Joshua 19:10–15 the site is not mentioned in connection with the tribe of Zebulun, although it does mention Japhia just three kilometres to the south-east (destroyed by the Romans in AD 67).

The word *Nazarene* derives from the Aramaic root *nazar*, which means something like 'to pick out', and thus both 'to discern', 'to observe', and 'to put to one side', 'to preserve'. In a figurative sense, the word can also be used to mean 'to be devoted' or 'to consecrate oneself to the service of God'. Used as a noun, it means 'diadem', the symbol of an anointed head. A Nazarene was therefore an observer and preserver of the sacred rites. The *Nazaria* constituted a branch of the Essenes, and must have been, with the Ebionites, among the original Christian communities which, according to the Talmud, were referred to as *Nozari*[5]. All these Gnostic sects (*gnosis* 'knowledge') used magic in their rituals. Their members were initiates and anointed ones who led ascetic lives dedicated to the community in godliness and righteousness. It is possible that the slightly different spellings of the adjectives that described them in fact relate to individual groups that differed from each other in their interpretation of the faith and in lifestyle, although all were described in terms deriving from the same etymological origin. The description *Nazarene* is also linked by etymological derivation to that of the Old Testament Nazarites, who existed at a time long before Jesus.

Hundreds of years earlier still, the mighty hero Samson was a *Nazoraios* or *Naziraios* who refused to cut his hair and who drank no wine (Judges 13:5–7) – in other words, an ascetic. According to John M. Robertson, contemporary non-ascetics deliberately described themselves as Nazarenes in order to distinguish themselves from 'nazirism' or asceticism.[6]

Jesus cannot be said definitively to have belonged to any of these various groups for he evidently refused to be categorically subject to any imposed laws, choosing, like Buddha, just 'to do the right thing at the right time'. The huge physical distance between Palestine and India had over the centuries widened the gulf in understanding between the leaders of the spiritual faith who subscribed to the principles of Buddhist philosophy in India and their equivalents in Israel. Jesus could for this reason be accurately described as a 'reformer' who was sent to re-establish a unity of belief among the 'lost sheep', to strengthen their resolve, and to give them spiritual and moral support in their struggle against Roman occupiers, Sadducees, Pharisees and Orthodox Jews.

Jesus was the Divine Messenger for whom many had earnestly longed during a time of tumult and confusion. The two disciples sent by John the Baptist asked him, 'Art thou he that should come, or do we look for another?' (Matthew 11:3).

John the Baptist was a prophet to the Nazarenes, and was known as 'the Saviour' in Galilee. Flavius Josephus describes the Baptist as

> . . . an honourable man, who inspired the Jews to do good and to treat each other well, and who urged them to receive baptism. Then, he declared, God would look with favour on the baptised – for baptism conferred physical healing and was not merely the washing away of sin. Atonement for sin must come beforehand, and must centre on the leading of a virtuous life. Massive crowds thronged around John, much moved by what he said . . .[7]

Ritual immersion in water originated in India and continues to be practised daily by the Hindus with the same devotion as it was thousands of years ago – a tradition as old as any mysteries. In Palestine the Essene rite of baptism marks a major point of departure from the dogmas of the Jewish tradition, and especially from the blood sacrifice, which was based on the crude premise that sins are forgiven if blood is shed. Ritual immersion is meant to symbolize release from all that is earthly, on the one hand, and the rebirth of the spirit in a pure body, on the other. The second Book of the *Laws of Manu*, which deals with the sacraments, contains the injunction to pour consecrated water over a newborn baby before severing the umbilical cord. Then a mixture of honey, clarified butter (ghee) and salt should be placed on the baby's tongue with a small, golden spoon, while auspicious prayers are continuously recited.

The Atharva Veda contains the passage, 'Whoever is not purified after birth with the water of the Ganges blessed by the holy invocations will be subject to as many wanderings as years he spent in impurity'('wanderings' refers to life either as a spirit or after a rebirth in another body).

John's form of baptism seems also to have constituted a token of belonging to a certain community, members of which were clearly distinguishable from non-members by their fulfilment of various ritual preconditions. This makes it clear that the Nazarenes were an independent sect who celebrated their own version of the mysteries of an established teaching. Meanwhile, esoteric sect-leaders who attract emotional crowds while yet keeping a low public profile have always been the target of distrust and persecution by the ruling authorities. Paul faced the same hostility when he was accused by Tertullus before the governor Felix of being 'a ringleader of the sect of the Nazarenes' (Acts 24:5).

According to Pliny the Elder and Josephus, the Nazarene sect had lived on the banks of the Jordan and on the eastern shore of the Dead Sea for at least 150 years before Christ's birth. Its followers were permitted to wear their hair long. Perhaps they never cut it at all, like many Hindu ascetics. John the Baptist is depicted with long hair, and wearing 'raiment of camel's hair, and a leathern girdle about his loins' (Matthew 3:4). A description of what Jesus looked like is given by a Roman patrician named Lentulus in a letter to the Roman senate. In this apocryphal document, known as the *Epistle of Lentulus*, Jesus' hair is described as 'flowing and wavy'; it fell loose over his shoulders, and was 'parted in the middle of the head after the fashion of the Nazaraians'.

It is not really possible today to form a detailed picture of the Nazarene sect from the few sources at our disposal because the references are so scanty. Nor would it be possible, therefore, to trace how the spiritual attitude of Jesus the Nazarene differed from that of his orthodox contemporaries – were it not for the discovery of a wealth of new information about the sect of the Essenes, in which the influence of Buddhist teachings is clearly visible. The Essenes differed from the Nazarenes only in a few external details: Jesus used oil, for example, whereas the Essenes used only pure water.

As long ago as the nineteenth century, those familiar with the accounts of the Essenes came to the conclusion that Jesus' community was an Essene group. The Jewish historian Heinrich Graetz even described Christianity as 'Essenism with foreign elements'.[8] The Essenes are also evidenced in indirect references to them made by ancient historians. The Jewish philosopher Philo of Alexandria called them 'athletes of virtue', and Josephus dedicated nearly an entire chapter to them in *The Jewish War* (II:8). Both estimated the total number of members to be about 4000 'men of excellent morals, who live throughout the land'. The Roman author Pliny the Elder also mentions the sect of the Essenes.

But it was not until the discovery of the famous Dead Sea Scrolls at Qumran in the twentieth century that people perceived the full significance of Essene teachings, which anticipated the teachings of Jesus and shed a completely new light on Jesus himself.

The Essenes: Christianity Before Jesus

In the summer of 1947, a young Bedouin came across the entrance to a cave while searching the cliffs beside the Dead Sea for a goat lost from his herd. His curiosity aroused, the youthful pastoralist entered, and discovered a number of earthenware vases sealed with lids among a whole lot of fragments of other vases. Hoping to find a treasure, the lad opened the sealed vessels, but to his great disappointment found just a few ancient scrolls in musty vellum.

Treasure it was, though, and the find was soon to prove the greatest archaeological sensation of the century. When the famous archaeologist William F. Allbright was shown the scrolls in 1948, he called them the greatest manuscript find of our time. He dated them to the first century BC, and had no doubts about their authenticity.

Over the course of the following years, researchers in the area of Khirbet Qumran discovered ten more caves and many more scrolls, a good quantity of which have still not yet been completely translated or made public. It was soon clear, nonetheless, how very similar the teachings of Jesus were to those of the Essenes. Indeed, some even said that the Essenes must have been the true precursors of early Christianity. The astounding similarity of the two movements is particularly evident in their parallel theological views and their religious institutions: all confirm the existence of a Christianity *before* Jesus.

Seven scrolls from the first cave are now on display in the Hall of Manuscripts of the Museum of Israel in Jerusalem. The most extensive manuscript is one known as the 'Isaiah scroll of St Mark'.[9] Its fifty-four manuscript columns of Hebrew contain the complete Book of the prophet Isaiah. The Isaiah scroll is the oldest of the finds (dated to around 150 BC), and bears an astonishing resemblance to early copies of Biblical texts. Fragments of a second Isaiah manuscript[10] and a commentary to the Book of the prophet Habakkuk[11] were also found.

The most important find, however, was a scroll almost two metres in length, which detailed the rules and regulations for a religious community. Today the document is called *Serek Hajjahad*, from its opening words, meaning 'The Rule of the Community', or *The Manual of Instructions*.[12] The first part describes a Covenant of Eternal Love which binds the members of the community to God. The second part describes 'the two spirits in the nature of Man': the spirit of light and truth, and its opposite, the spirit of error and darkness. (In Buddhism this is expressed as the contrast between Knowledge and Ignorance.) The regulations of the Order follow, giving a detailed description of conditions for entry and penalties for infringement against the Rule of the Community. The whole thing comes to an end with a final long hymn of thanksgiving.

In addition to the Rule for the celibate order of monks, a second manuscript was found that had been rolled up with (or possibly once even sewn on to) it. This scroll was entitled *Rule for the Whole Community*,[13] and was directed at the lay branch of the communty, for those members who were married.

There are very evident parallels here with the early Buddhist communities, which also made a distinction between the monks (in Pali *bhikkhu*) and the laity (*upasaka*).

Those who belonged to the 'worldly' branch of the sect were to be taught *The Manual of Instructions* with all the rules of the community from the age of eleven years. (Jesus, remember, was taken to Jerusalem from Egypt at about that age – and then disappeared, not to be seen there again until he was an adult man aged over thirty.) Men were not allowed to marry until they had turned twenty; at the age of twenty-five they were accorded a position and an authority in the community. It was actually possible to rise to any of the chief offices at the age of twenty, but it was still necessary then to render full obedience to the priests and elders of the community. Men of standing were expected to retire from office when they reached a certain age.

Towards the end of the scroll, there appears a description of the seating arrangements for the communal meal celebrating the life to come after death – it was these seating arrangements that became a topic of debate among Jesus' disciples at the Last Supper (Luke 22:24–27).

Another scroll, badly damaged in parts, contains both the biblical Psalms and some forty original Essene psalms, all of which begin with the words, 'I praise thee, Lord'; this scroll is accordingly known as *Hokhajot*: 'Songs of Praise'.[4]

The other writings brought to light are evidently the meagre time-worn remnants of what discoverers of bygone centuries had overlooked, for even Origen reports that a translation of the Psalms had been found together with other manuscripts in a vase somewhere near Jericho. And the Patriarch of Seleucia, the Nestorian Timothy I (*fl.* AD 823), in one of his letters described the discovery of some Hebrew scriptures laid up in a cave not far from Jericho.

Some of the texts were written in a secret code, but there are constant references to a 'New Covenant' (which of course is what Martin Luther and other reformers meant by 'New Testament') and a mysterious 'Teacher of Righteousness'.

In his *Historia Naturalis*, Pliny the Elder mentions a monastery that he had seen a short distance to the north of En-gedi on the western shore of the Dead Sea. He called it the Essene Monastery, and its members he described as ' . . . a reclusive group of men, one of the most remarkable in the world, without any women at all, who have renounced the baser passions and live utterly on their own resources under the palm trees' (V:17).

Less than one kilometre away from the cave in which the first scrolls were discovered are some ruins that have been known since ancient times as Khirbet Qumran ('the ruins of Qumran'), long held to be the remains of an early Roman fort. Excavations at the site began only in 1951, under Lancaster Harding of the Jordanian Office of Antiquities and Père Roland de Vaux, Director of the Dominican Institute of Theology in Jerusalem. What they found surpassed their greatest expectations – the Monastery of Qumran, in which the scrolls themselves had probably been written. Over the subsequent five years, labouring intensively, the researchers uncovered an extensive settlement protected by a well-fortified wall. A squarish building at the centre was adjoined by several smaller buildings, a large dining-hall, baptismal baths, and no fewer than thirteen wells from which a complex system of channels supplied water all round. There was also a cemetery containing more than a thousand graves, in which only men had been buried. And they found a scriptorium, a writing-room with carved stone tables in which ink-wells had been bored, where most of the manuscripts of the nearby caves had presumably originated. It is now known that the monastery had been inhabited from as early as the eighth century BC, but had been abandoned at the time of the Babylonian Exile, to be reoccupied once more only at around 175 (the second century) BC.

Josephus gives an account of how the monks lived:

They spurn worldly wealth; most admirable is how they own all things in common so that no one among them possesses more than anyone else. For it is their rule that anyone who wishes to join the sect must first donate everything he owns to the whole community. The result is that neither abject poverty nor excessive opulence is anywhere to be seen. Instead, they treat all property as for their common use – although originally collected from individual members of the order – very much in the spirit of brotherhood. Oil is regarded as dirty, however. If one of them has his body smoothed with oil against his will, he takes a thorough bath to get it off. For to walk around with skin in its natural state is as virtuously creditable to them as wearing clean white robes.[15]

There are obvious parallels between this description of the Essenes' way of life, the Buddhist monastic rules, and Jesus' own habits. Just as Buddhist monks owned no property beyond their clothing and a few minor nomadic necessities, Jesus led the existence of an itinerant teacher who possessed little or nothing. And just as Jesus required his disciples to renounce families and worldly goods, so the Buddhist rule required that followers joined the community by 'going out into the open' – by quitting their houses and families (and with them the trappings of lay life) to enter the brotherhood of monks wandering without permanent shelter, to be free of all earthly concerns, to meditate on the Teachings, and gradually to free themselves from mortal passions and worldly desires. Jesus said, 'It is easier for a camel [although he might have meant a camel-hair rope] to go through the eye of a needle, than for a rich man to enter into the kingdom of God' (Matthew 19:24).

The Gospels provide another example of Jesus' thoughts on freedom from earthly concerns:

> And a certain scribe came, and said unto him, Master, I will follow thee whithersoever thou goest.
> And Jesus saith unto him, The foxes have holes, and the birds of the air have nests; but the Son of Man hath not where to lay his head.
> (Matthew 8:19–20)

A further point of interest is the Essene ban on oiling the body. Buddha himself is said to have warned his followers against the practice because it corresponded to taking an inordinate pride in one's own body, amounting thus to a selfish desire. The Nazarene sect was apparently under no obligation to conform with this strict ordinance.

The Essenes wore white robes, which led some eighteenth-century critical philosophers to declare the Crucifixion and Resurrection of Jesus to be no more than an elaborate hoax staged by Essene monks. The critics said that the young man in white robes who announced the Resurrection to the women at the empty tomb was clearly proved by his white raiment to have belonged to the Essenes. During the nineteenth century the theory was also advanced that Jesus was the natural son of an Essene to whom

Mary had given herself by way of religious betrothal. The child was handed over to the Order, which, according to an account by Josephus,[16] genuinely was an Essene custom and practice.

As long ago as in 1831, August Friedrich Gfrörer, vicar of a parish in Stuttgart and teacher at the seminary in Tubingen, wrote: 'The Christian Church evolved from the community of the Essenes, whose ideas they developed, and without whose rules its organization could not have been established.'

Some linguistic historians believe the expression *Essene* basically to mean 'baptist'. Others relate it instead to a Syrian word *hasen* 'the pious', or to the Aramaic *assaya* 'healer', 'physician' (semantically comparable with the Greek *therapeut*). Many Essene monks dedicated years of their lives to ascetic practices of self-discipline and contemplation, and achieved astonishing powers of extrasensory perception and telekinesis just as the yogis and fakirs in India did and do. The Essene monastery was located near Jericho, among the mountains west of the Dead Sea – a region renowned for its mild and healthy climate since the days of the prophets Elijah and Elisha. This is the one and only part of Palestine where it is warm enough throughout the year to practise exercises like those of Indian yoga out in the open air. The mystical gifts described by the Essenes themselves are the same extraordinary powers to which the students of Kundalini Yoga attain in India; they include clairvoyance and precognition, levitation and teleportation, healing by the laying on of hands, and the restoring of the dead to life.

The fact that the New Testament observes complete and utter silence on the subject of the Essene Order – on a sect that was at least as significant in numbers as the Sadducees and the Pharisees (Josephus put their number at 4000) – implies that the omission was quite deliberate.

Simple geography shows that Jesus could not have been unaware of the monastery at Qumran. Indeed, the spot on the bank of the Jordan where Jesus underwent his ritual baptism at the hands of John (by means of which he was inducted into the moderate Nazarene sect) was within sight of the monastery, a mere seven kilometres away. To visit the place is to see how striking is the proximity of the baptismal site to Qumran; the clear air of the wide mountain wasteland seems to bring the two locations visibly even closer. At the same point there is also a clear view of the mountain on which, by tradition, Jesus was tempted by the devil during his period of isolation following baptism (Luke 4:1–13): the mountain is some fifteen kilometres distant.

John lived here in the desert, perhaps even in the caves of Qumran. Jesus spent forty days of isolation here in the desert immediately after being baptized. The reclusive inhabitants of Qumran certainly referred to the area in which they lived as 'the desert' in their writings. Jesus, in his sojourn, was 'with the wild beasts; and the angels ministered unto him' (Mark 1:13). But the word translated as *angels* need mean no more than 'messengers', and the Essenes preserved an extensive hierarchy of 'angel-messengers' that was part of their sacred mysteries. So if Jesus spent some time in a cave outside Qumran, perhaps as part of a period representing a novitiate, there may well have been some contact with the monastery – perhaps the 'angels' were actually monks!

In the chapter about the Essenes, Josephus wrote:

> Anyone who wishes to join the sect is not granted admission immediately but has first to spend a year outside the order, leading the same kind of life as the members. He is provided with a small axe, a loincloth and a white robe. If he passes this test of asceticism over the whole period, he takes one step closer to full membership: he may take part in the baptismal consecration with water but may not yet partake of the communal meals.[17]

Much the same procedure occurs in Tibet. Before an ordinary monk is consecrated as lama (meaning 'higher [one]'), he must undertake a series of exercises and tests. The aspirant is also expected to stay somewhere outside the community for a time, in a place where he can remain totally undisturbed so as to devote himself completely to meditation. The Hemis monastery in Ladakh, like all the larger lamaseries, has a second much smaller and simpler building for the purpose, on the peak of a high mountain some five kilometres distant from the main monastery. Immersed in deep meditation in their individual cells, the candidates receive only a little food twice daily from assistants.

An earthquake destroyed the entire community of Qumran in 31 BC. Rifts and cracks in the terrain are still visible, and the level of the floor varies by nearly half a metre at some points. Qumran remained uninhabited for almost thirty years after the earthquake, and it was not until about the time of Jesus' birth that the monastery was revived and endowed with a new spirit.

In addition to human graves, the buried remains of animals were also found in the grounds of the monastery. The bones of sheep, goats, cows, calves and lambs had been carefully laid to rest in earthenware vessels. It would appear, therefore, that although the Essenes put their domestic animals to good use, they did not kill or eat the animals themselves because they considered the taking of any life at all to be an atrocity, like the Buddhists. The monks cultivated fields and orchards. Countless date-stones confirm the existence of a plantation of palm trees just as Pliny the Elder described. Philo tells how bee-keeping was also one of the community's major pastimes – at which John the Baptist's daily fare as recorded in Mark's Gospel (locusts and honey) springs to mind.

Somewhat surprisingly, about 400 coins were also brought to light at the monastery, and from what they reveal the history of the community can be reconstructed with great precision. Quite a few of the coins date from 4 BC, when Archelaus succeeded his father Herod as governor of Judea. The gap in the sequence of coins prior to this date suggests that it was only on the accession of Archelaus that the monastery was permitted to reopen. Members of the community had had to keep well clear of their monastic centre for all the years that Herod, based in his luxurious winter palace in Jericho a mere twelve kilometres away, had been suppressing and expelling the Essene sects. Herod dead, the Essenes returned and began to rebuild their monastery. Qumran remained continuously inhabited from then on until the Jewish rebellion against Rome in AD 68. The grounds of the area display evidence of a violent final destruction. A layer of ashes indicates that the monastery was overwhelmed by fire.

The Teaching of the Essenes at Qumran

The members of the Essene community at Qumran did not ascribe any specific name to their sect in their religious writings. They called themselves 'the holy community', 'the chosen ones of God', 'the men of truth', or, most often, 'the Sons of Light'. In many respects the Essenes fulfilled the precepts inherent in Jewish Law to the letter, but they also deviated from it to such a degree in other respects that it is debatable whether the Qumran community should really be described as a Jewish sect at all.

According to the *Hokhajot*, the Songs of Praise (or Essene psalms) that were unearthed, the mission of the Essenes was to preach 'the Good News (*eu-angelion*) to the poor as a measure of God's mercy', and they themselves were to be 'messengers of the

Good News'. They perceived a need for a 'New Covenant' with God – in fact they sometimes referred to themselves as the New Covenant – as was later held to have been established in the person of Jesus. The New Covenant was to last 'from the day that the One Teacher departs until the coming of the Messiah of Aaron and Israel'.

But most astonishing of all is the fact that when the Qumran sect prayed as a community, as they did three times every day, they did not face in the direction of the Temple in Jerusalem (as did and do all Orthodox Jews) but eastwards. The focus of their prayer lay to the east, in the direction of the rising sun. Josephus writes that the Essenes 'speak only piously . . . before sunrise, offering up certain ancient prayers to the sun . . .' This shows that the Essenes regarded the sun as an acceptable symbol for God Himself. One of the Qumran psalms makes the point even more clearly, addressing God as '. . . the true aurora of Dawn [who] appeared to me at the break of day', and again: '. . . you have appeared to me in your might with the coming of the day'.

The Rule of the Community (or *The Manual of Instructions*) required the faithful of the New Covenant to recite a prayer at dawn and a prayer at dusk. The followers of Pythagoras – who was apparently taught by Brahmans in India – at his establishment in Crotona, southern Italy, and the adherents of the Gnostic sect of Hermes Trismegistos (based on worship of the Egyptian god Thoth but later much influenced by the Pythagoreans), observed an identical mode of worship. Both the easterly direction of prayer and the symbolic use of the sun are reminiscent of the Sun Temple of Martand in Kashmir.

The Essenes were just as remarkable in that they did not use the calendar sanctioned by the Temple authorities in Jerusalem, which was a lunar calendar. They had their own method of defining dates that was based on the solar year, which is somewhat more accurate, and which had been in general use in India since the beginning of Brahmin domination. Only during the time of Julius Caesar was the solar calendar promulgated for use throughout the Roman Empire, although it has still, even today, not been accepted by the Jews.[18] In the Qumran calendar, therefore, feastdays of the religious year always fell on the same day of the week, in contrast to official Jewish practice.

Nor is the practice of dividing the year into four seasons of Jewish origin. It was Pythagoras who introduced the quarterly arrangement from India, and before that, the ancient Greeks had really only thought in terms of three, or even two, seasons.

The spiritual background and original source of Essene philosophy is further revealed by another Essene teaching: like the Indian sages and the Greek philosophers they believed in immortality, a life after death – in other words, that the soul or spirit outlives and leaves its temporal prison, the body. In this respect it was Jesus who added a new element in his teaching of resurrection. He spoke of the resurrection of the dead, but without expressly referring to the resurrection of the body. So he was not necessarily talking about a resurrection in the flesh, but about the doctrine of reincarnation, transmigration, and the continuous cycle of rebirths until the end of *samsara* (the world of constant change, as described in the *Upanishads*) – a basic tenet of all forms of religion in India. The Pythagoreans, the cultists of the Orphic mysteries, Empedocles and Plato were all, well before the Essenes, acquainted with the doctrine of the cycle of rebirths by which the soul enters a new body. The notion of metempsychosis (the expression for it used by the ancient Greeks as well as modern English) has survived in the West to the present day chiefly through the Gnostic sects and a few non-Arabic sects of Islam, and the subject remains studied in university courses in theosophy and religious anthropology.

Even during the nineteenth century, commentators pointed out Buddhist aspects in the teachings of the Essenes.[19] Some saw them as intermediaries between rabbis, Gnostics, Platonists and Pythagoreans on the one hand, and Zoroastrians and Buddhists on the other, and suggested that the religion of the Essenes and Therapeuts evolved from the merging of Buddhism and Semitic monotheism, just as Buddhism had merged with shamanist Bon in Tibet, with the philosophies of Taoism and Confucianism in China, and with the Shinto religion in Japan.[20]

The Buddhists wore white robes like the Essenes – and like the early Christians. Catholic scholars were astounded on first noting the extraordinary similarity between the rituals and teachings of Tibetan Buddhism and those of the Catholic Church. The costume of the Tibetan lamas is virtually identical not only with the vestments worn by Catholic priests, but also with the clothing of the apostles and the first Christians, as depicted in contemporary frescoes, right down to the details. The hierarchical organization of the Tibetan and Roman Catholic monastic orders exhibit quite astounding similarities. Like the Catholics, the Buddhists say prayers of intercession and praise, and give alms and offerings, and in both religions the monks take vows of poverty, chastity and obedience. Buddhists use consecrated water and raise their voices in the celebration of a religious service in which the liturgy is very close indeed to that of the Eastern Christian Church. The rosary came to the Catholic Church as the Buddhist prayer-beads. The Buddhist depiction of the *aura* became the halo of Christian iconography.

The Doctor of the Church Jerome and the Church historian Eusebius state that Christian monasteries evolved along the lines of communities of Therapeuts in Alexandria. The three major 'ranks' of Christian clergy (bishop, priest and deacon) do in fact correspond to the three 'ranks' of the Therapeut monks. The first Christians are described by Epiphanius as *Therapeutae* and *Jessians* (the latter of which is presumably a corrupted form of 'Essenes'). The highest ambition for an early Christian initiate was to become a Therapeut, and much of the everyday organization of daily life in the first Christian communities was undertaken by seven elected deacons – a title that itself also derives from the monastic conformation of the Therapeuts.

Christians celebrate the Lord's day on Sunday, whereas Jews celebrate the Sabbath on Saturday. The Essenes likewise held the holy day to be Sunday, on which they started their Sabbath celebration. On the Sabbath, the Jews brought meat, wine and corn to the Temple to sacrifice, and the priests were allotted a proportion for their own use. The reason for the priests' bitter enmity with the Essenes is obvious: the Essene sect's refusal to have anything to do with blood sacrifice represented a considerable threat both to the priests' diet and, more significantly, to their main source of income (either in performing the slaughter of the animals, or in supplying or licensing the animals for sacrifice). This was surely the main cause of the plotting of the priests against Jesus, for as leader of a Nazarene-Essene movement Jesus was propounding a doctrine that would have eliminated many of the duties and most of the status of the priests. As far as they were concerned, Jesus had to be got rid of for them to be certain that their livelihoods were secure.

Philo describes Jewish mystics who were similar to the Hindu gymnosophists of India, who likewise rejected the sacrificing of animals.

The Essenes also believed in a doctrine of moral causation – that the deeds done in the present life strongly affect one's position in the next life: the Indian teaching of *karma*. Those who understood these mysteries had either to live righteous lives or continue to sin and stand condemned on the Day of Judgement. This was in the context of their fervent expectation of the apocalypse and of the imminent coming of the kingdom of God.

There were numerous points of contact in the outlook of Jesus and that of the Essenes, but that there were differences too should not be overlooked. The Gospels report that Jesus ate meat and drank wine. He grew up in an environment influenced by local Essenes, and most of his followers were Essenes. But although he had probably been a novice in an Essene monastery, he later made a distinct break with the rigidly mannered precepts of the sect because he felt – as had Buddha some 500 years before him – that blind adherence to strict rules and regulations was no way to attain personal salvation. And by taking an individual stand, Jesus created a new, tolerant version of the Essene-Nazarene faith, one that made room for ordinary lay people who were not in a position to follow the path of asceticism: one that welcomed anyone and everyone with open arms.

In particular, Jesus' approach to the Commandments and to the other requirements of Mosaic Law was much freer: 'Ye have heard that it was said by them of old . . . But *I* say unto you . . .' (Matthew 5:21–48). According to strict Orthodox Jewish law, those who disobeyed the restrictions on activity on the Sabbath, and who disregarded warnings, should be put to death. But the Damascus text of Qumran prohibits the execution of a person who breaks the Sabbath, and according to Matthew's Gospel Jesus said, 'For the Son of Man is Lord even of the sabbath day' (Matthew 12:8).

The disparity between the views of Jesus and those of the Essenes is especially evident in connection with the idea of loving one's enemy. Unlike Jesus, the Essenes felt no compunction about hating their enemies. On the contrary, the people of Qumran rather prided themselves on being at least aloof from, if not morally superior to, the rest of the world. Very different from this, it was Jesus' mission to make contact with sinners, to rescue those who had got lost: his words emphasized that he had been sent out to find 'the lost sheep of the house of Israel', and he expressly disapproved of religious bigotry, of any organization or institution that claimed to have exclusive access to righteousness.

Another sharp difference lies in the contrasting attitudes towards the use of oil or balsam. Jesus, after all, is the Christ, the Anointed, a description used as a title for him – and one that sets him quite apart from the Essenes. The ancient magical texts claimed that unction served the specific purpose of enchanting demons so as to grant protection from them, and on a medical basis it helped to heal wounds and drive away diseases of mind and body. In some way the unguent 'sealed' the body of a worshipper, so somehow assuring him or her of God's protection. Celsus says that the snake-worshipping Ophites possessed a magic ointment that transformed anyone who received it into a 'Son of the Father': 'I have been anointed with the pure white unguent of the Tree of Life'.[21] In the apocryphal *Gospel of Philip* there is a passage: 'The Tree of Life is in the centre of Paradise; it is the oil tree that yields the oil with which holy kings are anointed (*chrisma*), and by means of it resurrection [was made possible].'[22]

If it is the rebirth of a soul within a new body that is the overall idea here, it is evident what a decisive new element Jesus, the Anointed, introduced to the teachings of the different Essene groupings. As Irenaeus wrote, the sacrament of holy unction was a 'rite denoting salvation' for the 'one become perfect', and was consequently regarded as far more important than baptism. The anointing was generally on the temples and forehead, often in the form of a cross. The tradition of anointing has its origins in India, where Hindu ascetics (*sadhus*) may still be recognized by a small white circle, or white horizontal or vertical stripes, on the forehead, applied with a mixture of oil and holy ash (*vibhuti*).

Buddha and Jesus: A Comparison

The God of the Semitic tribes is, to pull no punches, a bloodthirsty and vengeful deity. Yahweh-Jehovah of the Jews tends to be depicted as a fearsome overlord seated on a throne above the clouds, violently chastising his Chosen People whenever they transgress his edicts and his restrictions.

The philosophy behind Jesus' Sermon on the Mount, as relayed by Matthew's Gospel, is illuminated by a totally different God. Christ's message is a message of love, a joyful message of forgiveness and reconciliation: love your neighbour as (you love) yourself; if anyone strikes you on one cheek, turn the other towards him too. There can hardly be a greater contrast with the attitudes revealed in the Old Testament. No other religion of the eastern Mediterranean area lays claim to the magnanimously loving Grace preached by Jesus. Where did Jesus learn the precepts he proclaimed in the Sermon on the Mount?

A possible answer to this question may be found in early (pre-Christian) Buddhist scriptures like the *Lalitavistara*, which is the Buddhist text that exhibits the greatest number of parallels with the tradition of the Gospels. Written in Sanskrit, the *Lalitavistara* is a biography of the Buddha that is linked in time and culture with the Sarvastivadins. Its most ancient sections, deriving from the Hinayana, date from the third century BC, although the full version in its present form was compiled in the centuries either side of Christ's birth, and was included in the canon of the Mahayana by edict of the Council of Haran in the first century AD – significantly, some years before the compilation of the New Testament.

In the *Lalitavistara*, Buddha says:

> The knowledge of the truth, the attainment of Nirvana – this is the supreme blessing. Through love alone can hate be vanquished; through perfect love evil may be overcome . . . Speak no harsh words to your neighbour, and he will respond to you in like terms.

A merchant from Sunapaortha asked the Enlightened One to teach him. 'People are violent,' said the Reborn. 'If they offended you, how would you respond?'

The merchant shrugged his shoulders. 'I would make no reply at all to them,' he said.

'And if they hit you?'

'I would not react then either.'

'And if they kill you?'

The merchant smiled. 'Death, Master, is no evil. Some even desire it!'

In the same way, Jesus enjoined his disciples: 'Whosoever shall smite thee on thy right cheek, turn to him the other also.'

Buddha said to his favourite disciple Ananda, 'Believe in me, Ananda! All those who believe in me will come to great joy.' Christ likewise instructed his disciples to believe in him, and not to waver in this faith.

On another occasion, the Buddha described the giving of alms as 'a seed sown on good ground, which brings forth fruit in plenty'. He also declared that 'Food that is eaten does not destroy a person . . . but the taking of a life, stealing, lying, adultery, and even thinking of doing these things, can certainly lead to a person's destruction.' And 'A man buries a treasure in a deep pit. But a treasure hidden away like this can be of no use to him. Now a treasure of love for one's neighbour, of piety and of moderation – that is a treasure that no thief can ever steal.' And 'Even when the heavens crash to the earth, even when the world is swallowed up and destroyed, even then, Ananda, the words of the Buddha remain true.' And in another place the Enlightened One referred to himself as 'a shepherd full of wisdom' who bends down to redirect those of the flock who are wandering towards the abyss.

All these sayings of Buddha are strongly reminiscent of Jesus' sayings, as contained in the Gospels. Could Jesus perhaps have been familiar with the words of the *Lalitavistara*?

John the Baptist baptized at the mouth of the River Jordan, where it flows into the Dead Sea, very near the place where the Essene community was based and where the Dead Sea Scrolls were discovered in 1947. John exhorted the people to repent of their sins and to receive baptism at his hands in the waters of the Jordan. After he was baptized by John, Jesus retired into the desert, where he was subjected to temptation by Satan. Five hundred years earlier, Buddha too was subjected to a series of temptations by Mara, the 'lord of sensory pleasures', as the *Lalitavistara* narrates. To Siddhartha in the middle of his fasting and meditation Mara offered delicious dishes and showed him the riches and distractions of this world, but the contemplative's concentration was not in the least disturbed. Jesus underwent the same test in the desert, with the same result. A similar story of temptation is told of Zarathustra (Zoroaster), and indeed the selfsame theme – relatively well attested in the East – plays a part in many stories of the lives of the Christian saints.

Jesus commanded his disciples to go out and proclaim the message of joy to the House of Israel. Like the Hindu *sannyasis*, the disciples were to take no gold or silver with them, nor any second set of shoes or clothing.

Five hundred years before Jesus, the Buddha used the same command in nominating his first disciples – the noble thirty – as Jesus was to use later: 'Come, follow me!' The disciples renounced everything on the spot and followed him, just as Peter, Andrew and the sons of Zebedee were to follow Jesus so long afterwards.

And like Jesus, the Buddha spoke in parables. Jesus once described how a blind man cannot lead another blind man without both falling into a ditch. In a similar passage the Buddha says: 'When blind people hold on to each other in a line, the one at the front sees nothing, the one in the middle sees nothing, and the one at the end sees nothing!' There is also an equivalent to the parable of the Prodigal Son in the Buddhist scriptures.

Other parables told by Jesus are represented not among the sayings of Buddha but in pre-Christian Hindu traditions and proverbs, including, for instance, the famous saying that faith can move mountains. In this way Krishna relocates the mountain Govardhana to protect its inhabitants from the wrath of the god Indra, and in the *Ramayana* the monkey god Hanuman carries a mountain to Sri Lanka. No such image was present in Old Testament traditions.

Attributed to Buddha are many miracles, a number of which are very similar to those described in the New Testament as being performed by Jesus. Buddha and his disciples were invited to attend a wedding in the town of Jambunada. The holy group sat down to a hearty meal but the food, instead of being rapidly reduced as it was consumed, actually increased in quantity and went on increasing, so that even though more and more guests arrived there was enough for the veritable multitude that was there by the end.

Like Jesus, Buddha was regarded as both divine and human. Before his arrival on Earth Buddha exists as a spiritual being among the divine entities in the spiritual world. Of his own free will he descends to Earth in order to benefit it. Like Christ's, his birth is the result of a miracle: angel messengers proclaim that he will be a saviour, and prophesy to his mother: 'All joy to you, Queen Maya, rejoice and be glad, for the child to whom you have given birth is holy!'

Just as the old and pious Simeon has been told he will see the coming of the Messiah, the birth of the Buddha is prophesied by the saintly old Asita who, shortly before he dies, comes to the newborn child, takes him in his arms, and declares:

> This is the peerless One, pre-eminent among men . . . He will attain to the ultimate height of enlightenment. He has knowledge of the supreme Will. It is he who will set the Wheel of Doctrine in motion. He has had compassion on the struggles of humankind. The faith he founds will spread all over the world.

Simeon, it will be recalled, likewise takes the holy child in his arms and says,

> Lord, now lettest thou thy servant depart in peace, according to thy word:
> For mine eyes have seen thy salvation,
> Which thou hast prepared before the face of all people;
> A light to lighten the Gentiles, and the glory of thy people Israel.

(Luke 2:29–32)

Even relatively cautious scholars are convinced that this speech has a direct precedent in Buddhism.

At school, the young Prince Siddhartha is somehow already familiar with all kinds of religious texts. He goes off on a short excursion of his own, is missed, and is then found deep in meditation. The parallels with the twelve-year-old Jesus' being discovered in learned debate with scriptural experts in the Temple while his parents have been looking for him are so obvious they cannot be mistaken.

Buddha begins teaching publicly at about the age of thirty, the age at which Christ began to do the same. Like Jesus, Buddha travels the country together with his principal disciples in voluntary poverty, instructing them meanwhile by using vivid imagery and parables. Like Jesus, Buddha has twelve principal disciples, and his first followers are two brothers – again in an exact parallel with Jesus' first followers.

When called by Buddha, his first companions are sitting under a fig tree, and it is when sitting under a bo or pipal tree (another species of fig) that Buddha attains enlightenment. To Buddhists the bo tree (*Ficus religiosa*) remains the most important symbol of the quest for enlightenment. Jesus too first lights upon the disciple Nathanael sitting under a fig tree. Both Buddha and Christ have one favourite disciple and one disciple who betrays him – and, like Judas Iscariot, Buddha's enemy Devadatta comes to a wretched end (although his plot fails, whereas Judas' does not).

As strongly as Jesus criticizes the Pharisees, the Orthodox Jewish believers who cling steadfastly to the letter of the Mosaic Law, Buddha criticizes the priestly caste of the Brahmans whose orthodoxy has been reduced to meaningless ritual and officious regulations. 'Like arrogant apprentices in a trade they are still learning, the priests are forever widening their web of regulations and are at the root of every evil scheme.' Of the Pharisees, Jesus similarly says, 'They bind heavy burdens and grievous to be borne, and lay them on men's shoulders; but they themselves will not move them with one of their fingers. But all their works they do for to be seen of men' (Matthew 23:4–5). In just the way that Buddha characterizes the Brahmans – 'Inside you are like rough wood, though your outer appearance is smooth' – Jesus lays open the hypocrisy of the Pharisees: 'You are like unto whited sepulchres, which indeed appear beautiful outward, but are within full of dead men's bones, and of all uncleanness' (Matthew 23:27).

Just as Buddha rejects the blood sacrifice performed by some

Brahmans, Jesus denounces the blood sacrifice of the Jews. And just as Buddha slates shallow notions of what is pure and what is impure and how ritual ablutions may or may not be efficacious, Jesus censures anything that is insincere and ostentatious.

Despite all attempts at obscuring the true origins of Jesus' teaching, and despite the compression of the Gospels into strict conformity along different lines, more than one hundred passages[23] in the New Testament may be cited that exhibit evidence of sources that hark back to a much older tradition: Buddhism.

Buddhist Thought in the Teachings of Jesus

Affinities between the ethical teachings of Jesus and of Buddha are well known. Both forbid murder, theft, bearing false witness and illicit sexual relations. Both insist that elders must be held in great respect. Both aim to overcome evil with good. Both preach love of one's enemy. Both value peace of mind and peaceable intent. Both advise against the laying up of futile 'treasures upon earth'. And both advocate mercy for sacrificial victims. The parallels are many, and some texts of both faiths coincide virtually word for word.

Like Jesus, Buddha called himself a 'Son of Man', and just as Jesus may be described as the Light of the World, so Buddha is acclaimed in the titles 'Eye of the World' and 'Incomparable Light'.

Buddha's understanding of himself and his role differs little from Christ's understanding of his own nature and place. 'I know God and the Kingdom of Heaven and the Way that leads there,' says Buddha, 'I know it as well as one who has entered the *Brahmaloka* (the Kingdom of God) and has been born there.' And 'Those who believe in me and love me are certain to reach Paradise. Those who believe in me can be sure of salvation.' This is remarkably similar to the promises of Jesus recorded in John's Gospel: 'He that heareth my word, and believeth on him that sent me, hath everlasting life, and shall not come into condemnation; but is passed from death unto life' (John 5:24). And 'He that believeth in me, though he were dead, yet shall he live' (John 11:25).

Buddha says to his disciples, 'Those who have ears to hear, let them hear.' He performs miracles: the sick are healed, the blind regain their sight, the deaf hear again, and the crippled walk freely. He steps across the Ganges in flood just as Jesus walks across the waters of the lake. And it is eventually given to Jesus' disciples to perform miracles, just like their predecessors, the disciples of Buddha.

On one occasion Buddha came to the bank of a river. From the opposite bank a disciple who had been unable to find a boat began walking across on top of the water towards him, just as Peter once approached Jesus by walking on the water. And in the same way that Peter began to sink when his faith started to waver, Buddha's disciple began to sink when his meditative concentration on Buddha was disturbed. Peter was saved by the supporting words and arm of Jesus, and Buddha's disciple was saved when he managed to regain his absorption in contemplating the Master. The people who witnessed the individual events were astounded. Buddha said, 'It is faith that leads us across the floodwaters, wisdom brings us safe to the other side.' Walking on water is a concept quite unheard of in Jewish traditions, but is a theme that is widespread in India: it is more than possible that the New Testament adopted the idea from there.

Like Jesus, however, the Buddha would have no truck with miracles designed merely to cater to people's craving for sensations. To a yogi who had spent twenty-five effortful years in trying to acquire the ability to cross a river without getting his feet wet, the Buddha said 'Have you really been wasting so much time on such a minor matter? All you ever needed was a small coin, and the ferryman would have taken you across in his boat.'

But at a later date, the miracle stories of Buddha in the tradition of Mahayana Buddhism were accorded a status equal in importance to the miracles of Jesus in Christianity. At all times and in all places, people have been more easily impressed by miracles, signs and magical spectacles than by spiritual truths, especially when the spiritual truths are difficult to take in.

There is one particular story that represents perhaps the most amazing parallel of all between the older Buddhist texts and the New Testament. In Christian terms it is the parable of the Widow's Mite. According to the Buddhist version, there is a religious assembly at which the faithful are required to make financial donations. The wealthier members of the congregation give generously and in valuable coin. There is a poor widow, however, whose total possessions amount only to two small coins, and these she duly gives, and with pleasure. The presiding priest perceives her noble gesture and publicly praises her for making it, saying nothing at all about the other donations.

The corresponding passage in Mark's Gospel tells it this way:

And Jesus sat over against the treasury, and beheld how the people cast money in the treasury: and many that were rich cast in much.

And there came a certain poor widow, and she threw in two mites, which make a farthing.

And he called unto him his disciples, and saith unto them, Verily I say unto you, That this poor widow hath cast more in, than all they which have cast into the treasury:

For all they did cast in of their abundance; but she of her want did cast in all that she had, even all her living.

(Mark 12:41–44)

Apart from the fact that the basic theme is identical in both versions, there are some especially striking coincidental details. In both versions the story is about a widow. Both make their offering at a religious assembly together with rich people. Both give all they possess, namely two coins. And each is subsequently praised by someone present who values her sacrifice much more highly than the donations of the rich. So close are the versions that it would be difficult to believe that the later (Christian) one was somehow invented quite independently of the earlier (Buddhist) one.

Parallels between Buddhism and Christianity are discernible not just in the words and deeds of their founders but also in other aspects of the two religions after their founders' respective deaths. Myth and legend surround the two central characters in such a way that, soon after they die, Buddha and Jesus are elevated above all the lesser deities and stories of miracles proliferate and spread. In both cases the disciples at first fail to establish any organized religious community for the faith, operating instead in small, scattered groups. Quite soon, theological disputes break out between groups with different backgrounds: between Sthaviras and Mahasanghikas, and between Jewish Christians and Hellenist Christians. In both religions Councils are convened, one in Rajagriha, one in Jerusalem. And just as the Orthodox Buddhists formalized their doctrine at the Council of Pataliputra (in 241 BC) 250 years after Buddha's death, so did the Christian Church at the Council of Nicea (AD 325), 300 years after Jesus was last seen in Palestine.

At the time Jesus was living and teaching in Palestine, the Mahayana school of Buddhism had just evolved from the rather self-oriented Hinayana. It was Mahayana that turned Buddhism into a universal religion, open to believers of every nation and background. Mahayana philosophy focuses on compassion for all beings, as embodied in the ideal of the Bodhisattva, a concept that took shape in the third century BC. The Bodhisattva is the Englightened One who defers his merging with the Universal Being, who postpones his entry into *nirvana*, for as long as it takes for him to lead every person and being to salvation. The earthly existence of a Bodhisattva has the single purpose of leading all souls on to the path of release (*moksha*), the path that constitutes liberation from the cycle of rebirths and from the distractions of the world and physicality.

All those qualities that characterize a Bodhisattva are to be found in Jesus, down to the last detail. Jesus is by himself the epitome of the Bodhisattva ideal.

Was Jesus an Orthodox Jew?

A Jew among Jews, Jesus is sometimes held to be representative of the Judaism of his time and local culture. But in no way can the epithets 'traditional' and 'orthodox' be applied to him in a religious sense. In regard particularly to the subjects of death, the family, the Law, and indeed Jewish tradition, there are fundamental differences that distinguish his outlook from Orthodox Judaism. It would not be unfair to say, even, that Jesus debunked all that was most sacred to traditional Jewish culture!

This is especially the case in relation to death and the family. In four successive verses Luke reports how Jesus considers personal freedom to worship and a love for God to be of more importance than first the conventional burial rites and second the duties inherent in being one of a family.

> And he said unto another, Follow me. But he said, Lord, suffer me first to go and bury my father.
>
> Jesus said unto him, Let the dead bury their dead: but go thou and preach the kingdom of God.
>
> And another also said, Lord, I will follow thee; but let me first go bid them farewell, which are at home at my house.
>
> And Jesus said unto him, No man, having put his hand to the plough, and looking back, is fit for the kingdom of God.
>
> (Luke 9:59–62)

Whenever Jesus' teaching and activities touch upon family matters, they tend 'to offend Jewish feelings', as the Jewish historian C. G. Montefiore has put it.[24] 'If any man come to me, and hate not his father, and mother, and wife, and children, and brethren, and sisters, . . . he cannot be my disciple' (Luke 14:26). 'He that loveth father or mother more than me is not worthy of me' (Matthew 10:37). Especially contrary – and incomprehensible – to the Jewish tradition is the passage in Matthew's Gospel in which Jesus verbally disowns his own mother:

> While he yet talked to the people, behold, his mother and his brethren stood without, desiring to speak with him.
> Then one said unto him, Behold, thy mother and thy brethren stand without, desiring to speak with thee.
> But he answered and said unto him that told him, Who is my mother? and who are my brethren?
> And he stretched forth his hand toward his disciples, and said, Behold my mother and my brethren!
>
> (Matthew 12:46–49)

The same Jesus in whose name 'crusades for the family' have been organized evaded his own family when they wanted to talk to him. And it is Matthew – the writer of a Gospel from a Jewish standpoint, of all people – who quotes Jesus as making a statement that is unique for the ancient world and particularly scandalous to the Jews: 'I am come to set a man at variance against his father, and the daughter against her mother, and the daughter-in-law against her mother-in-law.' And in a strange anticipation of Freudian theory, he adds: 'And a man's foes shall be they of his own household' (Matthew 10:35–36).

Viewed against the background of contemporary Jewish culture, such behaviour on the part of Jesus – casting off family ties and severing bonds held to be sacrosanct – may be considered nothing short of baffling even today. Yet this same attitude is precisely that of the Buddhist striving after complete liberation from the desires and distractions of the worldly self. To gain release from the sufferings of this earthly life, all personal attachments must be forgone, as must any cultural niceties that represent similar hindrances. The individual human person remains a prisoner of the cycle of rebirths for as long as he is unable to free himself from selfish desires. Jesus found himself constantly chafing against the Jewish Law, which seemed to him in any case to be expounded in futile and vacuous terms, and his decisive rebuttal of the importance of the Sabbath was enough finally to lead to his Crucifixion.

Had Jesus really intended to lead a godly life as understood by the contemporary Orhtodox Jews, or even to become a rabbi, he would have to have been married – especially at his mature age. Matthew, however, leaves no doubt at all that Jesus remained single (19:12).

And Jesus would have to have been circumcised, as required for all male Jews as the sign of the Covenant between Yahweh-Jehovah and Abraham.[25] Only circumcised men were permitted to take part in the meal commemorating the Passover, and no uncircumcised man was allowed to enter the Lord's sanctuary in the Temple.[26] Anyone who refused to be circumcised was held to be in breach of the Covenant and was expelled, 'cut off from his people' (Genesis 17:14). Yet the Gospels do not actually state whether Jesus was circumcised or not. Luke 2:21 merely says that when Jesus was eight days old and the statutory circumcision was due, he was given his name. There is no definitive declaration that he really was circumcised.

The apocryphal *Gospel of Thomas* relates a saying of Jesus on the subject of circumcision:

> His disciples asked him, 'Circumcision – is there any real point in it or not?' He answered, 'If it was really important, your heavenly Father would have seen to it that you came into the world already circumcised from your mother's womb. But certainly, circumcision in spirit may well be of great importance.'
>
> (Logion 53)[27]

The Essenes are known to have recognized only such a 'spiritual circumcision', and not to have required the physical removal of the foreskin. In this way Paul, who was strongly opposed to circumcision as a religious requirement, managed to override the objections of the Jewish Christians and to get the rescinding of the obligation affirmed by the apostles at the Council of Jerusalem.

Successors to the Essenes and Nazarenes

In the struggle for dominance that took place between the many Paulinist, Gnostic and Jewish-Christian groupings during the early centuries of the present era, it was the Church of Rome, as organized in hierarchy and in form by Paul, that finally emerged as the victor following the Emperor Constantine's conversion to Christianity in AD 313. Three hundred years later it found itself under pressure as a new religion pressed forcefully from the south into Asia Minor: Islam succeeded in winning over much of the population of the area within a surprisingly short space of time.

But what became of the groups who were unwilling to submit to the authority of the Pope in Rome and the Emperor in Byzantium – the Essenes and Nazarenes, the hard-core Jewish Christians (Ebionites), the Gnostics, Manicheans and neo-Platonists? Did they simply disappear, absorbed without trace either into the Church of Rome or into mainstream Islam?

A large number of different tribal communities, clans and sects still live today among the mountains of Asia Minor, Syria and Kurdistan, who are regarded as potentially trouble-making heretics by orthodox Muslims, and who, when not called simply Shiites, may be known instead under the collective name of *Alawites*[28] (because the cousin and son-in-law of the Prophet Muhammad, Ali, is accorded a special place in their beliefs).

These Alawites include, for example, the Bektashi dervishes of Anatolia and the Nusairis of the coastal mountains of Syria. The name of the latter group is thought by many authorities to derive from *Nazarene* or *Nazoraian*, or from the name *Nasara* or *Nasrani* that was applied to the first Christians in Palestine.[29] And there are the better-known Druse communities of the Lebanon mountains, and the Yazidi of Kurdistan, who are disparagingly called devil-worshippers by orthodox Muslims.

Until modern times outsiders, including scholarly researchers, knew virtually nothing about the religious beliefs of these groups, all of whom claimed to be dedicated Muslims, and all of whom swore those intiated into the mysteries of their faiths to absolute secrecy, on pain of the severest penalties. Only very recently did several of these tribal communities, particularly some groups in Turkey,[30] open their doors to the outside world to reveal an ancient tradition in which Mediterranean and Anatolian notions of Classical times have been preserved in combination with old Jewish, early Christian and Gnostic views, some of which bear unmistakable parallels both with the Essenes, Nazarenes and Therapeuts, and with ideals of religious life and thought in India.

All these sects typically divide the community into non-initiates (the laity) and initiates (monks). The monks are disposed in three ranks, just like the monks of the Therapeuts and the early Christian clergy.

In Anatolia, the monks who belong to the celibate branch of the Bektashi Order live either in monasteries or as wandering mendicants travelling from place to place on foot. Women too – who are accorded a much more independent mode of life than Muslim women – are accepted into the society of the initiates,[31] and are permitted to participate in the *Jem*, the most important rite of worship, which takes place in the monasteries or in the houses of devout believers. It features a communal meal with bread and wine (very similar to the *agape* meal at the assemblies of the first Christians), a confession of sins before the clergy, and a sacred dance undertaken in an ecstatic state by both men and women.

Candidates for initiation are sprinkled with water by twelve brothers of the Order, and symbolically hanged, as a sign of the death of the old person and the resurrection of the new. The Alawites of western Iran known as Ahl-e Haqq ('People of the truth') even conduct the novice to a spring in which he is then immersed.[32]

The philosophical precepts of these communities are strongly reminiscent of Indian traditions. The universe undergoes an endless cycle of formation and dissolution, called the cycle of being. From a Primary State called Haqq ('Truth') corresponding to the basic state of all things – comparable with the *brahman* of the Hindus, the *shunyata* of the Mahayana, and the Chinese *Tao* – there emanates a Deity in three Persons, who in turn brings forth the primal Logos or World-Intelligence, who is made incarnate among men in every age in order to show them the way to Englightenment. Particularly reverenced examples of such incarnate divinities are Ali and, notably, Jesus. The aim of human life is to gain Enlightenment and pass beyond the cycle of rebirths, so to become a 'person perfected' (*insan-i-kamil*), a reflection or image of God, like Ali or Jesus.[33]

An anthropologist from Luxembourg who had spent many years studying the Kurdish tribespeople of eastern Anatolia once told me that many legends continue to circulate about Jesus' residing in what is now south-eastern Turkey after the Resurrection. According to Persian folklore, he lived at the town of Nisibis, near Edessa, now called Nusaybin and on the Turkish border with Syria. Other scholars record a tradition among the Alawites of Anatolia that Jesus survived the Crucifixion, was nursed back to health by his disciples, and then forever left the territories that were under imperial Roman rule.[34] The lands north, west and south were all in Roman hands, so Jesus can only have migrated east.

Most authorities believe that these tribal communities represent direct descendants of the Essenes and Nazarenes who, after the time of Christ, merged with the Jewish Christians opposed to Paul's dominant Hellenist group, and who, in the interests of survival under Islamic rule, later assumed the guise of an Islamic sect.

There are many points of correspondence in addition to those already mentioned. All the groups celebrate Christian festivals, for example, and especially Easter. Revering Jesus, they also regard John the Baptist and Peter with particular respect, but have no time at all for Paul. They greatly esteem the Gospels of Matthew and John, but treat the (Hellenist) Greek Luke's Gospel with something approaching disdain.

What is even more interesting, perhaps, is that these tribes inhabit the very areas where some of the original Christian communities lived. The Alawites of Turkey, for example, occupy the territory that was once home to the Galatians – a people to whom one of the epistles ascribed in the New Testament to Paul was addressed.

Surely it is possible, then, that these remote communities living in inaccessibly mountainous areas might have preserved the original Christian doctrine in a far less adulterated form than did the Church of Rome with all its emperors, popes and cardinals.[35]

Chapter Six

THE SECRET OF JESUS

'What Manner of Man is This?'

The attempt to pin down the historical figure of Jesus Christ is rather like a physicist's attempt to prove the existence of a subatomic particle and to determine its charge. The particle itself cannot be traced by direct optical means, but over the course of a number of experiments it is possible to record the tracks of other, larger particles with which it has collided, and by following these tracks back to their source, to calculate the forces involved in the collision. The invisible subatomic particle is thus ultimately described by its effect.

In the case of Jesus, there are two additional factors that make the task more difficult. The first is that the Christian Churches have destroyed virtually all the evidence that might be used to reconstruct the events of Jesus' personal history. The other is that Jesus himself was compelled to preserve his secret (the secret of who he really was) throughout his life, in order to keep out of the clutches of his enemies as much as he could. Jesus the person is covered by a veil of mystery and secrecy. An obscuring cloud hangs over the events of his personal life, leaving all too much scope for speculation.

So much ambiguity only makes for eventual and complete bafflement. Our ideas on the nature and personality of Jesus Christ are based not so much on documented biography and historical evidence as on a truth that transcends history while being passed down through history. We inevitably come up against the limits of what seems natural and comprehensible. All our questions ultimately reduce to a single, central question – one that was indeed even posed by Jesus' contemporaries: 'What manner of man is this?' (Mark 4:41).

That there can be such differing perceptions of Jesus must be presumed to stem from the nature of the historical person – a remarkable and studiously maintained balance between openness and secrecy. Jesus' exhortations to others to keep silent about him, the incapacity of even his own disciples to understand him, and the fact that what the Son of Man actually said was relatively fleeting, have all played a role in this. Those same disciples who had been spending their lives accompanying the Master were able neither to understand him correctly nor to appreciate what he was about. He seemed eccentric and enigmatic, and he was apparently not too concerned about reducing this cryptic aspect to his public life. Even the disciples were expressly bound to silence.

After Peter's revelatory declaration, Jesus 'charged them that they should tell no man of him' (Mark 8:30), and when coming down from the mountain following the Transfiguration, he 'charged them that they should tell no man what things they had seen' (Mark 9:9).

There was the same enjoining to secrecy when Jesus healed people. Again and again, Jesus forbade those who were healed to spread the news about the event. He sent away a leper whom he had cured with the words, 'See thou say nothing to any man' (Mark 1:43). And to those present at the awakening of Jairus' daughter 'he charged them straitly that no man should know it' (Mark 5:43). Jesus sent home the man of Bethsaida whose sight he had restored, with the command 'Neither go into the town, nor tell it to any in the town' (Mark 8:26). In spite of all this, the miracles could not be kept secret and soon became very public knowledge. The result was that after the healing of the person who was deaf and dumb, for instance, 'he charged them that they should tell no man: but the more he charged them, so much the more a great deal they published it' (Mark 7:36).

Jesus even ordered demons who recognized him as the Holy One of God (cf Mark 1:24; 5:7). He 'suffered not the devils to speak, because they knew him' (Mark 1:34). 'And unclean spirits, when they saw him, fell down before him, and cried, saying, Thou art the Son of God. And he straitly charged them that they should not make him known' (Mark 3:11–12).

In this way, then, the disciples, those who were healed, and unclean spirits and devils were all forbidden to publicize his actions – indeed, they were given a formal instruction generally to keep very quiet about him. 'And he would not that any man should know it [was he]' (Mark 7:24; 9:30).

The command obviously also applied to the disciples. There seems to have been a great intellectual gulf between Jesus and his disciples, who were simply unable to fathom him at all. This is particularly evident in Jesus' expressions of exasperation at their total lack of comprehension. Aboard the ship tossed about on the lake by a storm, there came the stern words 'Why are ye so fearful? How is it that ye have no faith?' (Mark 4:40). And, following the miracle of the loaves, 'Why reason ye, because ye have no bread? Perceive ye not yet, neither understand? Have ye your heart yet hardened? Having eyes, see ye not? And having ears, hear ye not? And do ye not remember?' (Mark 8:17–18). And finally, 'How is it that ye do not understand [even now]?' (Mark 8:21). When the disciples' attempt to cure a boy possessed by a 'dumb spirit' turned out to be unsuccessful, Jesus admonishes them with the words, 'O faithless generation, how long shall I be with you? How long shall I suffer you? Bring him unto me' (Mark 9:19). The second of these two questions might be interpreted as implying that Jesus had always intended his mission in Palestine to be of limited duration, and that he could see approaching his return sometime soon to India.

The circumstances surrounding his final public entry into Jerusalem are also puzzling. Why should this son of the common people be hailed with such celebrity in the city if – as the official line goes – he had been sawing planks in his father's carpentry shop all his adult life until his thirtieth year, and so could hardly have been a stranger among the local population? The enthusiastic reception by the people of Palestine rather suggests instead that he had returned after a prolonged absence from far away, with strange and novel teachings, and with such supernatural powers as the ability to perform miracles and to heal the sick.

This also puts the question of the Nazarene Baptist, John, in a new light: 'Art thou he that should come, or do we look for another?' (Matthew 11:3).

Reincarnation in the New Testament

According to public opinion statistics gathered in research by the Gallup organization, some 23 per cent of North Americans in 1980–1, and around 21 per cent of Europeans in 1983, believed in the doctrine of reincarnation.[1]

Reincarnation is referred to quite specifically several times in the New Testament, although such references are most often ignored or (possibly deliberately) misunderstood. Belief in reincarnation was a matter of course to the early Christian communities, until it became the victim of a historic error perpetrated by the Ecumenical Council of Constantinople in AD 533. Declared heretical, it has since remained banned from 'Christian' doctrine to this day.

The idea of rebirth was widespread throughout the Graeco-Roman world of classical antiquity. The great Greek philsopher and mathematician Pythagoras (around 570–496 BC), a contemporary of Buddha, was a firm believer in the transmigration of souls, and there are quite a few legends that tell of his travelling to India.[2] Plato (427–347 BC) was likewise a disciple of reincarnation, and rebirth also plays a central role in the philosophy of the Stoics. The Roman poets Virgil and Plutarch, contemporaries of Jesus, believed that the souls of people who were somehow tied to the physical world of the flesh would be reborn in a new body when the old body died.

In ancient North Africa, in Asia Minor and in the Middle East, from Anatolia and Egypt to Persia, the notions of the transmigration of souls and rebirth were taken for granted. The Old Testament contains clear examples of a belief in the rebirth of the soul in another body. According to Psalm 90:3, God 'turnest man to destruction; and sayest, Return ye children of men'. Friedrich Weinreb even interprets a passage in the Book of Jonah as describing regressive reincarnation in the form of cattle, and also tells of a reincarnation of Nimrod. Weinreb explains the Jewish concept of the God-soul *nshamah*, the divine and perfect spirit that is equally in all humans, certain characteristic aspects of which from time to time make an appearance.[3]

By AD 30 the Jews were quite familiar with the doctrine of the transmigration of souls, which they called Gilgal ('Wheel', 'Cycle'). As Jerome, the Doctor of the Chuch, reports, the Gilgal doctrine was common knowledge among the first Christians. Under the heading 'Reincarnation in the Jewish Talmud', Meyer's *Konversationslexikon* – a standard German encyclopaedia published in 1907 – declares:

> The Jews of the time of Christ held a general belief in the transmigration of souls. The authors of the Talmud took it for granted that God had created a finite number of Jewish souls that would continue to return to an earthly existence for as long as there were Jews, if occasionally in the form of an animal in order to teach a soul a lesson. But all would be purified on the Last Day, and rise in the bodies of the righteous in the Promised Land.
>
> (*Konversationslexicon* Vol.18, p.263)

The Old Testament actually ends with a prophecy (made in about 870 BC) announcing the reincarnation of Elijah: 'Behold, I will send you Elijah the prophet before the coming of the great and dreadful day of the Lord' (Malachi 4:5).

Nearly nine centuries later, an angel appears to Zacharias and announces the birth of a son:

> But the angel said unto him, Fear not, Zacharias: for thy prayer is heard; and thy wife Elisabeth shall bear thee a son, and thou shalt call his name John.
>
> And thou shalt have joy and gladness; and many [!] shall rejoice at his birth.
>
> For he shall be great in the sight of the Lord, and shall drink neither wine nor strong drink; and he shall be filled with the Holy Ghost, even from his mother's womb.
>
> And many of the children of Israel shall he turn to the Lord their God.
>
> And he shall go before him in the spirit and power of Elias [*Elias* is just a Greek version of the Hebrew *Elijah*], to turn the hearts of the fathers to the children . . .
>
> (Luke 1:13–17)

Jesus himself was later to state that John the Baptist was Elijah/Elias:

> For this is he, of whom it is written, Behold, I send my messenger before thy face, which shall prepare thy way before thee.
>
> Verily I say unto you, Among them that are born of women there hath not risen a greater than John the Baptist: notwithstanding he that is least in the kingdom of heaven is greater than he. . . .
>
> For all the prophets and the law prophesied until John.
>
> And if ye wlll receive it, this is Elias, which was for to come.
>
> (Matthew 11:10–11, 13–14)

According to John 1:21, when asked by the priests and Levites, the Baptist replies that he is not Elias. Leaving aside for the moment any speculation on what might constitute a tangible reason for such a negative response by John the Baptist over whether he was or was not Elijah/Elias, the most significant thing about it is that the religious authorities evidently thought it quite possible that he was indeed the new incarnation of Elijah/Elias.

We are nowhere told how John the Baptist spent his youth – that is, where he was educated. There is only the one succinct sentence in Luke: 'And the child grew, and waxed strong in spirit, and was in the deserts till the day of his shewing unto Israel' (Luke 1:80).

It is not inconceivable, therefore, that John too was recognized as a reincarnation of a particularly holy soul, and likewise given direct monastic training in far-off India. If this were the case, 'preparing a path for the Lord' would have had a more than figurative meaning.

On another occasion, Jesus asks his disciples: 'Whom do men say that I the Son of Man am? And they said, Some say that thou art John the Baptist: some, Elias; and others, Jeremias, or one of the prophets. He saith unto them, But whom say ye that I am? And Simon Peter answered and said, Thou art the Christ, the Son of the living God' (Matthew 16:13–16).

And the disciples asked Jesus, 'Why then say the scribes that Elias must first come? And Jesus answered and said unto them, Elias truly shall first come, and restore all things. But I say unto you, That Elias is come already, and they knew him not, but have done unto him whatsoever they listed. Likewise shall also the Son of Man suffer of them. Then the disciples understood that he spake unto them of John the Baptist' (Matthew 17:10–13).

According to the Gospels, then, Jesus himself confirmed that the soul of Elijah/Elias had been reborn in human form as John. Elijah/Elias had tried to foster monotheism at the royal court, and had taught that God does not manifest himself in fire and destruction but in 'a still, small voice' – that is in reflective and patient calm.

The first Elijah dressed himself in the rags typical of a wandering monk, was nourished miraculously, and was permitted to perform miracles himself – notably to multiply quantities of food and to raise the dead to life. Given the mission of anointing others, he spoke of being a 'messenger' and attracted a vast flock of followers. Finally, he disappeared in so mysterious a manner (ascending heavenwards in a whirlwind) that he was sought by fifty men for three days but could not be found.

The followers of Jesus knew that Jesus was a reincarnation, but were still not sure about his identity and offered several suggestions. Jesus himself gives no direct reply to the speculations, but he does confirm the disciples' ideas indirectly by encouraging their enquiry: 'But who do you say I am?' There are also significant descriptions in the New Testament (Matthew 14:1–2; 16:13–14; Mark 6:14–16; Luke 9:7–9) of the conjectures of various people, including Herod, as to whose soul Jesus might represent the reincarnation of. All these passages definitively prove that reincarnation was a widespread belief at the time. According to Josephus, the Pharisees believed in 'the power of . . . those returning to life',[4] and that the souls of the good pass on to another body.[5]

In the account of Jesus' healing of a man blind from birth (John 9), the disciples expressly ask, 'Master, who did sin, this man, or his parents, that he was born blind?' The idea that someone could have been born blind because of sin committed previously natural-ly carries with it the implication of a life lived before and a subse-quent rebirth. A further and simultaneous implication in the question is the sublime concept of *karma* (the Sanskrit term for 'action' or 'causation'), by which the actions undertaken in one life profoundly affect the conditions and circumstances of the next life.

Again, the concept of reincarnation is evident in the third chap-ter of John's Gospel. When Jesus meets the Pharisee Nicodemus, he greets this 'ruler of the Jews' with the words: 'Verily, verily, I say unto thee, Except a man be born again, he cannot see the king-dom of God.' Taken aback, Nicodemus replies: 'How can a man be born when he is old? Can he enter the second time into his moth-er's womb, and be born? Jesus answered, Verily, verily, I say unto thee, Except a man be born of water and of the Spirit, he cannot enter into the kingdom of God' (John 3:3–5).

The clearest reference in the New Testament to reincarnation is found in the Epistle of James (3:6, quoted here in the *Jerusalem Bible* version), where it says that the tongue 'is a whole wicked world in itself: it infects the whole body; catching fire itself from hell, it sets fire to the whole wheel of creation'. The translation of the last phrase that appears in most English Bibles is 'the course of nature', 'the wheel of our existence', or some equally nebulous expression that distorts the sense of the original Greek words, which literally mean 'cycle of being' or 'wheel of living', and in which the word for 'being' and 'living' is *genesis*, related to the verb 'to come into being', 'to be born' – so corresponding exactly to the Indian doc-trine of the wheel of rebirth (*samsara chakra*), which is set in flames like the 'cycle of being' of James' Epistle. Most theologians inter-pret this passage in the text as 'showing Gnostic influence', and the doctrine propounded by the Gnostics – or so all the modern Christian Churches, denominations and authorities would have us believe – is not only non-Christian but fundamentally opposed to the teaching of Jesus . . .

Christianity and the Gnostics

In the theological writings of the early Christian Church, and in other contemporary documents, there are many examples of a relationship between Christian and Indian thought in the first centuries after Christ. Numerous references at the hands of the Fathers of the Church of the time may today be interpreted as demonstrating the doctrine of reincarnation, despite all the literary tampering that went on later.[6] Eusebius, the first writer of Church history, tells us that Pantainos – the founder of the famous theological school at Alexandria – had lived in India before beginning work as a theologian.[7]

Trade between the Roman Empire and India flourished during the first century of our era, and the centre for this trade was the city of Alexandria. Along with the wares of commerce, Indian ideas also found their way to Alexandria, so permeating local political and religious thought. By that time Christianity had not yet become the monolithic and highly stratified Church it was later to be; it was instead made up of many individual groups, each of which was affiliated to any of various schools of philosophy, and many of them to those that were eventually to be unceremoniously grouped within the description 'Gnostic'. Most of the Gnostic doctrines were later condemned as heresies by the Church Councils, but some sects still survived into the Middle Ages, until the last of their followers (the Cathars, the Albigensians and the Bogomils) were brutally eradicated by the autocratic Church of Rome. Common to all these Gnostic groups was a strong faith in Jesus and in reincarnation. Many learned authorities have contended that the very early Christians and the Gnostics were originally part of the same movement, and that the celebrated antagonism between the two groups was a falsification of history on the part of Church leaders at a much later date.[8] This contention has never convincingly been refuted. Indeed, a number of commentators even believe that there was a Buddhist colony in Alexandria at the time.[9]

Whether there was or not, at that very early stage, it remains an uncontested fact that in the second century AD a delegation of Buddhist monks from Egypt took part in a major Buddhist conference in Sri Lanka.

The followers of the Buddha in Alexandria during the decades either side of Jesus' birth, if there were any, certainly did not call themselves Buddhists. Instead, they would probably have used the name adopted by their brothers in India: the followers of the *Dharma* (the universal Law and the teaching of Buddha). In Greek, the word *Dharma* may be translated as *Logos*, 'Word', and adherents of this teaching could therefore be described as Logicians. One group of Gnostics was in fact actually known as the Logicians.

The famous introduction to John's Gospel – 'In the beginning was the Word . . .' – thus has a literary form that is by no means unlike a quotation from Buddhist scriptures, 'The essence [of all things] is the Dharma . . .', especially in that the Greek word used for 'beginning', *arche*, can have other meanings, notably 'origin', 'principle' and 'mastery', and that the Greek imperfect form of the verb 'to be' – translated simply as 'was' – suggests a continuation of the action through to the present.

The most sacred authority in Buddhism is the trinity represented by Buddha, Dharma, and Sangha. Christian theology has the Holy Trinity of the Father, the Son and the Holy Spirit, of whom the Son, the second Person, is equated with the Logos (that is to say the Dharma), and the third Person, the Holy Spirit, is active in the community of the faithful (the Sangha).

The concept of a Holy Trinity, a Deity in three Persons or manifestations, has existed in religious doctrine since the dawn of history, from Egypt to eastern Asia. It was in this mode that the ancient Egyptians of early dynasties conceived their prime trinity of a sun god, an earth mother and (a combined) sun-over-earth son. The Chinese equivalent was the trinity of Heaven, Earth and the human individual made perfect (represented by the Emperor, the Son of Heaven). The Hindu Trimurti of Brahma, Vishnu and Shiva, although it appears to have developed as such only during medieval times, is rooted in much older ideas of the Three. In Vedic philosophy, the core of modern Hinduism, God or the Deity is described as Sat ('Existence', pronounced 'saht' [see Appendix]), Chit ('Awareness') and Ananda ('Blessedness'), the three of which have clear parallels with the Persons of the Christian Trinity.

Gnostic thought is to be found everywhere in early Christianity, and notably in the letters of Paul – especially in the letter to the Ephesians (which may well not be by Paul, admittedly) – and in the Gospel of John. Because almost all the 'heretical' writings were destroyed by the Church, hardly any original texts outlining Gnostic beliefs have survived. What little does remain includes the *Pistis Sophia* (Greek: 'Faith Wisdom'), the Books of Jeu and the Coptic library of Nag Hammadi from the 4th century AD, which turned up in 1945 by means of a discovery much like that of the

Dead Sea Scrolls.

Despite the longstanding denial of any connection between the early Christians and the Gnostics by the historical authorities of the Christian Church, it remains an incontrovertible fact that a number of theological concepts that came to be part of the ortho-dox doctrine of the Church of Rome actually originated within the confines of the Gnostic culture resident in Alexandria, in which the first great Christian theologians Clement (around 150–214) and Origen (about 185–254) lived and worked. It has been proved that Clement of Alexandria was familiar not only with the spiritual cul-ture of India but even with the teaching of Buddha.[10] His under-standing of the transmigration of souls speaks for itself:

> Yet we exist before the foundation of the world, we who are already present even before then through our being in God; we, the creatures given the knowledge of the divine Logos, through whom we are most ancient . . .[11]
>
> For as each such birth follows the previous one, we are led in grad-ual progression to Immortality.[12]

Clement's pupil and successor was Origen, the founder of system-atic Christian theology, one of whose teachers was a mysterious individual named Ammonius Sakkas, or Ammonius the Saka. The Sakas were a people of northern India, and the Indian antecedents of Ammonius are beyond doubt, but many authorities today believe that the epithet *Sakkas* does not actually mean 'the Saka', but that it more probably refers to Sakya or Sakyamuni – to the fact that Ammonius was a Buddhist monk.[13]

If this is the case, then the most important theologian of early Christianity after Augustine was the pupil of a Buddhist monk from India, and many of the images and metaphors that he uses in his theological works ought to be viewed as taken directly from Buddhism. Unfortunately only a fragment of Origen's writings have survived. Most of his manuscripts were later destroyed pre-cisely because he was prepared to show great tolerance towards people of differing views, and especially because of his belief in reincarnation. What remains is his major opus *De Principiis*, an attempt at a systematic presentation of Christian teachings (in the edited Latin translation by Rufinus of Aquileia), his treatise *Contra Celsum*, and a 'Commentary on Matthew'.

Two passages from his writings suffice to demonstrate his belief in the existence of the soul before birth, and the influence of actions undertaken previously:

> Every soul . . . enters this world strengthened by the victories or weak-
> ened by the stumblings of its previous life. Its place in this world . . . is
> determined by what it has earlier gained or discarded.[14]
>
> Does it not make absolute sense that every soul . . . is guided into a
> body, and this in accordance with deeds done earlier? . . . The soul
> makes use of a body for a certain duration . . , but as it changes, the
> body becomes less suited to it and it then exchanges it for another
> one.[15]

Similar statements are made by many other Christian theologians
in the period prior to the Council of Constantinople in 553.
Gregory of Nyssa (about 334–391) was one:

> The soul needs to undergo a kind of healing process in order to be
> cleansed of stains caused by sin. In the present life, virtue is the reme-
> dy that is applied to heal these scars. If they remain incurable in the
> present life, then the healing treatment is continued in a future life.[16]

The Anathema of Justinian

Almost every Christian historian to date has put forward the view
that the doctrine of reincarnation was declared a heresy (anathe-
matized) by formal decree at the Council of Constantinople in the
year 553. A closer look at the real circumstances, however, reveals
that any idea of a formal decree by the Council just does not stand
up to investigation. The doctrine of reincarnation was in fact condemned by no more than a mere personal veto by the Emperor
Justinian, and the anathematization was never part of Council resolutions.

Justinian's wife (according to the historian Procopius) was the
ambitious, not to say power-crazed, daughter of a bearguard at the
amphitheatre in Byzantium. She began her meteoric rise, eventually to lead to her becoming ruler of the empire, as a courtesan. As
soon as she became Empress, in order to break the ties with her
ignoble past and to foster an austerely moral image, she ordered
the torture and execution of 500 of her erstwhile courtesan colleagues. Then, in an endeavour to avoid suffering the dread consequences of such cruel deeds in a subsequent life according to the
laws of *karma* and reincarnation, she set about applying all her
influence to have the doctrine of the cycle of rebirths formally
abolished. She was apparently quite convinced that an edict promulgated by the 'divine decree' of the Emperor anathematizing

the doctrine as a heresy would altogether absolve her from all cul-
pability. In addition, both the Emperor and his wife were intent on
bolstering Constantinople's supremacy of spiritual and temporal
authority over Rome and the Bishop of Rome – which also goes a
long way towards explaining how an imperial decree anathematizing the doctrines held by Origen and his counterparts came to be
promulgated without the endorsement of the Pope and the Roman
bishops of the West.

The Emperor Justinian had already declared war on the teachings of Origen in AD 543 when, without bothering to consult the
Pope, he had them condemned as heretical by a specially convened
synod. Ten years later he assembled a Council in Constantinople,
only afterwards to become known as the Fifth Ecumenical Council.
Hardly 'ecumenical', it could only just be described as a 'council',
for it was little more than an ego-trip for Justinian, who saw himself as the head of the Eastern Church and was trying to consoli-
date this claim to power in relation to the Bishop of Rome in the
West. Of the 165 bishops present, a mere dozen were from Roman
dioceses; all other Western bishops specifically refused to take part
in the Council. The Eastern (Orthodox) bishops who made up the
numbers were feudal vassals and in no position to resist the pressure the Emperor put on them. Pope Vigilius himself – although
he was visiting Constantinople at the time – also stayed away from
the Council in protest.

As had happened at the earlier synod of the Eastern Church in
543, the Emperor once more had Origen's teaching on reincarnation condemned at this assembly, and fifteen anathemata (ecclesiastical proscriptions) were issued against him.

The formal procedures, however, required that official protocols
of the eight Council sessions (which lasted four weeks altogether)
were presented to the Pope for his ratification. Constrained by the
Emperor, the ambitious Pope Vigilius (who had only been made
Pope at the insistence of the Empress in AD 537) finally wavered,
and appended his signature to the Council decrees laid before him.
The significant thing about this, though, is that the documents
given to the Pope for his signature concerned only an indictment
of three scholars who had been pronounced heretics by Justinian,
and against whom the Emperor had already issued an edict four
years before (an affair generally known as the 'episode of the Three
Chapters'). But there was no mention of Origen in them. The suc-
ceeding Popes Pelagius I (556–561), Pelagius II (579–590) and
Gregory I (590–604) were soon afterwards to speak of the Fifth

Council without referring once to Origen, even in passing. Somehow the conviction that Justinian's anathema – 'Eternal damnation to anyone who preaches the spurious pre-existence of the soul and its unnatural rebirth' – had been part of the Council's resolutions became lodged fast in ecclesiastical lore. A scrupulous examination of the historical events and the documentation pertaining to them makes it perfectly clear that the supposed ban on the doctrine of reincarnation is nothing more than an error of what is now well over a millennium's standing.

By about 1900, an American by the name of James Morgan Pryse had already come up with a complete list of references to the doctrine of reincarnation in the New Testament.[17] Pryse considered that the doctrine proceeded quite naturally from fundamental insights of the ancient world, through the teachings of the old philosophers, and so on (just as naturally) to appear in the New Testament. That the spiritual priciple behind human existence and the spiritual principle behind the existence of the entire universe (microcosm and macrocosm) are fundamentally one and the same means that all elements, forces and processes exist within the individual person, both in a physical and material sense and in a spiritual and divine sense. This concept reveals the spiritual unity of all beings: there is no separation between Nature and God. It reveals the Deity in all and as all, at all times, in each minute particle of the universe.

The human individual in physical form is a manifestation emanating from the realm of the undifferentiated, boundless and timeless Divine Unity which materializes Itself according to cyclical phases in various forms of being.

The essential and primordial Being is eternally changeless, whereas Nature – or the universe – is a Coming Into Being, a Being in continuous flux.

The soul – or the spirit – of Man is thus, in its deepest consciousness, everlasting, whereas in its constant coming and going (reincarnation) it is subject to a continuous sequence of action: of causes and effects.

In order to return finally to the divine state, Man must become aware of this principle, and take active steps to attain mastery over the material aspects of his existence. After a lengthy sequence of lives, a state may be reached in which all karmic suffering resulting from these periods of earthly existence is surmounted, and in ultimate perfection the inner or spiritual self merges into the Eternal Unity.

This is how the doctrine of reincarnation might be summed up in a few words.

Through knowledge, insight, meditation, asceticism, contemplative absorption, renunciation, and similar disciplines, it is possible to overcome the narrow restrictions of bodily life while still on earth, so to become aware of one's divine nature. Matthew's Gospel describes the goal in this way: 'Be ye therefore perfect, even as your Father in heaven is perfect' (Matthew 5:48). But the path to perfection is paved with many reincarnations, until the individual is fully awakened to being the child of God and performs the works of a Christ:

> Believe me that I am in the Father, and the Father in me: or else believe me for the very works' sake.
>   Verily, verily, I say unto you, He that believeth on me, the works that I do shall he do also; and greater works than these shall he do.
>
> (John 14:11–12)

Jesus, to me, is an ideal example of the Boddhisattva – that is, a Buddha in the making; a person who, standing at the gates of total Enlightenment, voluntarily returns to be born again out of compassion for human beings. Jesus is already very close to that divine state, having discarded all personal ties and selfish effort. He fully perceives that earthly existence, the cycle of rebirths determined by *karma*, is the cause of all suffering; he has preached to his disciples the conscious renunciation of worldly life; and he has shown them the way to Englightenment through 'right action' and the creation of good *karma*. 'The survival of Western humanity depends on the reintroduction of the concept of *karma* to the minds of the populace at large', as Paul Brunton said, and if we can become (once more) acquainted with the ideas of *karma* and reincarnation, it opens up completely new dimensions in understanding Jesus, showing us the way ahead, towards a coming age, even without a 'resurrection of the body'.

Miracles – of Jesus, and in India

To a casual observer, the miracles performed by Jesus may by themselves seem unique and without precedent. But behind many extraordinary, spectacular and inexplicable events throughout human history – some useful or even beneficial, others harmful or even catastrophic – people have tended to see the workings of a mysterious Force unknown in nature and beyond human understanding. From the very first primitive magical rites performed to appease deities of the earliest forms of religion, Man has interested himself in such inexplicable phenomena, and he continues to do so today.

Jesus' 'magical' powers were apparently considered nothing out of the ordinary enough to warrant mention by contemporary historians. During Jesus' lifetime wonder-workers, faith healers and outright charlatans were common everywhere. What was different about Jesus was primarily the fact that he did not practise his arts in a bid for fame and fortune.

The stories of the miracles in the New Testament – around thirty of them altogether – stem largely from the religious traditions of the contemporary communities of the area, and so are not verifiable historically. Reports outlining Jesus' activities as an exorcist are older, however, and were certainly current in Jesus' own time.

For thousands of years, whether miracles were actually possible was a question that was never asked. It first arose as a matter for speculation during the Renaissance, when a new scientific curiosity about the world started to manifest itself. Not until the seventeenth century did anyone attempt to find a rational explanation for some of the miracles described in the Gospels. Rationalists, however, are prepared to accept only phenomena that accord with natural laws and are intelligible to the scientifically enquiring mind. Miracles are thus phenomena for which causal relationships are neither understood nor explicable. Today, scientists are daily discovering completely new laws in the workings of natural processes, and constantly solving puzzles that were considered unfathomable, if not magical, the day before.

Theologians define a Christian miracle as 'the suspension of the action of a law of nature by God himself'.

In contrast, the occultist does not believe in the suspension of a law but maintains that miraculous phenomena are subject to higher laws that have not yet been discovered and defined. Everything that happens in our universe occurs in accordance with law and can be explained. The so-called magical powers of the initiate are therefore no more than the natural consequence of his better knowledge of how natural laws and these higher laws that derive from the inner realm of consciousness may be played off against each other.

Neither in the Old Testament nor in the New (in the original languages) is the term 'miracle' used. The scriptures instead speak of 'signs', 'power' or the 'marvellous deeds of God'.

The most important Hebrew word *el* (and *elohim*), for example, which derives from the Semitic root *alah* 'to be strong', means 'the great Power'. The word that describes this holy miracle-working power is thus derived from the same source as the word for 'God'.

There are similar connections in Indo-European languages. The first element of the Sanskrit word *brahman* can be traced back to the triconsonantal root *brh* 'to extend', thus 'to expand', 'to radiate (light)', 'to have power over', and 'to be strong'.

The miracles of Jesus seem to have been performed largely on compassionate grounds: the healing of the sick, the mentally deranged and the physically handicapped. But he evidently performed other types of miracle when necessary: he transformed water into wine, multiplied quantities of food, made himself invisible, raised the 'dead', and walked on water (levitated).

As with the other stories about Jesus, there are of course parallels and literary precedents for the miracle stories in both European and Asian traditions. Pliny tells of the miraculous cures of the Greek doctor Asclepiades (124–about 60 BC). Tacitus and Suetonius report on miraculous healings performed even by the Emperor Vespasian. The early Christian apostles were also able to heal the sick and perform various different miracles, and during the first century AD Apollonius of Tyana worked similar and other wonders.

But for the earliest reports of miracles identical to those performed by Jesus, the prime source comprises the stories of Krishna in the post-Vedic literature of India, the *Puranas* (especially the *Bhagavata Purana* and the *Mahabharata*). Krishna is the eighth avatar of the god Vishnu, and to the majority of Vaishnavite Hindus who worship Vishnu (Sanskrit root *vish* 'to pervade') as the supreme Lord, his incarnate form Krishna is the Saviour. The Rig Veda is too early a work for Vishnu to be depicted as deity made human, so he is there a manifestation of solar energy. In later Hindu theology, however, Vishnu is the Sustainer of the Universe in the divine Trinity, alongside Brahma the Creator and Shiva the Destroyer. An avatar (Sanskrit *avatara* from *ava* 'downwards' and *tri* 'to cross over') represents an incarnate form of God. The divine Higher Being takes on a mortal body out of compassion, in order to help suffering humanity to attain liberation and perfection.

The story of Krishna's birth, childhood and life contains many parallels with accounts of Jesus in the New Testament, even in the details (as for instance in the occurrence early on of a massacre of infants). Krishna and Christ are the two most prominent performers of miracles in the holy scriptures of the Hindus and Christians respectively. Bhagvan Dass divides Krishna's miracles into seven types:[18]

1. the granting of visions;
2. visual perception over an extraordinary distance;
3. the multiplication of small quantities of food or items;
4. appearing simultaneously at many places in a less than fleshly body;
5. the healing of the sick by the laying-on of hands;
6. the raising of the 'dead' to life; and
7. the destruction of demons and the exorcism of the possessed.

Some miracle-workers can perform only one or two kinds of miracles, others more. There have always been mystics, holy men or seers of different powers and reputations. And India has always been the home of the miraculous, the land of the phenomenal. In his treatise *The Holy Science*, Sri Yukteswar[9] sees the purpose of earthly existence as the aspiration and attempt to unite the inmost self with God. For Yukteswar regards Creation as 'substantially nothing but a mere simulacrum of Nature imposed over the only Real Substance, God, the Eternal Father, who is Guru – the Supreme – in this universe'. This means that all things are composed of the same one Entity. And God himself, who appears as a multiplicity because his essence is expressed in a variety of ways, is everywhere and everyone. The Bible says exactly the same thing in Psalm 82:6, 'I have said, Ye are gods; and all of you are children of the most High.' The passage is quoted in John's Gospel: when the Jews accused him of trying to make himself out to be a God, Jesus replied, 'Is it not written in your law, I said, Ye are gods?' (John 10:34).

Yukteswar goes on to explain that initiates who have attained perfect mastery over the world of matter find their God or ultimate fulfilment in their inner self and not in the external world. These 'divine humans' finally obtain mastery over life and death, virtually able to shape the world around them, capable of absolutely anything. They achieve the eight ascetic attainments (Aishwaryas), through the power of which they can

anima: shrink matter (or one's body) down to whatever size they want;

mahima: enlarge it up to whatever size they want;

laghima: make it weigh as little as they want;

garima: make it weigh as much as they want;

prapti: possess anything and everything that they want;

vashitwa: gain power (*vasha*) over anything and everything they want;

prakamya: fulfil all desires through the strength of the will;

ishitwa: become the Lord (*Isha*) of all things.

When Jesus' disciples failed to exorcise an unclean spirit, they asked him why, and he explained that it was through lack of faith: 'For verily I say unto you, If ye have faith as a grain of mustard seed, ye shall say unto this mountain, Remove hence to yonder place; and it shall remove; and nothing shall be impossible unto you' (Matthew 17:20). The related phenomena of teleportation and levitation have had an uninterrupted tradition both in and outside the Christian Church. No fewer than around 230 Catholic saints are recorded as having possessed the ability to levitate more or less voluntarily.

During the nineteenth century, the medium Daniel Douglas-Home successfully convinced thousands of spectators on various occasions of his ability to 'fly'. Witnesses included such notable celebrities as William Makepeace Thackeray, Edward Bulwer-Lytton, Napoleon II, John Ruskin, Dante Gabriel Rossetti and Mark Twain. Such performances took place over a period of nearly forty years, and were repeatedly investigated and confirmed.

In his reports on all the different forms of psychic phenomena, Francis Hitching cites more than twenty-five case of levitation.[20] Examples of levitation have certainly been reported right up to the present day. Swami Rama gives an eyewitness account in his collection of talks, *Living with the Himalayan Masters*. The phenomenon has been photographed and even filmed.

Levitation seems to be produced by a greatly heightened control over bodily processes, for example by concentration and meditation, or through the effects of religious ecstasy that permit moments in which the force of gravity somehow no longer applies.

Such 'minor miracles' can even be performed for money or to satisfy sensation-seekers. But the true masters only perform these 'miracles' for altruistic purposes.

The miracle-working holy man of India Sai Baba says, like Jesus, that every person has divine powers that can be brought into play through training and mental discipline. But whoever uses the powers to sow evil will reap evil. And whoever uses the powers selfishly and to his own advantage will lose them altogether. Sometimes these powers are limited in their efficacy or duration, particularly when used without altruism, wisdom and spiritual awareness.

Today, as thousands of years ago, 'miracles' remain a legitimate method of bringing the divine message closer to the doubters and those who are hemmed in by the material world. Almost everything reported about Jesus has a parallel in the ancient Indian legends. One of the reasons that this similarity between Indian and Christian stories remains so little known is the fact that very few Europeans are in a position to read the Sanskrit of the ancient texts: only recently have translations begun to arouse the interest of the Western world.

None of the known 'divine-human' representatives of God on Earth seems to have been able to convince the unbelieving masses of his divine authority without recourse to miraculous signs and wonders. Every Son of God has had to be able to demonstrate his status to sceptics by means of superhuman attributes.

Krishna is an avatar – a mortal form descended to Earth – of the god Vishnu (the second element in the Hindu Trinity, the Sustainer of Creation). It would seem that Krishna and Christ might well have more in common than miracles: it is certainly possible that the two expressions are etymologically cognate. The title 'Christ' (Latin *Christus*) comes from the Greek *khristos* (*christos*), the 'anointed' (Greek *khriein* 'to anoint', but also 'to dye', 'to colour'; *khrisma* 'ointment'). The Sanskrit name *Krsna* (pronounced 'Krishna') means 'the black' or 'the blue'. Both terms, Christus and Krishna, may well also be related to the Sanskrit root *krs* (pronounced 'krish') 'to attract', and based on this etymology the name Krishna is often translated as 'The all-attracting One'. This person who attracts all Creation is the highest form in which God has been seen on Earth.

Following Brahmin tradition, Brahma is viewed as the Creator of the Universe, and sometimes even called 'Father'. Vishnu, who became incarnate as Krishna, is occasionally called 'Son'. And Shiva, the third Person in the Hindu Trinity, who is Spirit, corresponds thus to the Holy Spirit, 'who directs the eternal law of formation and dissolution, indwelling in all living creatures and all Nature . . .'

Krishna is the eighth avatar or incarnate form of the god Vishnu, following seven earlier avatars. The ninth appearance of

Vishnu on Earth is in the form of Gautama Buddha (Prince Siddhartha, Sakyamuni 'the sage of the Sakyas').

Krishna and Christ

According to the most ancient of sources, some 5000 years ago the Lord Vishnu appeared in the form of a man in the presence of the maiden Devaki ('Made for God'), a member of the royal household. Devaki fell into an ecstasy and was 'overshadowed' by the spirit of God, who came to her in the splendour of his divine majesty, so that she conceived a child. The tradition tells of an annunciation:

> Blessed art thou, Devaki, among women. Welcome art thou amid the holy Rishis. Thou hast been chosen for the work of salvation . . . He will come with a luminous crown: heaven and earth will be full of joy . . . Virgin and Mother, we greet you; thou art the mother of us all, for thou shalt give birth to our Saviour. Thou shalt call him Krishna.

But the King of Mathura had been warned, in what to him was a nightmare, that a king would be born to his sister's daughter, who would be more powerful than he. The maiden Devaki hid in the fields with the newborn child in the company of some cowherds, and miraculously the child escaped the soldiers who had been despatched by the king to kill all newborn male babies.

According to another version of the tradition, King Kansa of Madurai saw a shooting star and asked a Brahman about its significance. The wise man replied that the world had become wicked, and that people's greed for gold together with their burdensome life had moved God to send a Redeemer. The star was the sign of Vishnu, who had been made flesh in the womb of Devaki; the avatar would one day restore righteousness and lead humanity on new paths. Beside himself with rage, the king had the Brahman killed along with all newborn males.

There are many tales of Krishna's childhood, glorying in his power and knowledge.

Like the boy Jesus in the apocryphal Gospels, Krishna was able to perform every conceivable miracle even as a little child. It was thus he was able to survive the many dangers prepared for him by his uncle Kansa. At one point a snake crawled into his cradle to strangle the child, but was itself killed by the lad with his bare hands (an exact parallel with the myth concerning the young Herakles/Hercules). Later, Krishna fought the multiple-headed snake Kaliya, defeated it, and compelled it to leave the River Yamuna. The heroic deeds performed by the Indian superboy were enough to fill any number of volumes. When he was sixteen, Krishna left his mother to spread his new teaching throughout India. He spoke out against corruption among the people and the princes, everywhere supported the weak against oppression, and declared that he had come to Earth to release people from suffering and sin, to drive out the spirit of evil, and to restore the rule of righteousness. He overcame tremendous difficulties, fought alone against entire armies, performed a wide range of miracles, raised the dead to life, healed lepers, gave sight to the blind and hearing to the deaf, and made the lame walk.

Eventually he amassed a large number of disciples, who supported him zealously and were to continue his work. Everywhere people came to him to hear his teachings and to marvel at the miracles he performed. He was honoured as a god and acclaimed as the true Redeemer who had been prophesied by the fathers.

From time to time Krishna would go off by himself for a while, leaving his disciples to their own devices in order to test them, and returning when they got into difficulties. The growing movement was watched with suspicion by those in authority, and they tried to suppress it, but without success.

Krishna did not wish to propagate a new religion but simply to renew the religion that already existed and cleanse it of all its follies and abuses. His teachings are in the form of poetic parables, aphorisms and similes very like the recorded words of Jesus. They are contained in the *Bhagavad Gita*, which presents the lofty, pure morals of the sublime view of life in a way simple enough for all to grasp. Krishna thus teaches his followers to love their neighbours; he lauds respect for the individual, calling upon all of us to share what we have with the poor, to do good deeds out of pure altruism and righteousness, and to believe in the ever-dependable goodness of the Creator. He instructs us to repay evil with good, to love our enemies, and he forbids revenge. He consoles the weak, condemns tyranny, and helps the unfortunate. He himself lives in poverty and devotes himself to the poor and the downtrodden. He is devoid of personal ties, and advocates chastity.

Krishna also undergoes a Transfiguration. The Son of God shows himself in a thousand different divine forms simultaneously to his favourite disciple Arjuna, and tells him,

Who doeth all for Me; who findeth Me
In all; adoreth always; loveth all
Which I have made, and Me, for Love's sole end,
That man, Arjuna! unto Me doth wend.

(*Bhagavad Gita*, Canto 11, tr. by Sir Edwin Arnold)

Finally, Krishna allows an arrow to strike him in the foot, marking the end of his ordained life on Earth. But when his followers search for his body it is nowhere to be found, for he has ascended to heaven.

The legend of Krishna is probably the oldest source that contributes to the mystical Christ figure. But similarities with the legends of Dionysos/Bacchus (dating from around the eighth century BC) are equally astonishing. And in addition to the lofty cultures of ancient Greece and Rome, that of ancient Persia – which also had its Saviour-Redeemer personalities – equally decisively influenced the eschatological and apocalyptic notions of the Christian religion.

Chapter Seven

THE SHROUD – A LEGACY
OF JESUS

Accusation and Trial

The political situation in Judea at the time of Jesus was extremely turbulent, and was regularly punctuated with dramatic
events.

Herod the Great (37–4 BC) had had to deal with persistent civil
unrest, sometimes outright revolt, throughout his reign. Fighting
against him and his successors was a guerrilla army, nationalist
fanatics to a man, determined to do everything they could to
undermine Roman rule. Josephus makes a reference to the leader
of the troublesome 'gang of bandits', one Judas of Galilee, but the
'bandits' would seem rather to have been men of strong religious
convictions, who were basically just trying to defend the faith of
their forefathers against foreign domination.[1]

Among these rebel groups – which included the Pharisees, the
Sadducees and the Rechabites – the Essenes were given special
place, being formally organized as an Order, and having an 'élite
corps' in the form of the Nazarenes (Nazareans). The Sadducees
and Pharisees were eventually to come to a compromise with
Herod's successors, accepting the lure of high office. The
Rechabites, on the other hand, utterly rejected the 'civilization' that
Rome sought to impose on them, and continued to live in tents
outside the towns, as their forebears had done for centuries.

It was probably when Herod's son Archelaus was deposed in
the year AD 6 that the Essenes and Nazarenes returned from exile
in and around the city of Alexandria. Certainly, the monastery of
Qumran was reoccupied from that time.

But it was also at that point that nationalist resentment of imperial Roman domination flared up into guerrilla warfare, particularly in the area administered by Herod Antipas (Archelaus' brother).

The resistance struggle was mostly conducted in great secrecy by Essene partisans who could melt invisibly into the countryside. And so it was that the Essenes and the Nazarenes were actively and bravely taking on the full strength of the mighty Roman overlord even while the conformist Pharisees and the Sadducees were becoming integrated into the overlord's political system.

After the death of Herod the Great, the country lurched from one crisis to the next. Many of the native Jewish population were desperately hoping for a Messiah who would revive the Kingdom of David and Solomon, and free the land from the hated foreign dictator.

According to the Gospel texts of Mark, Matthew and Luke, the period during which Jesus was publicly active lasted for about one to two years at the most. Only the latest Gospel, John's, refers to three Passovers in Jerusalem at which Jesus was present. All in all, it has to be assumed therefore that Jesus stayed in the area for between two and three years.

During this time, Jesus often crossed the borders of the various provinces into which Palestine was divided, each time thereby leaving the jurisdiction of the local religious and secular authorities. Why he should then go to Jerusalem, and by so doing give himself up to his persecutors, remains a mystery.

And his entry into Jerusalem was particularly spectacular: Jesus was jubilantly feted as the king who would establish the 'Kingdom of God'.

By Christian tradition, the 'Kingdom of God' is a state of heavenly perfection, to be understood in a purely spiritual sense: all may attain to it through God's own grace and assistance. But what the masses in Jerusalem were looking for was something of a rather more worldly nature. Jewish Messianism anticipated a Kingdom of God that was a new, purified and powerful state of Israel, and its leader (the Messiah) was expected to be an invincible military commander and statesman, as King David once had been, and to free the land from the Roman yoke.

Jesus' view of such hopes is recorded in the Gospel of Luke: 'The kingdom of God cometh not with observation: Neither shall they say, Lo here! or, lo there! for, behold, the kingdom of God is within you' (Luke 17:20–21).

The entry into the city of Jerusalem was an act of unprecedented provocation. Up to that point, the resistance had operated as an underground movement: they had not dared to show themselves openly in the capital. About a week before the great festival of the

Passover, Jesus decided to leave his place of hiding in the mountains of Ephraim (John 11:54), and journeyed with his followers by
way of a detour through Jericho to the capital, some 40 kilometres
away (Luke 19:1,28).

Mark's Gospel tells of the dramatic decision:

> And they were on the way going up to Jerusalem; and Jesus went
> before them: and they were amazed; and as they followed, they were
> afraid. And he took again the twelve, and began to tell them what
> things should happen unto him,
>
> Saying, Behold, we go up to Jerusalem; and the Son of Man shall be
> delivered unto the chief priests, and unto the scribes; and they shall
> condemn him to death, and shall deliver him to the Gentiles:
>
> And they shall mock him, and shall scourge him, and shall spit
> upon him, and shall kill him: and the third day he shall rise again.
>
> (Mark 10:32–34)

Five days before the great festival, they reached Jerusalem.
Entering through the city gates, Jesus was noisily acclaimed by the
crowds. But although Jesus was riding a donkey as a gesture of
humility, meekness and peaceful intent, the acclamation was later
to be tragically misunderstood. 'The whole city was in turmoil'
(Matthew 21:10, *Jerusalem Bible* version). Jesus' strongly-worded
statements, and the equally forthright, not to say violent, methods
he used in driving the traders out of the Temple, might perhaps in
a different atmosphere have been understood as being allegorical –
but they were certainly open to being interpreted as a clarion call
to the people to rise up. Some of Jesus' words were the very opposite of conciliatory: 'Think not that I am come to send peace on
earth: I came not to send peace, but a sword' (Matthew 10:34).[2]
And 'I am come to send fire on the earth; and what will I, if it be
already kindled?' (Luke 12:49).

The very first thing Jesus did in Jerusalem was to mount an
attack against the authorities, an attack such as no one had dared
to attempt before. With unmistakable directness Jesus remonstrat-
ed against the guardians of the Law in the Temple. His pointed
and barbed denunciations (Matthew 23) were a public settling of
accounts with his antagonists in front of a great number of enthusiastic pilgrims. According to the Gospels, he even went so far as to
drive the traders and moneychangers out of the place of worship.
Of course, such an attack on the authority of the Temple officials
could not be allowed to pass unchallenged – but care was required,
for in such a tense situation any untoward action was liable to trig-

ger a mass uprising. 'And the scribes and chief priests heard it, and sought how they might destroy him: for they feared him, because all the people was astonished at his doctrine' (Mark 11:18).

There was always the possibility of riots and other forms of civil unrest during the holy days of the festival, and Pilate (the Governor, as representative of the Emperor in Rome) had marched in from Caesarea with his cohorts (each of 500 legionaries) to be ready to intervene if necessary. Such disturbances are only briefly alluded to in the Gospels. According to Mark, a certain Barabbas was taken prisoner together with 'them that had made insurrection with him, who had committed murder in the insurrection' (Mark 15:7). Mark also says that the chief priests and scribes 'sought how they might take [Jesus] by craft, and put him to death. But they said, Not on the feast day, lest there be an uproar of the people' (Mark 14:1–2). If Jesus was to be liquidated, both great speed and great caution were called for.

The Pharisees first tried to get Jesus to incriminate himself in a public discussion. They asked him whether it was right to pay taxes to the Roman Emperor. If Jesus had replied in the negative, he would have been open to the charge of high treason; had he replied positively, he would have lost all the support and most of the interest of the people. Instead, he got out of the predicament by a stroke of genius (Mark 12:14–17). The Sadducees then attempted to ridicule his doctrine of reincarnation. This attack too he parried skilfully (Mark 12:19–27).

The date of the events in Jerusalem still poses a considerable problem. Neither the month nor the year of the event is to be found in the Gospels. Current speculations range from the year 30 to the year 33.

Although all the Gospels agree that Jesus was crucified on a Friday, there are two different suppositions about what date of the month it was. According to the Synoptic Gospels, Jesus celebrated the Last Supper with his disciples on the Thursday evening. By the Jewish calendar, Thursday was the 14th of Nisan, the day on which the Paschal Lamb was to be eaten. The Friday after, 15 Nisan, was the first holy day of the Jewish festival of Passah-Mazzoth. But it is quite unthinkable that Jesus was arrested and interrogated before the entire Sanhedrin (comprising seventy-one Jewish citizens) on that very holy night. Such a violation of Jewish Law by its own guardians is simply not credible.

An alternative solution is to be found in the gnostically influenced text of John's Gospel. Here, the Last Supper is not specified

as the Passover meal of the Jews, and Jesus has already been crucified by 14 Nisan. If this is the way it really was, Jesus must have
celebrated without the prescribed unleavened loaves and ritual
utensils, because these are (even now) only prepared for use on the
day immediately preceding the Passover, which is actually called
the Day of Preparation. John's version of events seems logical
enough, but it relies on the assumption that on this occasion Jesus
did not observe the Jewish customs anchored in the Law (although
there were certainly other occasions on which he deliberately
ignored them).

Even the place chosen for the Last Supper suggests the influence of the Essenes: 'Behold, when ye are entered into the city,
there shall a man meet you, bearing a pitcher of water; follow him
into the house where he entereth in' (Luke 22:10). But in the
Jerusalem of those days, the fetching and carrying of water was
done only by women. So in this particular house the usual customs
obviously did not apply. And in fact the meal did not proceed at
all according to the prescribed rite, but entirely in the Essene manner. They did not eat the sacrificial lamb, but bread, like the
Essenes, who of course did not eat meat at all. In the apocryphal
Gospel of the Ebionites, when the disciples raise the question of
where they should prepare the Passover meal, Jesus tells them, 'I
do not want to eat meat with you this Passover!'[3] The disciples
then have an argument about their places at the table because,
according to the Rule of the Essene Order, each person was
assigned a fixed place according to rank, designated by proximity
to the Master (1QSa). 'And there was also a strife among them,
which of them should be accounted the greatest' (Luke 22:24). So a
kind of Passover meal did take place, but not on the prescribed
day, without meat, and without the usual ritual.

At this point, a question arises that has caused the experts considerable soul-searching – a question to which they have as yet
been unable to come up with an answer: how to establish the date
of the Last Supper. But the problem is solved automatically if it
was the Essene calendar that was used to set the date for the festival. Because the solar calendar made it possible to divide the year
(counted as 364 days) into 52 weeks, there was no remainder in
days left over at the end of each year (as there was with the Jewish
calendar). New Year's Day always fell on a Wednesday in spring.
Accordingly, the Essene Passover on 14 Nisan regularly occurred
on a Wednesday, and so must have taken place two days before
the orthodox Jewish Passover that year. John's Gospel is thus also

correct in saying Jesus was crucified on 14 Nisan, for what he has in mind is the official calendar, which put the Crucifixion on the day before Passover.

The entire sequence of events in Jerusalem now takes place over a period of three days and can be established logically and conclusively:

Tuesday evening:	the Last Supper
	arrest at Gethsemane
	preliminary hearing by Annas
	threefold denial by Peter
Wednesday morning:	the beginning of the trial before the Sanhedrin
	examination of witnesses by Caiaphas
Wednesday night:	Jesus kept in custody overnight
	receives ill-treatment in Caiaphas' prison
Thursday:	the Sanhedrin reconvenes to announce judgement
	Jesus handed over to Pilate and interrogated
	Jesus is passed over to Herod Antipas
Friday:	the political trial continues before Pilate
	the scourging, the crowning with thorns
	the sentencing
	crucifixion at about the sixth hour (12 noon)

An unusual incident took place during the arrest of Jesus by the Temple guards after the meal: 'Then Simon Peter having a sword drew it, and smote the high priest's servant, and cut off his right ear. The servant's name was Malchus. Then said Jesus unto Peter, Put up thy sword into the sheath: the cup which my Father hath given me, shall I not drink it?' (John 18:10–11). Why was Peter carrying a sword?

Since the second century BC, the Sanhedrin (Greek-derived Hebrew: 'Assembly') had represented the highest Jewish authority not only in matters of religion but in all secular, national and judicial affairs to which there was a religious aspect. Before rule by Rome, the Sanhedrin also wielded considerable political power. It was composed of seventy members – priests, elders and scribes – under its president, the current chief (or high) priest, at this time Joseph Caiaphas. Among the elders of the assembly was Joseph of Arimathea, a rich and influential land-owner who voted against the decision of the High Council to put the Nazarene to death (Luke 23:50–51).

After detailed cross-examination of the witnesses, the chief priest, Caiaphas, concluded by posing the crucial question: 'I adjure thee by the living God, that thou tell us whether thou be the Christ, the Son of God' (Matthew 26:63). When Jesus answered, 'Thou hast said [it]', Caiaphas took this as a Yes – from which there was no turning back. According to Jewish Law, anyone who arrogated divine honours to himself was a blasphemer, and was liable to immediate capital punishment. Actually, the Jewish Law stipulated execution by stoning, but Jesus could not be taken out and summarily stoned to death because the Sanhedrin had only recently received an order from Rome that no one was to be put to death without the prior approval of the Roman procurator. Another factor was that all business before the Sanhedrin had to be concluded during the hours of daylight (between dawn and dusk). If all the seventy council members had been summoned and the trial had taken place at night, the entire proceedings would have been illegal from the start. In Luke's Gospel there is confirmation that the session took place during the day (Luke 22:66). The assembly did not reconvene until the following morning (Thursday) to announce its judgement: 'When the morning was come, all the chief priests and elders of the people took council against Jesus to put him to death: And when they had bound him, they led him away, and delivered him to Pontius Pilate the governor' (Matthew 27:1–2).

Pilate seems to have been unhappy with the case from the very beginning (John 18:31) because, as he said himself, he could find no count on which Jesus might be guilty. He tried to get him set free but, failing, in a demonstrative gesture washed his hands of the matter to preserve his 'innocence' (Matthew 27:24). Pilate's attempt then to pass the delicate matter on to the local Jewish ethnarch, Herod Antipas – who happened to be present for the festival – also failed, for Jesus would say nothing at all. He was sent back again to the procurator (Luke 23:6–16), who at last gave in to the will of the mob that had been stirred up by Caiaphas and the priests, and turned the Nazarene over to them for execution as they demanded.

To bear in mind that Jesus the Nazarene belonged to the New Covenant of the Essene movement, presumably as one who observed the Community Rule without actually belonging to the enclosed community, is to be able to find an explanation for quite a few of the contradictions and puzzles of the Gospel stories that is relatively straightforward and makes perfect sense. It certainly explains how Jesus could be prosecuted by the Orthodox Jews and yet find himself on trial for his life in the secular and political courts at the same time. Indeed, considering the scant nature of the historical sources at our disposal, it is *solely* in this light that the events surrounding the end of Jesus' ministry in Palestine can be convincingly and satisfactorily accounted for.

Problems arising from the popular understanding of the 'Resurrection from the dead' and the 'bodily Ascension' of Christ are rather more difficult to solve. The available literary sources do not explain why Jesus was declared dead just a few hours after his crucifixion. His legs, after all – unlike those of the two men crucified with him – had not been broken. (Fracturing the legs would have decisively shortened the torment, which could otherwise last up to five days.) No wonder Pilate was very surprised when he was asked to release 'the body': 'And Pilate marvelled if he were already dead' (Mark 15:44).

No one saw the Resurrection – or, at least, we are told of no one purporting to have seen it – which means the Resurrection of Jesus from the dead has to remain purely a matter of faith. So the Church's teaching on the critical subject of the Resurrection must be regarded as an inference after the event, an interpretation.[4]

The matter might be left to rest there: either one believes in Jesus' Resurrection or one does not. Surely it would in any case be impossible now, so far ahead in time, to turn a critical spotlight on a historical event two thousand years ago and find out exactly what happened. It would indeed be quite impossible – were it not for an amazing piece of evidence that enables us to examine the events surrounding the Crucifixion in great detail, even while using the most modern tests technology can devise: Jesus' shroud.

The Turin Shroud

And now when the even was come, because it was the [Day of] Preparation, that is, the day before the Sabbath,

Joseph of Arimathea, an honourable (a wealthy: Matthew, Luke) counsellor (who was a disciple of Jesus: Matthew, John) (although a secret one for fear of the Jews: John) (who had not agreed to their decision and action: Luke), which also waited for the kingdom of God, (Luke) came, and went in boldly unto Pilate, and craved the body of Jesus (Matthew, Luke, John).

And Pilate marvelled if he were already dead: and calling unto him the centurion, he asked him whether he had been any while dead.

And when he knew it of the centurion, he gave the body to Joseph (Matthew, John).

And he bought fine linen, and took him down, and wrapped him in the (clean: Matthew) linen (Matthew, Luke) (linen wraps: John), and laid him in a (his: Matthew) (new: Matthew, John) sepulchre (in which no body had been laid before: Luke, John) which was hewn out of a rock (Luke), and rolled a stone unto the door of the sepulchre.

(Mark 15:42–46)

The linen mentioned here is today preserved in Turin, constituting an authentic document that has virtually by a miracle captured one of the most important moments in the history of the world for posterity, and this in something approaching a three-dimensional representation.

The famous Shroud of Turin is 4.36 metres long and 1.10 metres wide, and shows with astonishing clarity the impression of a man that has recently been crucified. One half of the shroud shows the back and, because the shroud was wrapped around the man's head at about its middle, the other side shows the front. The head, the face, the thorax, arms, hands, legs and feet of the man are easy to recognize within the impression. The colour on the fabric is for the most part sepia in tone, although grey in some areas. Traces of blood are clearly visible, and appear as a very pale crimson.

On first looking at the Shroud as a whole, one's eyes are first led to two dark stripes running vertically down the length of the Shroud, which extend to two larger, rhomboidal spots. These are burn marks that have been repaired with lighter-coloured stitches. Their peculiar shape arose as a result of the shroud's almost being lost in a fire in the Chapel at Chambéry, in France, in 1532, when lying folded in 48 layers in a silver casket. In the heat of the blaze, the silver container began to melt on one side, until streaks of molten silver left the geometrical pattern of scorch-marks in the folded material (Plate 29).

If it is really Jesus' image on this piece of material, and the authenticity of the cloth can be proved, then this document not only represents a scientific sensation of the utmost importance, it can also serve as the only acceptable scientific basis on which the question that has occupied so many for so long may be settled once and for all: did the Resurrection of Jesus actually happen?

There may be initial reservations over whether any length of fabric could really survive a period of time amounting to almost two millennia while suffering so little evident damage. Yet it is a fact that there are many pieces of linen that are considerably older and better preserved than the Shroud of Turin. Well-preserved exemplars are to be found in the collections of the Egyptian National Museum in Cairo, the Egyptian Museum of Turin, and the Egyptology departments of historical museums in London, Paris, Berlin, Hildesheim and elsewhere, some specimens going back 3500, even 5000, years. The dry climate of the Near East is particularly favourable to the long-term preservation of textiles and scrolls. In each case the vegetable substance is mainly cellulose, a very stable molecule.

The Greek word *sindon* (sometimes translated in English as 'muslin') in the Synoptic Gospels refers to a length of linen. The Shroud is of linen, the fibres twilled together in a ratio of 3:1, creating a fishbone weave. In Jesus' time this was an extremely rare form of loom work, requiring a great deal of expertise, and probably very expensive. The only surviving examples of this kind of material woven in the first century come from the Roman province of Syria, to which Palestine then belonged. (Twilling was introduced in western and northern Europe only in the fourteenth century AD.)

On using an electron microscope to examine the strands in 1973, Professor Raes of the University of Ghent in Belgium discovered a few traces of cotton, a plant that was not under cultivation in the Near East at the time of Jesus. In contemporary Syria and Mesopotamia, however, cotton imported from India was occasionally used for weaving, although the cotton had to be processed beforehand on a special loom.

The Swiss botanist and forensic scientist Dr Max Frei made use of complex techniques of pollen analysis to arrive at some sensational discoveries. Dr Frei took twelve samples, each ten to twenty square centimetres in area, from different parts of the Shroud's surface, on adhesive tape. Under the scanning electron microscope, he found, in addition to dust and the linen fibres, between one and four grains of plant pollen per square centimetre. Grains of pollen are between 0.0025 and 0.25 millimetres in size, and are therefore not generally visible to the naked eye. But the tiny grains are surrounded by a double skin, the chemical composition of which has not been fully determined even today. The external shell is by itself so durable that under certain conditions the pollen can survive intact for several millions of years. Moreover, every species and variety of plant has tiny pollen grains of an appearance quite distinctive from those of any other, so that it is possible to tell quite easily which grain originated from which plant.

In a report on his research published in March 1976, Frei announced that he had been able to identify a total of forty-nine different types of plant from the pollen he had found on the Shroud. Many of the plants still grow in all the areas in which the Shroud is said to have been kept during the course of its history: one such is the cedar of Lebanon (*Cedrus libani*). But the sensational news was that there was also pollen from eleven types of plants that do not grow at all in central Europe, but are halophytes deriving from the Near East. Halophytes are plants that flourish only in soils containing an unusually high proportion of salt – like the soils of the region surrounding the Dead Sea. Among them were special desert varieties of tamarisk (*Tamarix*), seablite (*Suaeda*) and artemisia (*Artemisia*) species.

The history of the Shroud had until this point been traced back only as far as the fourteenth century, and some researchers had therefore assumed that it was at that date that the Shroud had been produced, in France, since when it had always been kept within the borders of France or Italy. The pollen analysis now offered clear proof that the linen must have been in Palestine earlier than this. In addition, it turned out that the kinds of pollen identified on the Shroud were also to be found in relatively high concentrations in those layers of sediment in the Sea of Galilee which date back to the time of Jesus.

Grains of pollen from eight other varieties of plants were characteristic of the steppes of Asia Minor, particularly the area around Edessa (today Urfa in Turkey). Dr Frei could not have imagined how significant this fact was to prove to be.

The Portrait of Edessa

That it is now possible to trace the history of the Shroud all the way back to its origins[5] is in large measure due to the research of the English historian Ian Wilson.[6] From the great quantity of historical evidence at his disposal he was able to show that the Shroud corresponds to the so-called Edessa Portrait, of which there have been accounts from as early as the first century, and which has been known as the Mandylion since the sixth century. The story of the Holy Shroud has all the thrills of a good novel.

According to the apocryphal *Gospel of the Hebrews*, which was used by the Nazarenes, Jesus gave the shroud described in the Gospels to the 'servant of the priests' after the Resurrection.[7] It is logical to assume that the recipient of so marked a favour was not one of the mortal enemies of Jesus. The 'servant of the priests' was most probably given the priceless gift as a token of gratitude for some special service rendered. But no matter who took possession of the sheet after the Resurrection, it was most probably then preserved by followers of Jesus, the most likely candidates being Joseph of Arimathea and Nicodemus who had arranged for the body to be removed from the Cross and placed in the tomb.

But the cloth could not be allowed to remain in Palestine: the continual and vicious infighting with the forces of the hated Roman overlords presented too much of a threat. And so the followers of Jesus arranged to get the Shroud out of the country. Only the large, well-established Christian communities to the north could provide a secure haven for it, such towns as Antioch, Corinth, Ephesus and Edessa, which lay far from the areas in which Jesus had worked.

In about AD 325, the Church historian Eusebius (260–340), Bishop of Caesarea, reported that there had been an exchange of letters between Jesus and the King of Edessa, Abgar V, known as Ukkama ('The Black'), who ruled AD 15–50.[8] Eusebius says that he himself translated this correspondence, allegedly taken from the archives of the Edessan king, from ancient Syrian (Aramaic) into Greek. Known and accepted as genuine from very early times in the West,[9] albeit disseminated in a multitude of variants, this Legend of Abgar evidently represented a deep-rooted documentary constituent of early Christian faith, which in turn rather supports the presumption that it is based on actual events.

In those days Edessa was an important centre of commerce not far off the old Royal Road, which led from Ephesus in the west to Susa in the east, crossing the old empires of the Lydians, Medes and Persians, and linking Edessa directly with India and eastern Asia via the Silk Route. The most valuable commodity of trade in Edessa was silk from the Far East, and it was in this trade that members of the large Jewish communities of the town, most of whom were merchants, were very actively involved. Politically, Edessa was ruled by the Abgar dynasty from 132 BC to AD 216.

An organized Christian Church was established in Edessa only during the middle of the second century, under Abgar IX Ma'nu. According to historical sources, however, it is likely that there was a fairly sizeable Christian community in Edessa long before this, and that Abgar V Ukkama, even before the correspondence, already had some knowledge of Jesus' message.

Eusebius describes how King Abgar Ukkama sent a messenger to Jerusalem to ask Jesus to come to Edessa and heal him of a chronic rash. Jesus was unable to make the trip himself, but sent a disciple by the name of Thaddeus (called Addai in the Syriac texts) – not the apostle of that name but one of the seventy disciples mentioned in Luke (Luke 10:1) – with a letter for Abgar. In it, Jesus tells the king that the disciple will cure him, and that the letter will afterwards continue to protect the town from harm.

Sometime around 1850 a number of early Syriac manuscripts were discovered in a monastery near Wadi el-Natrun (the Natron valley) in the desert of Lower Egypt. Among them was another version of the Abgar story now known as *Doctrina Addai*,[10] that tallies exactly with the version noted down by Evagrius Scholasticus (527–600) at the end of the sixth century. And the same version of the tradition is recorded in the famous festive sermon delivered in the year 945 to mark the occasion on which the Edessa Portrait was installed in the Pharos Chapel at the court of the Byzantine Emperor Constantine VII Porphyrogennetos.[11] According to all these sources, Jesus sent not only a letter to Abgar but also a miraculously-formed portrait of himself. The king is said to have been cured at once by the miraculous power of this picture. And immediately after this spectacular miracle, Thaddeus-Addai preached in Edessa, whereupon Abgar and most of the citizens of the town were converted to the Gospel faith. The *Doctrina Addai* gives the date of Thaddeus' sermon as the year 343 by the Edessan reckoning, which corresponds to the year AD 33 – the very year in which Jesus was crucified.

Because a burial shroud was in those times considered to be contaminated with the 'impurity' of death, King Abgar would have been deeply offended if Thaddeus had handed him what evidently was one. Probably for this reason, Thaddeus folded the cloth to look more like a portrait on linen, and had it framed in gold by his Edessan co-religionist Aggai – a man who, according to Syrian and Armenian sources, was the leader of the Christian community of the town. It was a task for which Aggai was well suited: a goldsmith by trade, he was used to fashioning costly chains and had been responsible for crafting the king's own diadem. In the *Acta Thaddaei* of the sixth century (an attempt to explain how the image had been imposed on the cloth, from a contemporary viewpoint), the term *tetradiplon* is used to describe the Shroud, and is probably intended to mean 'folded in four double layers'.[12]

If the unwieldy, more-than-four-metre-long Shroud is folded in the middle, and then again, three times, what is left can certainly be described as four double layers. The resulting rectangle of cloth, now a much handier 110 centimetres by 54.5 centimetres, simply displays the head of Jesus, impressively framed, without giving any grounds for suspecting that it is not the true size of the *sindon*.

According to the text of the festive sermon delivered at Constantinople in 945 (referred to above), Abgar Ukkama set the portrait, in its gold frame, above the town gates of Edessa.

Abgar died in AD 50. He was succeeded for only seven years by his eldest son Ma'nu V, before his second son Ma'nu VI came to the Edessa throne. He, however, reverted to paganism, and brutally persecuted the burgeoning Christian community there. It was at this time that the portrait disappeared and no more was heard of it for five hundred years. The festive sermon of 945 reveals what actually happened. Aggai, who by this time had been Bishop of Edessa for twenty-three years (by the reckoning of the Chaldean patriarchs), spirited the sacred relic away to a place of safety, out of the grasp of the inimical king. He immured it within the town wall, in a recess above the west gate. In response, Ma'nu had Aggai cruelly executed, on 30 July 57 according to Mares Salomonis.

The first indication that the Shroud had once more come to light is found in a document written by the Church historian Evagrius in the year 593. He dates the event to some fifty years earlier, in May 544. The festive sermon of Constantinople similarly reports that the picture was rediscovered in Edessa in the sixth century, and that it was the same picture of Christ that a disciple had brought to Abgar. According to Wilson, the linen cloth was rediscovered when the buildings of Edessa were being repaired, by order of the Emperor Justinian I, after a catastrophic flood in the year 525 – specifically when the town gate was being dismantled. The picture was evidently identified at once as the original portrait brought to Abgar. In 544, Bishop Eulalios wrote that the image discovered was an impression genuinely 'not made by human hands': in Greek, *acheiropoieton*.[13] The rediscovered picture was brought to 'the great church' (the cathedral of Hagia Sophia), where it was kept in a locked silver casket. From this time forward the cloth became known as the Mandylion, and was considered so sacred and precious that it was brought out for public veneration only on the most important feast days.

In 639 the Arabs captured Edessa and so acquired the Shroud. A wealthy Christian, Athanasius of the Gmea family, bought back the linen cloth from the Arabs and concealed it in a crypt in one of the many churches in the town.

The term Mandylion, used in relation to the picture from this period, is thought by most authorities to be derived from the Arabic *mandil* (a word itself derived from late Latin *mantelium*), meaning 'a length of cloth' such as might be used as to make a veil, a short cloak, a turban or a hankerchief. Personally, I would suggest instead that the title is somehow connected with the Sanskrit term *mandala*, which signifies 'a circle', and specifically a mystical diagram in circular form. Mandalas were much used in Tibetan Buddhism. They represent a religious experience in symbolic form, indicating particular spiritual relationships in the symmetry of their design, and assist in the meditative disciplines that lead to Enlightenment.

After the discovery of the Edessa Portrait in the sixth century, there was a great upsurge in image worship in Christianity. Many reports of other images of Christ 'not made by human hands' did the rounds at the time (such as the *acheiropoieta* of Memphis and Camuliana). And along with this development, a sudden and marked change in what Christ was believed to have looked like became evident. Up until the rediscovery of the Shroud image, Jesus had been portrayed on classical lines, as a philosopher or emperor, as a teacher of truth, a good shepherd or a beardless, boyish youth like Apollo – youth being a symbol of the divine. As veneration for the Mandylion became established, there suddenly appeared a form of portrayal that was strikingly similar to the three-dimensional face-on picture on the cloth. A good example of this is to be seen on the sixth-century picture of Jesus on the silver vase of Emesa. From then on Jesus was mostly shown in frontal view, with large, wide-open eyes under pronounced brows, long wavy hair parted in the middle, divided beard, long aquiline nose, and of mature age.

The image quickly became accepted with almost doctrinal unanimity throughout the whole Christian world. At the Synod of Constantinople in 691–2 it was decreed that from then on Jesus was only to be represented in his 'human form', only 'pictures true to life' were permissible. At about the same date, Justinian II (ruled 685–95 and 705–11) minted his coins with the portrait of Christ for the first time, and on these too the visage of Jesus was similar to the 'Shroud' image. The result is that although the literary tradi-

At least fifteen different and unmistakable features can be identified on the face on the Shroud that are also to be found on the portraits of Jesus painted by Byzantine artists.

tion has bequeathed us no information whatsoever on what Jesus looked like, he has been portrayed so consistently from the sixth century onwards that anyone who sees a portrait never has any doubt about who the subject is![14] Historians have listed totals of between fifteen (Wilson) and twenty (Vignon, Wuenschel)[15] conspicuous features in the Shroud portrait that can be recognized in images of Jesus from the sixth century onwards.

Until the tenth century – when the Mandylion was moved to Constantinople – this image of Christ's face was typical in Byzantine sacred art, along with other elements of the Shroud picture. Many portrayals of the time present a face-on view of Jesus, without the neck, within a rectangle that is longer horizontally than vertically, and that appears to have a grid pattern superimposed on it like a net of diagonal lines, the face itself framed by a circular opening. The general layout of these depictions corresponds precisely with that of the cloth 'folded in four double layers'. And besides, a portrait within a horizontally-based rectangle may be considered to offend normal aesthetic sensibilities, and is accordingly most unusual in all forms of visual representation.

Wilson suggests that the Edessa Portrait, the Mandylion, is the authentic 'original' which set the course for the history of art.

In the eighth century, the movement known as the Iconoclasts (the 'image-breakers') came to power in the Eastern Roman Empire under Emperor Leo III. Everywhere, religious images and icons were torn down and destroyed – but the Mandylion, already hidden away from the equally image-hating Muslims then ruling Edessa, survived this period unharmed. Sixty years later, when the Iconoclasts had officially been discredited, efforts began in Constantinople (continuing over the following decades) to have the precious image brought to the capital of the empire. The project finally met with success under Emperor Romanus I Lecapenus (ruled 920–944) who, in 942, sent his most able man, the general Curcuas, to collect the Christ portrait. It was not long before the imperial Byzantine army laid siege to the town of Edessa and demanded the surrender of the Mandylion in exchange for the release of 200 prisoners and the sparing of the town. To avoid bloodshed, the Edessans yielded to the Emperor's terms, thereby gaining both immunity for their town and twelve thousand pieces of silver. Even then, according to contemporary sources, the Edessans seem to have tried to fob the Emperor's men off with a replica twice before they relinquished the real Shroud.

On 15 August 944 the Shroud finally arrived in Constantinople, greeted by jubilant crowds. And there it was probably kept for the next two and a half centuries, in the Blachernai church. (The pictures and 'shrouds' produced for the Pharos Chapel must be assumed to be copies.) Either during the surrender of the Mandylion at Edessa or while it was in transit to Constantinople, the picture had apparently come loose from its frame and been revealed as the complete Shroud. At any rate, Gregory – archdeacon of the Great Church of Constantinople – gave a sermon at the triumphal reception of the cloth, in which he mentioned the '. . . drops of blood, which had flowed out from his side . . .', that had left their impression on the cloth. And in this statement, at least, lies proof that the Mandylion of Edessa and the Turin Shroud are the same cloth. If the stab wound from the centurion's spear was visible, the cloth was no mere towel containing the image only of a face. The cloth must have originated in the brief period immediately following the Crucifixion.

The text of a sermon first given by Pope Stephen III in 769 had a passage inserted into it during the twelfth century to the effect that Jesus had lain stretched out with 'his whole body' on a white cloth '. . . on which the glorious countenance of our Lord and the full length of his body were thus miraculously impressed . . .'.[16]

Similar references are to be found in the ecclesiastical history of Ordericus Vitalis (around 1141)[17] and in the *Otia Imperialia* of Gervase of Tilbury at the beginning of the thirteenth century.[18] Over all these years the Shroud was evidently displayed in its full length on a regular basis in Constantinople. In 1203, the French crusader Robert de Clari wrote that he had seen the cloth in the Church of St Mary the Madonna at Blachernai in Constantinople: '. . . the Sindon, in which our Lord had been wrapped, which was displayed every Friday so that the figure of Our Lord could be clearly seen'.[19]

The Mysterious Templars

Robert de Clari had come to Constantinople as a knight on the Fourth Crusade. After a long siege, the crusaders finally sacked the wealthy city in April 1204. They destroyed everything that was of no value to them; everything in the city that was precious and costly they looted and took away with them, including, without compunction, the treasures and holy relics belonging to the

Christian Church. Amidst such chaotic turmoil the Shroud disappeared, not to emerge again until 150 years later in France, in the possession of members of the de Charny family, who displayed it in the West for the first time.[20]

A number of theories, some of them pretty far-fetched, have been put forward to explain how the cloth came to disappear from Constantinople, and how it ended up in France. Because the cloth disappeared for more than a century at a stretch, it was most probably in the possession of the same owners throughout the period – presumably a group closely linked with the crusaders, who were rich enough not to have to raise revenue by selling the relic, who could guarantee its security in absolute secrecy, who had a motive for keeping it, and who were also connected in some way with the de Charny family. All these clues point towards the mysterious Order of the Templars.

The Order of the Poor Knights of Christ and of the Temple of Solomon, better known simply as the Templars, was founded in 1119 by a group of crusaders led by the French knight Hugues de Payns. In addition to the standard vows of poverty, chastity and obedience, Templars swore to protect pilgrims in the Holy Land and actively to help in the struggle against the Muslims. The Order soon became extraordinarily powerful and influential. In the late thirteenth century, however, rumours began to circulate that the Templar knights were given to worshipping a mysterious icon at secret meetings. Contemporary accounts and the records of the Court of the Inquisition state that the Templars' icon was an image 'on a board' depicting a 'very pale and colourless' version of a life-sized male head 'with a divided beard, such as the Templars wear'. The Templars revered the icon as the 'unveiled face of God'. Copies of the icon were kept in some of the Templar centres. (A copy of this type was found in 1951 in a former seat of the Order at Templecombe in Somerset, England.) The icon matches the Mandylion image in every detail! The Templars had quite obviously come into possession of the Shroud and had made its image the focus of their religious worship. But how had they managed to remove the Shroud from Constantinople unnoticed and bring it to the West? Elmar R. Gruber has found a solution to this historical puzzle.

The Templars did not take part in the conquest of Constantinople because it had nothing to do with their duties in the Holy Land, but immediately after the city had been taken some of their agents went there on a secret mission. Only the grounds of

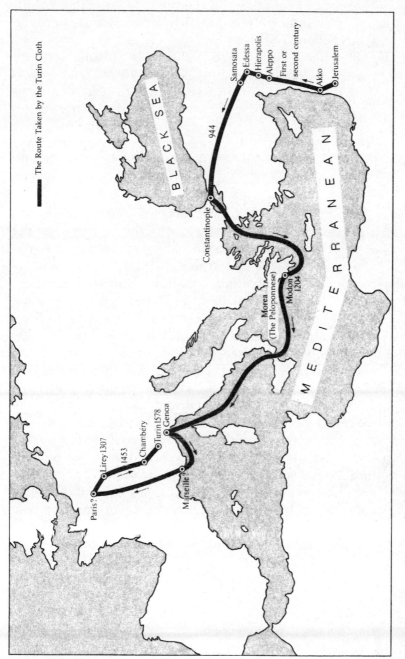

The Route Taken by the Turin Cloth

the Bucoleon and Blachernai palaces had not succumbed to the looting of the crusader soldiery, and then only because the crusader leaders had chosen the palaces for their own residence once the attack had succeeded. The treasures and relics the palaces contained were therefore distributed to high-ranking secular and religious dignitaries. In May 1204, Count Baldwin IX of Flanders was crowned Holy Roman Emperor in Byzantium. To relay this news to Pope Innocent II, the new Emperor chose the Master of the Templar court in Lombardy, one Brother Baroche, who may well have convinced Baldwin that to remove the Shroud from the Blachernai church and donate it to the Pope would undoubtedly secure the Vatican's favour. The mission was kept secret, however, for fear of possible unrest among the Greek population.

Brother Baroche transported his charge on a ship laden with riches on a course for Rome. Off the coast of the Peloponnese the vessel was suprised by six Genoese galleys, and was looted.[21] Strangely enough, the Genoese pirates then let the ship and its crew proceed on its way unscathed – captured ships were usually sailed back to Genoa – so that Brother Baroche reached Rome unharmed in autumn 1204, and delivered Baldwin's letter to Pope Innocent. Perhaps the Templars had made a secret deal with the Genoese by which the ship was robbed of its treasures but no harm came to the crew, the ship, or the 'worthless' old cloth. Or perhaps Baroche had in any case removed the cloth from the ship at some port of call – the Templars owned an estate on the Peloponnese – and then allowed himself and his vessel to be taken by the Genoese. At any rate, the Shroud had disappeared, and in a letter of 12 November 1204 Pope Innocent threatened the Genoese with excommunication unless they returned the stolen relics at once.[22]

The whole affair was extremely embarrassing for both Emperor and Pope, and it was hushed up. The Shroud had 'mysteriously disappeared'.

In 1307, Philippe le Beau of France used the rumours concerning the heretical icon-worship of the Templars, along with with other charges – such as homosexual practices, and secret deals with the Muslims and with the Cathars (who had been wiped out a hundred years earlier) – as a pretext to smash the Templars, and to embezzle the Order's extensive assets.

Two of the last remaining leaders of the Templar Order were burned at the stake in Paris for heresy in March 1314, even though they professed the Christian faith to the end, and protested their innocence. One was the Grand Master of the Order, Jacques de

Molay; the other was the Master of Normandy, Geoffroy de Charnay. Despite an intensive search, the prosecutors were unable to find the 'icon' of the knights anywhere.

A few years later, however, the cloth turned up again, and in the possession of a Geoffroy de Charny,[23] no less, who, from genealogical research, could well have been a grandnephew of the Templar knight who had forfeited his life, although having no overt connection with the Order himself. It would appear that the Templar leaders had hidden the cloth with a relative of Geoffroy de Charnay (the Templar) who was free of suspicion, in order to protect it from the persecution of Philippe. This would also explain why the de Charny family was unable to give any account of how they came to possess the cloth when they were later accused by the two bishops of Troyes, Henri de Poitiers and Pierre d'Arcis, of having displayed a forgery, following a public exhibition in the collegiate church at Lirey. Although the bishops had never seen the cloth themselves, they consistently opposed any public exhibition of the relic. A series of plots were then laid against the de Charny family, to which Margareta de Charny was able to put an end only by sending the cloth out of the country. She bequeathed it to the pious Duke Louis of Savoy, and in return received a rich reward for her 'valuable services'. The Duke gave the canons of Lirey 50 gold francs by way of recompense.

The history of the Shroud is well documented from here on,[24] and can be quickly summarized. In 1502 the cloth was deposited in the chapel of Chambéry Castle where, in 1532, it nearly succumbed to the fire that left the burn marks visible today. In 1578 the cloth was finally brought to Turin, where it was kept as a family heirloom of the House of Savoy for four centuries, until Umberto II of Savoy, ex-king of Italy, made it over to the Holy See in his will on 18 March 1983, shortly before he died. (Only two weeks earlier, Pope John Paul II had travelled in person to the Lisbon residence of the exiled monarch to persuade the old man to bequeath the cloth to the Holy See.)

Scientific Analysis of the Shroud

On the occasion of the fiftieth anniversary of the state of Italy in 1898, the Shroud was once again exhibited to the public. The amateur photographer Secondo Pia then had the opportunity to photograph the Shroud for the first time in its history. After several attempts, Pia succeeded in taking a reasonable picture of the Shroud. As he developed the exposed glass plates in his dark room, he made a sensational discovery: the negative on the photographic plate showed a natural likeness of Jesus, pretty well as he must have appeared in real life. The face familiar to us as the portrait of Jesus on the Turin Shroud is produced by the reversal of light and shade. (The bloodstains, on the other hand, appear as bright marks on the negative.) This fact alone demonstrates that the image cannot have been painted by an artist. To create such a perfect inversion by hand would take more than even the most modern technique is capable of. The negative of the photograph taken by Pia was the starting-point for the modern debate on the authenticity of the linen.

More recent photographs taken by Giuseppe Enrie in 1931 confirm that there is nothing to suggest that the image was painted on the shroud: no paint, no brush-strokes, no outlining. The body's impression gradually merges into the cloth: there are no distinct contours to be seen. These more precise photographs led to a whole list of new discoveries:

1. The body shown in the illustration is unclothed, just as criminals were when punished and executed under Roman law. An artistic representation of Jesus completely naked would have been inconceivable, a blasphemy of irredeemable proportions.

2. The image is very obviously of someone who was crucified by being nailed to a cross, rather than by being attached to the cross with thongs (as was also standard practice). Because crucifixions were frequent, this does not in itself serve to prove that the body is that of Jesus. It was the first Christian Roman Emperor, Constantine, who abolished this barbaric method of execution, so the cloth must have originated prior to AD 330.

3. The beard and hairstyle of the person portrayed were not usual in the Roman empire except in Palestine. The length of the hair and the central parting suggest that the victim was a member of the Nazarene community.

4. The Shroud bears clear evidence of six of the Stations of the Cross described in the Gospels. Firstly, medical specialists confirm the presence of a severe contusion under one eye and other superficial wounds apparently caused by punches to the face administered by the soldiers.

16 The 'Bath-Place of Moses' in Bijbihara (46 kilometres south of Srinagar), and a stone lion said to be around 5000 years old.

17 A stone bearing an Aramaic inscription, found at Sirkap near Taxila.

18 The 'Stone of Moses' or Ka-Ka-Bal, with which Moses is said to have demonstrated his magical skills.

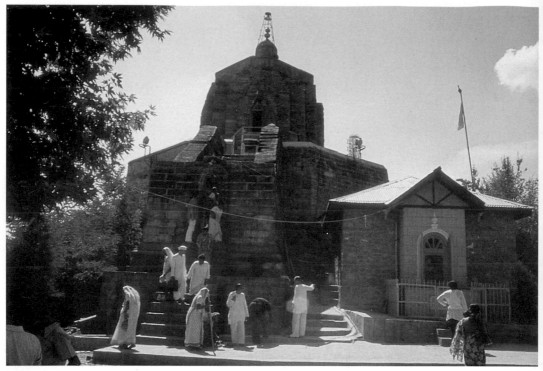

19 Takht-i-Suleiman, the 'Throne of Solomon', on the slopes of Barehmooleh, overlooking Srinagar; which was restored in AD 78 by King Gopadatta of Kashmir.

20 The profiles of these two young men clearly show the two different races of northern India: Semitic descent (left), Indo-Iranian descent (right).

21 *The Sun Temple of Martand (65 kilometres southeast of Srinagar), a temple with a Jewish ground-plan in Kashmir. Is this the Temple to which Ezekiel was referring?*

22 *The author on the temple walls at Martand. Behind structures added in the eighth century, the considerably older foundation walls are clearly visible.*

23 *The Buddha figure found in Marseilles and dating from the second century BC.*

24 *A Bodhisattva as the Good Shepherd.*

25 *The Temptation of Jesus in the Wilderness by A. D. Thomas.*

26 *The three Wise Men from the East, here represented as Buddhist monks, by Friedrich Hechelmann.*

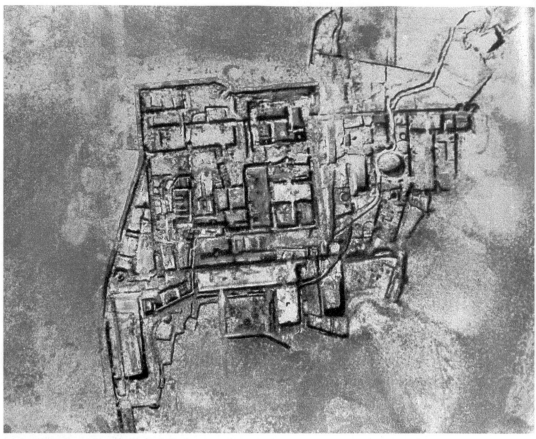

27 *An aerial photograph of the monastery at Qumran after excavation.*

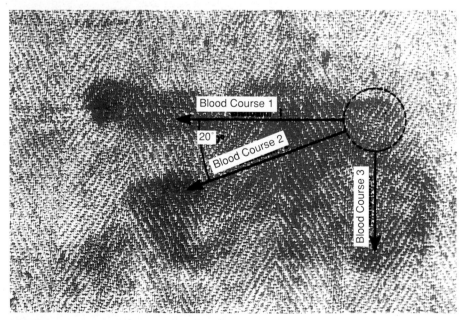

28 *The wounds in the hands: blood trails 1 and 2 are well dried (with correspondingly sharp edges) and originated during the actual Cruxifixion; but trail 3 was formed only after the body had been placed in a horizontal position.*

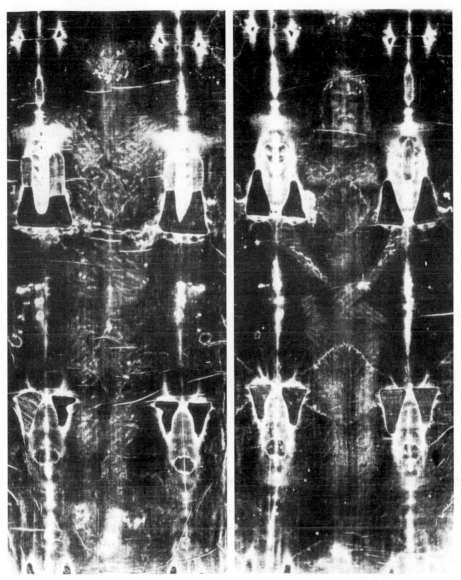

29 *The complete Shroud as a photographic negative. Only in the negative do all the details become clearly visible.*

30 *The face of the portrait radiates nobility and dignity.*

5. Secondly, small dumbbell-shaped marks are clearly visible all over the back of the body, and in some places on the front. There are more than ninety such wounds in all, from which it is possible to tell not only how many lashes were delivered during the scourging, but also that the Roman *flagrum* was the implement used. This special kind of whip had three leather straps fitted at the ends with pairs of small balls made of lead or bone.

6. The evidence for the third Station of the Cross is that the lash wounds in the shoulder region were evidently aggravated by the later application of a heavy weight – an indication that the victim of the crucifixion did indeed have to carry (at least) the horizontal beam of a cross.

7. The fourth Station of the Cross is visible in the irregular spots and streaks of blood on the forehead and the back of the head: evidence of a crown of thorns It was not, however, a plaited coronet or tiara, as depicted in Christian iconography by almost all artists, but must have been a 'cap' that covered the whole of the top of the head, much like Oriental crowns. Any counterfeiter would simply have produced a copy of the conventional circlet of thorns.

8. The fifth Station, the nailing to the cross, is visible in the streaks of blood on the hands and feet. From the direction of the larger trails of blood, it is not difficult to work out that the arms were outstretched at an angle somewhere between 55 and 65 degrees. Although artists and iconographers had always assumed that the nails were hammered through the palms, the bloodstains on the cloth show that the nails actually went through the wrists. Experiments by the French pathologist Barbet proved that the palms could not support a body weight of more than 40 kilograms (88 pounds) without tearing. What forger would have known that?

9. The last of the six Stations of the Cross is represented by a wound some 4.5 centimetres long on the right side of the body between the fifth and sixth ribs. The wound seems to have produced a fair amount of blood, which fits in with the account in John's Gospel of a spear injury from which 'blood and water' immediately flowed out.

10. Neither thigh nor calf show any signs of a major injury, which suggests that the legs were indeed not broken.

The points enumerated above, all of which coincide with the Gospel narrative, indicate that this was not just any crucifixion victim. The Jesuit and historian Herbert Thurston, who was convinced that the Shroud was a forgery, wrote, '. . . If this is not an impression of Christ, it was painted to look like one. These features, taken together, have never been exhibited by anyone else since the beginning of the world.'[25]

An even more thorough examination, using the most up-to-date scientific instruments, was possible only after a Commission had been set up for the scientific investigation of the Shroud. In 1969, Cardinal Pellegrino of Turin appointed a number of scientific specialists who, together with a panel of doctrinal experts, were to carry out a systematic examination of the Shroud. The group initially comprised only eleven specialists, but in the course of the following years so remarkable were the finds that entire institutes and universities, and even National Aeronautics and Space Administration (NASA) in the United States, became involved in the analysis of the linen.

Until then, research had centred on the photographs of the Shroud, but in 1969 the Shroud could at last be examined directly, over a period of two days. It seems extraordinary, but the Commission and its task were kept strictly secret; the names of the members were not made public until 1976. The results of these first experiments were very meagre. A number of colour photographs were produced, and parts of the Shroud were examined under the microscope, in normal, ultraviolet and infra-red light. A final report recommended that future research should snip off a number of small samples on which a full range of scientific tests might then be performed.

The ex-king of Italy, Umberto II of Savoy, who at that time was still the legal owner of the Shroud, agreed to the requests of the experts. In 1973, he permitted it to be systematically examined and tested for three days, after which it was shown on television to an audience of millions while Pope Paul VI talked about it.

Was Jesus Entombed Alive?

Since the 1950s, a German called Hans Naber (but also using the names Kurt Berna and John Reban), specializing in writing about the Shroud, had been gaining some celebrity by producing publications in a somewhat sensational style. He declared that the Shroud proved beyond doubt that Jesus could not really have been dead when he was removed from the Cross, because a corpse would not have continued to bleed in the manner that the body under the linen of the Turin Shroud evidently had.[26] Naber said he had had a vision in 1947 in which Jesus appeared and asked him to testify to the world that the man who had undergone Crucifixion had only appeared to be dead, but was in fact in a kind of trance from which he awoke after three days. Publication of the research results and photographs of the Shroud finally gave Naber the opportunity to try to prove his theories, and he managed to find a number of accredited Shroud experts prepared to support his attempt. Needless to say, the doctrinal authorities of the Church had no sympathy at all with his argument – but there came a day when, amid spectacular press coverage, Naber revealed that he had received a letter from an anonymous member of the Roman Catholic clergy, saying that it was not possible on the one hand to teach that Jesus had died on the Cross for the salvation of mankind, and on the other hand to revere a shroud which had never held a corpse. The Vatican found itself obliged to make an official statement on the affair, and determined at the same time that a radical and final solution had to be found.

To Professor of Theology Werner Bulst, Naber's claims were 'pure fantasy': Naber was accused of not knowing what he was talking about, and of having no 'scientific background' to boot.[27] But Naber could not just be ignored, because he was able to arouse worldwide interest. Nonetheless, the antagonism that Naber aroused by being persistent finally led to his physical, mental and financial ruin.

In 1973, when the latest results of the research came out, it looked as if the widespread doubts brought to prominence by Naber had been exploded. It is fairly simple, after all, to determine the presence of even minute quantities of blood by means of chemical analysis in a laboratory. The most common method by which this is done is what is called the peroxide reaction: even the merest trace of the red blood pigment haemoglobin releases oxygen from hydrogen peroxide, which in turn causes the colourless basic reagent benzidine to oxidize, so turning the solution blue. Haemoglobin and the product of its decomposition, haem, are very stable molecules that may continue to react normally even after many centuries.

Several threads from various bloodstained areas were carefully plucked from the material and examined by two independent laboratories in Italy. The result seemed to be a major setback – all the results of the tests proved negative. It seemed as though the spots that looked like blood were not blood at all!

The bloodstains on the feet (had it actually been blood) were of course enough to confirm Naber's theory that blood had flowed after Jesus was removed from the Cross. But now it was much easier for everyone involved to claim that the Shroud was the work of an ingenious forger, and there was no need to have to admit that Jesus was still alive when he was removed from the Cross.

Publication of the Commission's report in 1976 caused the news of the 'forgery' to spread like wildfire. What was not published, however, was the fact that there was no known substance that could have been used for any such forgery, and that haem, although relatively stable, loses its stability, decomposes, and so becomes untraceable if exposed to high temperatures – as the Shroud had been in the fire of 1532.

Whether the blood was real or not was a question not satisfactorily answered until several years after the investigations of 1973. In 1978, the Shroud had been in Turin for exactly four hundred years, and to celebrate the occasion it was once again exhibited to the public. From 28 August to 8 October, more than three million pilgrims gazed at the most valuable relic in Christendom, probably the authentic image of Jesus. Then, before the evening of the last day of exhibition was ended, the linen was removed from its bulletproof display frame and laid out on an adjustable bench. In a room in the Palazzo Reale, which adjoins the cathedral, two teams of top scientists were waiting to begin a research programme that was to last for two weeks. One group was predominantly European, and included Turin's microscopy specialist Giovanni Riggi, the pathologist Baima Bollone of Milan, the physicist Luigi Gonella of Turin, and the forensic scientist Max Frei of Zurich. The other group consisted of twenty-five American specialists in the fields of photography, spectroscopy, radiography, computer technology, organic chemistry and physics, equipped with an extraordinary array of sophisticated instruments, some of which had been specially constructed for the planned analysis of the Shroud.

In the days that followed, using a time-consuming but rigorous working procedure, a great number of photographic negatives, special types of photographs, graphs and tables of data were prepared, which were then evaluated with the help of large computers in the United States. The Shroud was first divided into a grid of sixty individual sections in order to carry out a precise photometric survey. Each of these sections was then carefully photographed, using a whole range of different filters. The negatives then served as the basis for a number of optical experiments. In NASA's photographic laboratory, the tonal (light-dark) values of the photographs were digitized (converted into computer data), which made it possible to enhance small areas of contrast in the picture, revealing fine details otherwise invisible to the human eye. The method even made it possible to reconstruct a life-size, three-dimensional relief of the body in the picture. If it had been a forgery, the proportions would have come out all wrong. On the basis of the relief it was possible to determine the actual height and weight of the body: about 1.80 metres tall and 79 kilograms in weight.

It was also possible to calculate the distance between the body and the cloth at every point, using the tonal values. The impression was darker at the places of direct contact between body and Shroud, and the greater the distance between the Shroud and the body the lighter the tone on the Shroud. The researchers then found that there was a direct relation between the image on the Shroud and the distances between the Shroud and the body: this confirmed the long-held assumption that the image must somewhow have been formed by contact with the body. And investigations of the fibres under the electron microscope revealed that the image was not produced by any detectable particles of substance, but that the fibres of the Shroud where the image was visible are themselves darkened on their surface, unlike those in non-image areas.

One experiment that was performed directly on the cloth itself, X-ray fluorescence spectroanalysis, finally provided proof that the the bloodstains do actually derive from the presence of blood. In this test a part of the linen was subject to a high dosage of radiation for a short period, and thus induced to fluoresce. Because every molecule fluoresces in its own unique way under the influence of high radiation levels, the atomic structure of a material can be determined from its fluorescence spectrum. The marks showed significantly large amounts of the element iron, which is a major constituent in blood, and specifically in haemoglobin.

For the American chemist Dr Walter McCrone, the presence of iron was proof in itself that the Turin Shroud could not be genuine, as he declared very publicly at the annual meeting of the American Association for the Advancement of Science at the end of 1971, and repeatedly thereafter. He regarded the iron in the marks as a sure indication that paint containing iron oxide had been used – a type of paint that had not been invented until the fourteenth century.

Dr McCrone had never even seen the Shroud at first hand!

The paint hypothesis was refuted by a different experiment in which particles of the Shroud were treated with hydrazine and vaporized formic acid, and then subjected to ultraviolet light. Under such conditions, porphyrin molecules turn a bright red, and the technique showed they were present on the Shroud. Porphyrin is a precursor in the metabolism of haem, and is an established indicator of the presence of blood in cases where the haem itself has been destroyed by high temperature.

This method of ultraviolet fluorescence photography also proved that there were two different types of burned areas. In 1532, the Shroud smouldered in its casket in the palace chapel of Chambéry, confined in an atmosphere containing little oxygen. The reddish fluorescence of the singe-marks confirmed the smouldering fire in the silver casket, as known in its history. Other burn marks show a fluorescence of a different colour, suggesting an unknown second episode of burning, in an 'open' fire. (This evidence also refutes the hypothesis that the body in the Shroud somehow left its image on the cloth by some process of irradiation.)

The experiments of the US researchers show that the differing degrees of sepia coloration in the image is due to a change in the chemical structure of the cellulose of the linen. In laboratory experiments it was possible to simulate the same differences in colouring by using various oxidizing agents to decompose the cellulose of the linen. Oxidation images grow more distinct as they age.

As early as in 1924, the French biologist Professor Paul Vignon had achieved great success with his experiments in what was then termed 'vaporographic theory'. Vignon proved that a sweating body placed on a linen that has been soaked in a mixture of light oil and tincture of aloes (*Aloe medicinalis*) produces the same coloration as that on the Shroud, because the sweat decomposes to form ammonia vapours, which then cause an oxidation process in the cellulose to take place. This coloration is strongest at the point of contact between the linen and the body, and becomes weaker as the distance between the body and the linen increases. (This also explains why the impression resembles a photographic negative.) Vignon explained that the impression on the linen is principally caused by the ammonia vapours released during the evaporation of uric acid from a feverish body. The solution of aloes and myrrh adsorbed in the linen reacts with this, and ammonium carbonate is formed, the vapours of which colour the linen fibres. And in the damp atmosphere between the skin and the linen, the degree of coloration is in direct proportion to the proximity of body and linen.

The rather more prominent coloration of the bloodstains is the result of a stronger chemical reaction. John's Gospel describes how large quantities of aloes were used in the burial of Jesus 'He came therefore, and took the body of Jesus. And there came also Nicodemus, which at the first came to Jesus by night, and brought a mixture of myrrh and aloes, about an hundred pound weight. Then took they the body of Jesus, and wound it in linen clothes with the spices, as the manner of the Jews is to bury' (John 19:38–40).

Vignon's experiments, though convincing, became the target of severe criticism in 1933, for the simple reason that the body salts and body heat necessary for the chemical reactions and evaporation could not have been present in sufficient amounts in a corpse. Nonetheless, it had been established that mixtures of aloes and myrrh in humid conditions could indeed create permanent impressions of a body on a fabric. Vignon showed that even the very brief exposure time of forty-five seconds could leave a faint impression, forming a clearly recognizable positive image when seen on a photographic negative.

Proof that the impression on the Shroud was of vaporographic origin could have put an end to virtually every other speculation – but the Christian Church objected to this neat solution on three counts:

a) According to the strict regulations involved in an orthodox Jewish burial, the corpse would have had to be physically and ritually cleansed before being embalmed. Marks such as bloodstains would have been impossible.

b) If the body had been properly wrapped up in the Shroud as prescribed, an overall impression that was somewhat misshapen and distorted across its width would have been produced, quite unlike the impression on the flatter lower surface, completely altering the image. This argument can be safely dismissed, because the soaked linen becomes rather stiff, so the material would not fold around every contour of the body, but only touch it on the more prominent parts.

c) Corpses do not sweat and do not emit body heat.

Professor Vignon's theory, the result of forty-six years of research, was discarded on the strength of this last objection – because corpses do not sweat. But had Jesus still been alive, the high body temperature caused by his wounds would have made him sweat more profusely than ever!

The Radiocarbon Dating of 1988

Today there is a simple test to determine the age of all organic material, by measuring the levels of the radioisotope carbon-14 (chemically the same element as common carbon, C^{12}, but with two extra neutrons in the nucleus, which makes the atom so unstable that after a while it decays radioactively). Living organisms absorb carbon dioxide from the air, incorporating the carbon in their structure. When the life of the organism comes to an end, the radioactive carbon continues to decay at a very slow and constant rate (at the rate of about half of all the material every 6000 years, its 'half-life'). Because the proportion of C^{14} in the atmosphere is constant (replenished by radiation from space), all that has to be done is to measure the ratio of C^{14} to C^{12} in what is left of the old organic material, do a simple calculation in relation to the half-life, and the age of the archaeological find can be determined with a precision of close on 10 per cent.

Before the 1980s, however, a large sample of the material under examination was required – and in the process completely destroyed by fire – and no Church authority was going to allow Christianity's most important holy relic to be mutilated or even visibly damaged in such a way. But for some years now it has been possible to date even the tiniest quantities of a material, and in April 1988, once Umberto II of Savoy had been persuaded by the Pope to bequeath the cloth to the Holy See, the Vatican (forced into action by Naber's spectacular publications) ordered a radiocarbon examination of the Turin Shroud in the hope that it would show once and for all whether the relic was genuine or not.

Three laboratories specializing in the dating of archaeological material – in Zurich, Oxford and Tucson (Arizona) – were given postage-stamp-sized samples of the Turin cloth. Six months later, in October 1988, the sensational result was announced to the public: the examination had shown beyond doubt that the cloth originated in the Middle Ages (somewhere around 1260 to 1390).

This finding, which contradicted all previous research results, at once aroused my suspicions about how carefully the radiocarbon dating had been carried out. I had studied the history of the Shroud for many years: I knew for certain of many things that actively proved that the cloth had existed before the Middle Ages. I had to look into the testing procedure. It was the start of three years of detective work which took me to all the places that figured in the radiocarbon testing.

As I tried to track down clues and find out more about the circumstances, I discovered that a multitude of contradictions and inconsistencies lay like a cloak over the course of the testing procedure. Soon it became apparent that the scientists who took part in the testing had something to hide. Questioned about details, they became entangled in contradictions and even resorted to falsification when they realized the official version of the events of the procedure was in jeopardy. The director of the investigation, Dr Michael Tite, was donated a million pounds for a new institute by unnamed 'friends and sponsors' (ironically, Dr Tite received the money on a Good Friday!), and Cardinal Ballestrero of Turin suddenly and unexpectedly went into retirement shortly after the publication of the test results, and was no longer available to answer questions on the subject.

By devious means and with great difficulty, I was finally able to obtain greatly magnified photographs of the pieces of cloth that the laboratories had been sent to put a date to. I had these photos examined by several institutes specializing in such work, and compared the digitized images on a computer with a photograph of each original fragment directly before it was cut off. The results were conclusive: the cloth pieces dated in the laboratories could not have come from the original cloth!

Pursuing my investigations I found out that the samples examined by the radiocarbon technique had been taken from a vestment that had been kept since 1296 in the basilica of Saint-Maximin in southern France, the cope of Saint Louis d'Anjou. This proved once and for all that the dating of the Turin Shroud had been manipulated: the idea was to present the cloth as a medieval forgery, and so put an end to all the discussions about whether Jesus had survived the crucifixion – discussions that were rocking the Christian Church to its foundations.

The full story of my astounding exposure of this massive fraud perpetrated on the public is to be found in *The Jesus Conspiracy: The Truth about the Resurrection*,[28] a book I wrote in conjunction with Dr Elmar R. Gruber.

The radiocarbon dating of 1988 has turned out to be no more than a cynical attempt at criminal deception. It certainly does not prove the Shroud to be a mere 700 years old – in fact, the intentional and fraudulent falsification of the test results is yet one more proof that the Turin Shroud really is the shroud in which Jesus was once wrapped, and that Jesus was still alive when he was 'laid to rest' in it.

Chapter Eight

'DEATH' AND 'RESURRECTION'

Two Burials in John's Gospel

(Many of the ideas put forward in this chapter are based on the work of Elmar R. Gruber, as published in the sections he contributed to *The Jesus Conspiracy*, which we wrote in conjunction with each other.)

L et us go back once more to that dramatic hour on Good Friday, when Jesus was nailed to the Cross and on the same day hastily put in the tomb.

The story of the Crucifixion comes down to us via the three Synoptic Gospels, the Gospel of John, and several apocryphal texts. Reading all four Gospel texts in parallel, which is quite an effort in itself, it is possible to discern a whole collection of points of variance in addition to all the points of agreement – a situation that makes it difficult to form a clear and consistent overall picture of events.

It is John's Gospel that generally exhibits the greatest divergence from the three other Gospels. The Gospels of Matthew, Mark and Luke are for this very reason described as 'synoptic', meaning 'from the same viewpoint': the many points of agreement in the texts can be listed in order and compared side by side – a correlation that suggests they derive mainly from one identical source. John does not fit into this pattern. Although the text of John was completed in Ephesus towards the end of the first century, and was the last of the four Gospels to be written, it is considered to be the most authentic of all four narratives. In particular it includes such episodes that do not occur in the other Gospels as the wedding at Cana, the conversation with Nicodemus, and the raising to life of Lazarus. Its detailed and historically accurate descriptions of topographical features (notably the layout and landmarks of Jerusalem before the Revolt of AD 66) lead to the conclusion that John himself, or the informant using his name, was personally present in these places at the time of Jesus. The strikingly mystical and Gnostic tone of his account, and the immediacy of his personal relationship with Jesus, suggest that John ought to be the most reliable witness not only to the events but also to the teachings of his master.[1]

Reading the text, we are at once given the impression that it is an eyewitness account we are hearing. Whereas the Synoptics merely state that Jesus received a burial according to Jewish custom, John tries to present the burial in the context of the discovery of the graveclothes on Easter morning, as actually seen by him or told to him at first hand. The Italian professor of literature Gino Zaninotto highlights this in an excellent piece of linguistic analysis – although he then comes to the somewhat audacious conclusion that John was an eyewitness also of the 'Ascension'.

In the middle of John's Gospel is one story that can perhaps be said to represent the crux of the entire Book: the account of the raising to life of Lazarus (John 11:1–45) – an episode that does not appear in any other biblical Gospel. A version of it was apparently once included in an early form of Mark's Gospel, but was later removed, evidently at the behest of Bishop Clement of Alexandria.[2]

The Lazarus story is of great significance to us here because, in telling it, John provides a detailed description of the burial customs of his time. Although the narrative is ambiguous on many points, with the result that there have been many different interpretations, one thing it states positively is that Lazarus was well and truly dead. He is described as being bound hand and foot in graveclothes, and the description in the original Greek includes the word *keiriai* (elsewhere in English translated as 'swathing bands'). This is where we encounter the first problem in translation: how are we to understand 'bound hand and foot'? The Jews are not known to have bound the limbs of the dead, except perhaps in order to transport the corpse to the grave.[3] The word *keiriai* refers to bands of linen long enough to wrap around the whole body. So we should not take this passage to mean that Lazarus was tied only at the wrists and ankles, but rather that his whole body was wrapped in linen bands *up to* the wrists and ankles, and *excluding* the hands and feet. Indeed, had Lazarus' feet been tightly tied, it is hard to see how he could have come out from the grave by himself when Jesus commanded him to (John 11:44). In addition, Nonnos, the celebrated Greek epic poet of the late classical period, used the same word in his paraphrase of the Gospel of John, describing Lazarus as having been 'wrapped in linen bands from head to foot'.

Interestingly, John uses a quite different word for the cloths in which Jesus was wrapped in the tomb: *othonia*. The plural of *othonion*, it has no connotations of any specific part of the body, and is much more an equivalent of the generic term 'cloths' than of the more descriptive 'swathing bands'.

Lazarus' face was 'bound about' (*peridedemenos*) with something called a *soudarion* (literally 'a cloth with which to wipe away sweat', Latin *sudarium*). In this case it was probably being used as a chinstrap, bound around the head of the corpse to hold the lower jaw tight to the upper.

John again finds different words to describe the burial of Jesus. The face of Jesus was not bound about with a *soudarion*, but was instead 'wrapped' (*entetyligmenon*) in one. Indeed, he says quite clearly that the cloth was placed 'upon the head' (*epi tes kephales*), presumably to exclude other alternatives, particularly that the cloth was used to hold the mouth shut. In all the literature on the Turin Shroud – the works of Barbet, Bulst and Currer-Briggs, for example – there are constant references to the idea that a chinstrap can be seen in the image on the Shroud.[4] But there is actually no visible trace of any such band. It would at the very least have made some lasting impression on the hair of the beard and on the sides of the face. The 'chinstrap' is one of those odd vagaries superimposed on the folklore of the image by being somebody's pet hypothesis.

In using different vocabulary for different events, it would seem that the author of John's Gospel fully intended to draw a marked distinction between the burial of Lazarus and the burial of Jesus, and so point up the differences between two incidents that were superficially similar. He was in this way making it quite clear to any reader attentive enough that the two events were utterly and fundamentally incomparable. The raising of Lazarus from the dead is described in words and images all to do with the normal burial of a dead body. In Jesus' case, however, everything suggests that it was not an ordinary burial at all.

In the Lord's Tomb

Let us continue our examination of these differences. Lazarus came forth (*ex-elthen*), and the word that is used implies that he came forth without any help. He made his way out of the cave that was being used as a grave, and was thereupon released from his linen wrappings so that he could move freely. Typically, a Jewish tomb consisted of a cavern excavated in a rocky hillside, in which shelf-like chambers about 50 centimetres wide, 80 centimetres high and 2 metres deep (*kôkim*, the plural of *kôk*) were cut. Corpses in their wrappings were deposited lengthways, head first, in these chambers.[5] Every indication, explicit and implicit, in the narrative supports the understanding that Lazarus' burial was in truth a final interment.

The burial of Jesus, however, is described in quite a different way. Jesus was not deposited in a chamber cut perpendicularly into the rock wall of a tomb, but set down on a stone surface or open ledge. On the morning of the 'resurrection', Mary Magdalene sees the 'angels in white', as they are called, 'the one at the head, and the other at the feet, where the body of Jesus had lain' (John 20:12). Jesus was not deposited lengthways into a *kôk*, for if he had been, no one could have sat at the head end.

At this point one possible objection is that Jesus could have been buried in what is called an Arcosol tomb. This form of tomb architecture is characterized by a large recess or vault carved at a height above the floor into the side wall of the burial chamber, above a stone platform or sarcophagoidal trough. In this case it would be quite possible for the 'angels' to sit at both ends of the corpse. But archaeological evidence is against this. Arcosol tombs were developed only during the early Byzantine period, some 200 years after Jesus' burial. Prior to this there was a short period when late Roman shaft tombs were in use. But the most widespread and typical tomb structure of Jesus' time was the chambered *kôkim* tomb, and quite evidently the tomb in which Jesus was placed was also of such construction.

The interior of a *kôkim* tomb was reached via an entrance below ground level, which was often closed with a movable stone. The tomb consisted of a large main cavern, in the sides of which a number of *kôkim* had usually been carved, each to take one body. At the centre of the cavern there was a square depression in the floor, which served as a drainage area. Each side of the depression, and at the same level as the entrance from outside, there was a surface on which a corpse could be laid out for washing and oiling.[6] Even in the daytime it was dark enough in the tomb to require the use of lanterns set in niches: Jewish law did not permit burial after sunset or before dawn.

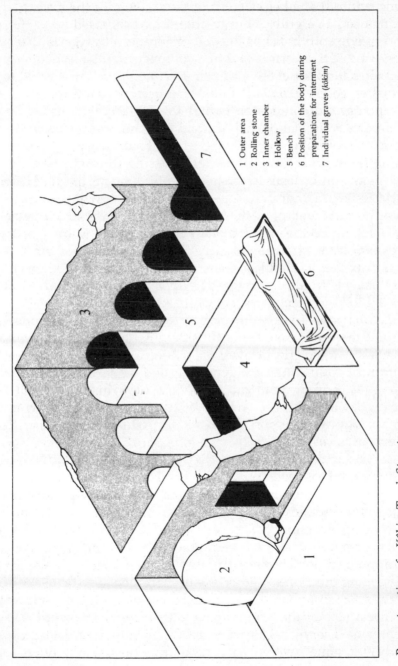

1 Outer area
2 Rolling stone
3 Inner chamber
4 Hollow
5 Bench
6 Position of the body during preparations for interment
7 Individual graves (kôkim)

Reconstruction of a Kôkim Tomb Structure

John tells us that Jesus' favourite disciple ran to the grave (20:5) and 'stooping down, and looking in' saw the linen clothes. Mary Magdalene 'stooped down, and looked into the sepulchre' (20:11), and saw the two 'angels' at the place where Jesus had lain. Two conclusions may be derived from these statements. One is that the plan of Christ's tomb as reconstructed by Brother Hughes Vincent, and often reproduced, is altogether wrong. It suggests that Jesus lies in an Arcosol tomb, and in a chamber that is reached by passing right through another one first. It would be impossible to see the place where Jesus lay by stooping in front of the entrance.

The second conclusion is that these statements support our assumption that the burial of Jesus was not completed. If he had already been lying in a *kôk*, the place would again not be visible from the tomb entrance. The light passing through the very low doorway only reaches to the middle of the main cavern. The body of Jesus could therefore only have lain somewhere around the middle of the cavern, on the ledge around the central depression in the floor, and certainly not inside one of the tomb *kôkim*.

Now let us look more closely at the Greek text of John: 'Then took they the body of Jesus, and wound (*edesan*) it in linen clothes (*othoniois*) with the spices (*meta ton aromaton*), as the manner of the Jews is to bury (*entaphiazein*)' (John 19:40).

For various reasons the interpretation of this sentence has caused many commentators considerable difficulty. The verb *deo*, of which *edesan* is a derivative, ordinarily means 'to tie up', 'to bind fast'. But things are generally tied up with strips of fabric (*spargana, keiriai*), with ropes (*desmoi*) or with thongs, not with cloths. Savio avoids the problem by translating *deo* as 'to wrap up', on analogy with certain Greek texts in which it is used with the preposition *en*.[7]

In Mark (15:46) the verb used instead is *eneileo* a word that while it describes Jesus as covered with a cloth also emphasizes that the body was wrapped up quite tightly, almost done up like a parcel. But it still does not suggest a complete bandaging process as used to enwrap a mummy. The verb *kateilisso* would be more apt in expressing that, as used, for example, by Herodotus to describe the wrapping of an Egyptian mummy and on another occasion the bandaging of a Greek soldier's injury. But one specific usage of the verb *eneileo* in ancient Greek texts has to do with a certain way of preparing food: first 'wrapping' it in fig leaves.[8] The word was evidently used as the preferred term by which to describe how Jesus' body had been covered, in particular to make some reference to the tight (perhaps because damp) binding caused by the aromatic substances absorbed in the cloth.

In order to justify the unusual terminology in this description, several linguistic commentators have suggested that some kind of embalming process was intended. They refer to the hundred pounds of aromatic substances procured by Nicodemus: 'And there came also Nicodemus, which at the first came to Jesus by night, and brought a mixture of myrrh and aloes, about an hundred pound weight' (John 19:39). One hundred pounds – forty-five kilograms – is an enormous weight of relatively light materials! If the aloes and myrrh were in dried or powdered form, the quantity making up that weight would have occupied a whole palette of sacks, and Nicodemus would have needed a number of assistants to help in transporting the load. Transport would have been even more difficult if the substances were in suspension in wine, vinegar or oil.

The theologian Paul Billerbeck describes the event as if an embalming was to take place, using the aromatic substances suspended in oil.[9] But Rabbinic texts refer only to the external oiling of the bodies of the departed. The addition of spices is nowhere mentioned, let alone in these quantities: it was never part of Jewish customs, and nor was embalming.[10] It would be pointless, in any case, to perform an embalmment in the way described. To prevent the gases of decomposition from distending and then rupturing the body, the entrails would have had to be removed via an incision that was repulsive to the Jews on both aesthetic and religious grounds, and these substances if applied would not by themselves have been effective in halting further decomposition. Many biblical authorities in consequence find this passage in John's Gospel both incomprehensible and perplexing. One commentator, Haenchen, can only conclude, 'The writer of this verse had no idea of Jewish burial rites, and knew nothing about embalming either.'

But let us pause a moment to consider the matter. We have already seen that John makes a clear and deliberate distinction between the burials of Lazarus and of Jesus, and it is most likely that he chose his words with equally careful deliberation to disclose to those who could read between the lines a situation that is not readily apparent in a superficial understanding of the text. The attentive reader would already have been alerted to the greatest difference between the burial of Lazarus and the burial of Jesus – that the first burial had been completed and the second remained unfinished. But why would Jesus' believers and followers have given their beloved master a half-finished burial after being in such a hurry to get him into the nearby tomb? It makes no sense at all.

Scriptural commentators have a lot of difficulty with this strange 'burial' of Jesus. They often try to sidestep it by saying that Jesus' burial took place in untoward circumstances: at twilight on Good Friday just as the Sabbath was about to begin, a day on which interment was not permitted, causing everything to have to be done with undue haste. The burial of Jesus was thus undertaken at such speed as only to fulfil the minimum of the customary burial rites, and to leave the actual interment incomplete. But this idea makes little sense, and for a number of reasons.

For one thing, it is just not accurate to claim that complete burial was not permitted on the Sabbath. The Rabbinic texts state no such thing in specific terms. One text says that complete burial is allowed on the Sabbath as on any other day; another says that in such cases the corpse should first be covered with sand to preserve it until the Sabbath is over, when the burial can be completed.[11] At the same time, by following Jesus Joseph of Arimathea and Nicodemus had already taken up a stance that represented the abrogation of their former adherence to Jewish customs and tradition, so it seems unlikely that they would be particularly concerned to observe such customs when it came to events and actions of such momentous importance.

There was no need, then, for a curtailed, hasty burial rite performed simply to comply with the customs. Nonetheless, there is every indication that Jesus' followers acted with maximum speed and maximum efficiency following a well thought-out plan. So what really happened in the tomb cavern?

Let us read the crucial sentence again in the light of the conclusions we have already come to: 'Then took they the body of Jesus, and wound it in linen clothes with the spices, as the manner of the Jews is to bury.' The spices were aloes and myrrh, this much we know. Myrrh was used as an ingredient for embalming by the Egyptians, but did not feature in the burial rites of the Jews. Instead, Jewish custom prescribes that the body of the deceased should be washed and oiled, the hair cut and tidied, and that the body should then be dressed again and the face covered with a cloth. Washing the body was of such critical importance that it had to be done even on the Sabbath day.[12] Yet there is no mention of any of this in John's Gospel. Nor was there any oiling of the body. Instead, as we are told, the women came to the tomb on Sunday to oil Jesus' body. Whatever Joseph and Nicodemus were doing, it had absolutely nothing to do with Jewish burial rites. John says that they buried Jesus in a way that was customary to the Jews – and then goes on to describe a burial which directly contravenes the custom!

Now why should he do this? Did he really not know the burial rites? Of course he knew them, because he described a standard burial in the story of Lazarus. Here too, then, just as we had to discern a deeper truth in the comparison of differences in the descriptions of Lazarus' and Jesus' burials, we have to discern what John was really trying to get across by obviously contradicting himself. So what happened in that rock-hewn tomb if it was not a burial?

The Mysterious 'Aromatic Substances'

The most unexpected feature of all that is described in connection with the burial and the tomb is the laying in of that extraordinarily large quantity of herbs. What was the point of them – for they had nothing to do with a burial?

Contrary to the view of some authors that the species of aloe mentioned by John is *Aloe perryi*,[13] it makes more sense to assume that the species used was instead *Aloe vera*.[14] *Aloe vera* is a plant native to the south-western portion of the Arabian Peninsula and to the offshore island of Socotra (which is why it is occasionally called *Aloe soccotrina*), where it grows together with over a dozen other types of aloe. Its south-west Arabian habitat was not far from the trade route that led from southern Arabia to the Mediterranean in classical times. A fleshy, juicy plant, it could quite easily survive the long caravan and sea trade routes without drying out, and it is well known that a brisk trade in plants from south-west Arabia with dealers in Palestine and the adjoining areas took place. Aloes were used in medicine and to make incense as far back as in the second and third millennia BC. A sticky gel taken from the plants was used for various purposes in antiquity, notably for healing wounds, topical inflammations and burns. The gel can be obtained by scraping off thin cells of leaf pulp (parenchyma) from the harder outer layers. The yellow resinous exudate that oozes from cut stems dries to form a waxy mass. In the ancient medicinal herb markets this was sold under the name bitter aloes, a compound rich in phenols, especially aloin.[15]

The second type of spice applied by Nicodemus was myrrh, a

gum-resin derived from shrubs of the genus *Commiphora*, which belongs to the family Burseraceae. The aromatic fragrance of myrrh played an important part in ancient rituals in India and the Orient. The holy oil with which the tabernacle and the ark of the ancient Israelites were anointed also contained myrrh, as one of the 'principal spices' (Exodus 30:23). Records in ancient Egypt describe how myrrh came from the legendary land of Punt (which was probably located on the coast of what is now Somalia). Hippocrates praised the disinfectant power of myrrh. It was used from very early times for the medication of wounds. In the Middle Ages myrrh was considered to be extremely important in the treatment of plague and other forms of infectious disease.

Both substances, aloes and myrrh, were commonly used in the treatment of large areas of injured tissue because they could easily be compounded as ointments and tinctures. Some specialists claim that the Jews often mixed myrrh with ladanum, the resin of the rock rose (*Cistus* species, not to be confused with the opiate laudanum).[16] This was used especially for plasters and bandages.[17] It is evident that such mixtures represented the universally trusted means of achieving the most rapid and effective healing of wounds, combined with the greatest possible protection against infection, at the time of Jesus.

There can be no doubt that Nicodemus procured a truly amazing quantity of highly specific medicinal herbs for the sole purpose of treating the wounds on Jesus' body. Such spices could have had no other function.

The realization gradually dawns that John's style of writing was very carefully cryptic enough both to reveal a great deal about a singularly important event to readers who have their wits about them, and to conceal that same information from the eyes of people who do not know enough to look for it. Jesus was not described as being buried – could not be buried – because he had not died on the Cross!

The author of John's Gospel, who was an eyewitness of the events at Jesus' tomb (or got the details from someone who was) and was also fully briefed by Joseph of Arimathea and Nicodemus, wrote in a way that would tell anyone who knows how to read between the lines what really happened during and immediately after the Crucifixion. He makes it quite clear, therefore, that while the outward trappings of an ordinary Jewish burial were maintained and kept visible, in reality there were efforts behind the scenes to 'bring Jesus back to life' in the privacy of the tomb cavern, under the direction of Joseph and Nicodemus. And the loyal friends of Jesus did not attempt this by endeavouring to perform a miracle like those he had performed himself, but by applying the art of medical healing.

Crucifixion: The Medical Facts

The events that took place in the rock tomb, not far from the site of execution, must be interpreted as an attempt by members of an Essene community to treat the seriously wounded Jesus with medicinal herbs. Why Mark should employ the verb *eneileo* now becomes clear: the word was generally used in connection with the cooking of food wrapped in leaves, as we have seen. To treat Jesus, the Therapeuts evidently packed him round with a fairly tight, sweat-promoting poultice that incorporated a large quantity of herbs, in overall effect not too unlike the culinary method. John's *edesan othoniois* ('and wound it in linen clothes') has to be seen in this context for its true meaning to be recognizable. What was meant was not a mere covering or wrapping, but an actual bandaging in strips that went around the whole body, tightly encasing it. Dioscorides, the Cilician physician of the first century AD, also used both the verbs *deo* and *eneileo* to denote wrapping in linen cloths.[18]

There was obviously no intention of burying Jesus. Instead, he was to be brought to a safe place where he could rest in peace while he healed. What better place for someone to 'rest in peace' than the tomb of a person believed dead! Of course we are not told anything about washing the corpse, a procedure so important in Jewish burials. Joseph did not wash Jesus, because he was not dead. In medical terms, washing was certainly not a good idea anyway. The act of washing would only have caused the numerous wounds caked with dried blood to start bleeding all over again. Joseph and Nicodemus must have applied the curative herbal solution to the body with the utmost care, to make sure that this did not happen.

In the face of such radical conclusions, it is right to wonder how possible it is for a person to survive crucifixion at all.

Death on a cross was considered by the Romans to be the most demeaning and frightening method of execution. Cicero called it the 'most horrible and repulsive form of capital punishment'. Only in exceptional cases were Roman citizens ever sentenced to this punishment, and they were always citizens of the lowest social class. But in territories occupied by the Romans, crucifixion was as much a medium of execution as a deterrent, keeping the potentially rebellious peoples docile and subservient. Palestine had long been notorious as a hotbed of nationalist fervour. Between the time of the Maccabees in 167 BC and Bar Kochba in AD 134, there were altogether some sixty-two episodes of revolt, war and rioting against domination by faithless outsiders, first by the Greeks, and then by the Romans. All but one of these disturbances started in Galilee – Jesus' home area. It is therefore hardly surprising that crucifixions were an almost routine affair there.

Crucifixion was alien to the Jews. For them the lawful means of capital punishment were stoning, burning, beheading and strangling. But according to Mosaic Law it was permissible to hang up a criminal who had already been executed 'on wood', as an additional punishment and humiliation: 'For he that is hanged is accursed of God' (Deuteronomy 21:23). The crucifixion of a criminal was therefore under no circumstances to be allowed to defile the Sabbath, the beginning of which is represented by twilight on the preceding day, the Day of Preparation.

In order to avoid provoking even worse civil unrest, the Romans made sure they did not wilfully offend the religious sentiments of the Jews. Once the official Roman death sentence *ibis in crucem* ('you shall go to the cross') was passed, care was taken to see that the execution was completed before the Sabbath. In the case of Jesus' crucifixion, therefore, the greatest haste was called for because it took place on the Day of Preparation. It had to be over before sunset. But that was not easy to arrange, because the special feature of crucifixion was that its agonizing torture was protracted over time. It was carried out in such a way as to extend the pain and misery of the guilty usually over a period of some days until they eventually expired.

There was considerable variety in the actual structure of the cross and the way the the victim was attached to it. If the full body weight of the crucified person was suspended solely at the wrists, death would occur within five to six hours through gradual suffocation, and not through blood loss or other any cause. In this extreme posture, breathing is so severely curtailed that the body is no longer properly supplied with oxygen. After a relatively short time, unconsciousness results, and the consequent hanging forward of the head then further reduces air intake.[19] To prevent such

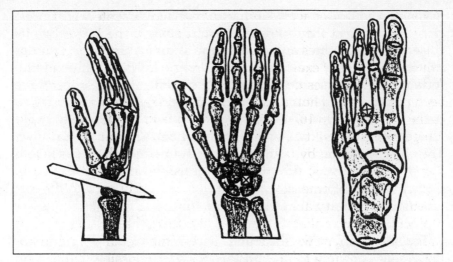

Nails through the hands and feet do not necessarily damage any bones or major blood vessels. Without some form of analgesic these injuries would certainly have been very painful, but in no way fatal.

an 'easy' death, a small wooden cross-piece called the *suppedaneum* was often fixed to the vertical post of the cross, on which the victim might prop himself up for as long as his strength allowed. This cross-piece should not be imagined as a short plank nailed on at an angle, as is depicted in Byzantine crucifixion scenes. The suppedaneum was a small, horizontal crossbeam, which the crucified person was able actually to stand on.

Not for nothing do the oldest pictures show the crucified person standing, as for example in the 'mock' crucifixion of the Cappella Palatina.

Attachment to the cross was by binding with thongs or by transfixing with nails at the hands and feet. The crucified person could then delay his death by his own effort, by supporting his weight with his arms at the point of attachment or with his legs on the crossbeam at the feet. Occasionally a piece of wood to sit on (*sedile*) was also fixed at the appropriate height, which presumably also alleviated the pain somewhat while yet prolonging the agony even further. As Nero's personal philosopher Seneca wrote in a letter, 'The life of the person sentenced to this punishment trickled away drop by drop.'

The Gospels report that Jesus was nailed on the cross at the sixth hour (12 noon) and gave up his spirit at the ninth hour (about three in the afternoon). Towards evening, the man taken for dead was removed from the cross. This unexpectedly rapid death on the cross was of concern to Pilate himself: obviously extremely surprised, he asked the leading centurion if everything was in order (Mark 15:44). That same concern and surprise is still in evidence today. Many authorities, especially expert medical ones, have undertaken considerable experimentation and research to try to come up with an explanation for the rather suspiciously rapid 'death' of Jesus. No author has found the problem easy to solve. The most common idea is that the harsh treatment of Jesus before his crucifixion must have been responsible: it had so severely undermined his physical condition that he succumbed to the torture of crucifixion after only a short time. Such explanations are pretty flimsy.

For one thing, unlike the strictly ascetic monastic community of the Essenes, Jesus was no frail ascetic,[20] but relatively tall, strong and robust (according to the Shroud, about 1.82 metres tall and 79 kilograms in weight), a man 'in his prime'. After a night of ill-treatment he nonetheless talked to the court the next day in a very clever way, obviously in full possession of his mental faculties, as would not be possible in a state of exhaustion. Moreover, Jesus was relieved by Simon of Cyrene of the burden of having to carry the crossbeam (*patibulum*) of his cross for much of the distance of about 550 to 650 metres from Pilate's Praetorium to the site of execution.

That Simon of Cyrene was co-opted at all has been taken by many commentators as proof that Jesus was in a very weakened state, no longer able to bear the weight of the beam. This too has to be queried. As for the scourging, Jesus was treated no differently from any other sentenced person. Everyone sentenced to death by crucifixion first endured such torture. Under Jewish law, thirty-nine lashes were the maximum that could be administered; a third of these on the chest or front side, the remainder on the back. The priest carried out this punishment in the synagogue with a three-thonged whip of calfskin. Of course we are not told whether they kept to the correct number of lashes in the case of Jesus. In the *Gospel of Peter*'s description of Jesus' being nailed to the cross it says, 'But he kept silent, as if he felt no pain.' It is probable that during his training Jesus became adept in the art of mastering pain through meditation, just like Indian yogis. Exercises that lead to this ability are practised by a great number of religious sects throughout the East: they have been scientifically investigated and are well documented.

In most cases, the arms of the sentenced person were first fixed to the *patibulum*, which he then had to carry on his shoulders to the place of execution. The weight of this crossbeam varied between about 18 and 30 kilograms. So considerable strength was needed to be able to carry the heavy load. The Gospel accounts tell us that Jesus was only nailed to the cross at the site of execution. He was laid naked on the ground, where his wrists were nailed to the *patibulum*, and the *patibulum* was nailed to the upright post (*stipes*). Then the whole construction, with him on it, was raised to the vertical.

Strange, is it not, that the death throes of other victims of crucifixion lasted so much longer than in Jesus' case, considering his well-trained and strong constitution. In the autobiography of Flavius Josephus, whose writings tell us so much about the customs and events in Palestine at the time of Jesus, there is an informative passage concerning a crucified man who recovered after being taken down from the cross:

> I was sent by Titus Caesar with Ceralius and a thousand riders to a certain town by the name of Thecoa, to find out whether a military camp could be established there. On my return I saw many prisoners who had been crucified, and recognized three of them as former companions of mine. Much affected, it was with tears in my eyes that I went to Titus and told him about them. He at once gave the order that they should be taken down and given the best treatment so they might recover. But two of them died while being treated by the doctor; the third did get better.[21]

It is difficult to see how Jesus could have given up the ghost so early, and that 'with a loud cry', a departing gesture which to the medical experts is both incomprehensible and perplexing. A closer study, however, shows that this too is a significant indication that Jesus was taken unconscious from the Cross.

The way the two men crucified next to him died is described in graphic detail in John's Gospel:

> The Jews therefore, because it was the [Day of] Preparation, that the bodies should not remain upon the cross on the sabbath day, (for that sabbath day was an high day,) besought Pilate that their legs might be broken, and that they might be taken away.
>   Then came the soldiers, and brake the legs of the first, and of the other which was crucified with him.

(John 19:31–32)

So the two criminals crucified with Jesus, who had certainly

undergone the same sort of ill-treatment he had beforehand, were
still alive. Their legs were broken so they could no longer take
their weight on their legs and straighten up, and so they painfully
suffocated to death within a few hours.

'But when they came to Jesus, and saw that he was dead
already, they brake not his legs' (John 19:33). This is very strange, if
not inexplicable, behaviour by the Roman soldiers. Why did such
hardened soldiers not break Jesus' legs too, to make sure of his
death? The scriptural interpretation provided – that the word of
the prophet in Exodus 12:46 had to be fulfilled ('. . . neither shall ye
break a bone thereof') – is no help at all. The question has to be
asked instead what the roughnecks could have been thinking of to
exempt Jesus from the usual cruelty. They must – and rightly –
have had their doubts about whether Jesus was really dead; they
must at the very least have viewed his unconsciousness form with
scepticism. Otherwise they would not have bothered to thrust the
spear in his side. Surely it was only to be expected that the brutal-
ized soldiers would break the legs of all the crucified men, to be
sure that they were all dead. Up to this point, moreover, Jesus had
apparently been treated with even more than the usual contempt,
suffering blows to the face, given the mock sceptre, and having the
crown of thorns put on his head. Why this sudden change of mood
– this 'privileged' and unreasonably compassionate treatment?

The Gospels provide no consistent answer to this question. The
only point they agree on is that Jesus died as early as the ninth
hour, uttering a loud cry, while those crucified next to him visibly
lingered on in their wretchedness. According to John (19:34), one
of the soldiers drove his spear into Jesus's side, and blood and
water flowed out. Luke and Matthew contribute nothing to this
scenario because neither of them mentions this event. Mark, however, leaves us an interesting clue (15:44–45). Pilate, surprised that
Jesus is already dead, summons the centurion, who confirms the
death, and Pilate then releases the body of Jesus. The centurion,
who has obviously checked the death of Jesus to his satisfaction, is
the same one who, moved by the events during the Crucifixion,
praises Jesus as the true Son of God (Mark 15:39; Matthew 27:54;
Luke 23:47). Who was this centurion?

In the apocryphal literature surrounding Pilate he is called
Longinus and represented as the captain of the guard in charge of
the Crucifixion. And according to a tradition to which Gregory of
Nyssa himself testified, Longinus was said later to have become
the bishop of his home territory, Cappadocia. This 'change of

heart' may mean that he had some connection with Jesus and his followers before the Crucifixion, and may even have been a secret believer in Jesus himself. Many of the problems surrounding the events of the Crucifixion would then instantly be resolved. Joseph of Arimathea, Nicodemus and the centurion Longinus were among the secret followers of Jesus. Influential in position and rank, they were informed well enough in advance about what the publicly seditious advent of Jesus would lead to. Joseph was highly respected as a member of the Jewish Sanhedrin. Since the second century BC this had been the supreme High Council, with authority over all affairs of state in which the Jewish religion was involved, including judicature. It consisted of seventy members under the chairmanship of the High Priest. Nicodemus, who was initiated by Jesus under cover of night (John 3:1–22), was also a Jewish councillor. Thanks to these offices, Joseph and Nicodemus had doubtless been kept well informed about the time and place of the execution, and were thus able to plan the rescue of their master. There is an echo of the advance infomation given to Nicodemus to be found in a much revered medieval legend that is part of the stories of the saints: it tells how Nicodemus, in a letter sent to Mary Magdalene, warns Jesus of an attack by the Jews while he was in Ephraim (John 11:53–54).[22]

Joseph and Nicodemus knew that the crucifixion itself could not be avoided. But if they could manage to get Jesus down off the cross early enough, and provided everything else went as planned, it would be possible to keep him alive, and he would probably be able to continue his mission under cover. It was crucially important to the whole operation that the apostles were not involved. They had gone into hiding in fear of persecution. No action would be taken against the respected councillors Joseph and Nicodemus or the Roman centurion. So there was just a short time in which the risky venture might be carried out successfully.

The Wound in the Side and the Potent Drink

Let us return to the spear-thrust into Jesus' side. A close look at the original Greek reveals that the verb used to describe the thrust of the soldier, *nyssein*, has the meaning 'to prick', 'to puncture', and does not really apply to a thrust with full force, let alone deep penetration. In the Vulgate (the universally known Latin translation of the Bible), the verb used is *aperire*, an inaccurate translation basically meaning 'to open up'. But the fundamental meaning, the intended meaning, is something different again. The action was a procedure that served as a kind of 'official confirmation' of death: if the body showed no reaction to a superficial stab, it could be assumed that the person was dead. It was probably the centurion mentioned in the Gospels who performed this test himself. It was certainly not meant to be a death thrust – after all, Jesus was believed to be dead already, and so much so that his legs were left unbroken. An experienced soldier would in any case hardly have intended to kill by thrusting a spear into the side: for that it should have been from the front, through the heart. The Roman soldiers of the day generally used the type of spear called a *hasta* or *pilum*, with a thin, tapering blade about 25 to 40 centimetres long, broadening just before the shaft. Like a stiletto, the blade was just right for scratching the skin a little to see if the crucified person showed any reaction.

Scriptural authorities find it difficult to explain the discharge of blood and water. Some can only regard it as a miracle, in consideration of how the circulation stops at death. Others discern more significance in a symbolic interpretation of the elements blood and water. Scientific explanations have also been educed, notably to the effect that the 'water' was in fact blood serum, which separates as blood coagulates. But decomposition of the blood in that manner only begins six hours after death, at the earliest!

But we must not discard this passage of John's Gospel as of no significance. We must assume instead that our eyewitness informant meant to lay special emphasis on the blood and water. For the sentence that follows this passage runs, 'And he that saw it bare record, and his record is true: and he knoweth that he saith true, that ye might believe' (19:35). This is crucial, and fits nicely with what we already know of John's style of writing – a depiction on two levels, as it were: an outwardly obvious description for undiscerning readers, and a number of cryptic references strewn throughout the text for those who know how to read between the lines to discover for themselves. The special emphasis so evidently put on testifying to the blood and water that flowed from Jesus' side is actually intended to make it clear that Jesus was still alive.

Even if many centuries were to pass before the circulatory nature of the human blood system was discovered, it was common knowledge at the time of Jesus that corpses do not bleed and blood serum is not seen on the wounds of a body that has just died.

Origen (185–254) himself, who believed for a fact that Jesus was dead at the time the blood and water issued from the wound, felt obliged to point out that corpses do not bleed.

The expression *blood and water* occurs as an idiom in other languages. In the ornate Arabic language, for example, it is used to emphasize the force of an event. In modern English we can say that someone 'sweats blood' when making a great effort (without meaning that blood actually oozes through the pores of the skin), but the German equivalent is 'to sweat blood and water', *Blut und Wasser schwitzen*. It might well be, then, that the same expression used in describing a wound means no more than that a considerable amount of blood is visible. Jesus was obviously only apparently dead. The quantity of blood discharged, and the emphasis put on it by immediately asserting that it was a true observation, were meant to point to this very fact.

Everything that was to happen, once the spear-thrust had confirmed death, had been carefully arranged beforehand by Joseph and his assistants. But the man from Arimathea had begun making the necessary preparations a long time before.

The first action the wealthy Joseph had taken was to purchase a garden in the immediate vicinity of the Crucifixion site.[23] With wise foresight, he decided to have a new tomb excavated from the rock on the estate – somewhere to which a supposedly dead body could be brought quickly for safety. That it should be a tomb unused till then was essential: to lay Jesus to rest in a tomb in which others were already buried would have given rise to strong legal and moral objections, for the presence of the body of an executed criminal would normally be taken to dishonour the bodies of the faithful who already lay in the tomb. There could be no objection to a 'burial' in an empty tomb, particularly since, as Josephus reports, political criminals who were executed by the Romans – as Jesus was – might certainly be afforded an honourable burial such as was denied to an ordinary criminal.[24] Naturally, Joseph of Arimathea could not say that he was busy preparing a tomb for Jesus. The Gospels therefore have it that Joseph brought the body of Jesus to lie in his own new family grave.

The Gospel passage stating that it was a tomb for Joseph's own use was intended to be taken literally by undiscerning readers who would not think twice about it.[25] Actually, the new tomb constructed in the garden near Golgotha was not meant for the dead at all, neither Joseph and his family nor anyone else. It was intended solely as a practical precaution, to avoid having to move the seriously wounded Jesus very far should they succeed in getting him off the Cross soon enough. Jesus' persecutors would meanwhile contentedly think him dead and buried.

The fact that the Crucifixion took place on the Day of Preparation was, if anything, an advantage, because it meant they could greatly speed up the 'burial' without arousing suspicion. Of course they had to make sure that Jesus really did seem to have died. This too they could not just leave to chance.

The Gospels tell of one other thing that happened just before Jesus is described as dying on the Cross:

> Now there was set a vessel full of vinegar: and they filled a spunge with vinegar, and put it upon hyssop [a plant used for ritual daubing], and put it to his mouth.
> When Jesus therefore had received the vinegar, he said, It is finished: and he bowed his head, and gave up the ghost.
>
> (John 19:29–30)

How did Jesus come (apparently) to die immediately after he had taken the bitter drink? Was it really vinegar that he was given? It was fully in line with Jewish custom to offer a person sentenced to death wine spiced with myrrh or incense in order to alleviate the pain with its slight narcotic effect. A passage in the Talmud states, 'The one on his way to execution was given a piece of incense in a cup of wine, to help him fall asleep' (Sanh. 43a). But there is no mention in the Gospels of a spiced wine. All the evangelists agree that it was a liquid with a very bitter taste. In Latin, 'vinegar' is *acetum*, closely related to the old stem *ac-* 'sharp', and *acid* in English. The Roman soldiers not only allowed Jesus to be given the drink, one of them even helped Jesus to take it (Matthew 27:48; Mark 15:36; Luke 23:36; John 19:29).

Let us look more closely at how it happened. The sponge was offered to Jesus on a hyssop stem. Hyssop is a plant with a weak stem hardly suitable for holding up a wet sponge with. Even a bundle of hyssop stems might not have sufficient rigidity to make it possible, although Jesus on the Cross may not have been very high off the ground. On some crosses, the sentenced person was fixed with the feet only just above the soil, and in such a case the sponge would not have to be lifted up to any real height to be offered. But perhaps the instrument used to offer Jesus the 'vinegar' has been subject to a simple linguistic mistake – *hyssos* 'a short spear' has all this time been understood as *hyssopos* 'hyssop'. It is a soldier who offers Jesus the sponge, according to the Synoptic authors, so that it is more than merely possible, it is likely, that some such verbal error occurred. We might even have reason to suppose that it was the centurion Longinus who raised the sponge to the lips of Jesus on his spear.[26]

The drink of vinegar is mentioned in John's narrative in a way that makes it look as if the vinegar had been brought to the site of the Crucifixion for the very purpose. It was a part of the preparations that Joseph, Nicodemus and the centurion had made in order to carry out their plan. What the bitter liquid actually was can only be guessed at. In those days there was a wide assortment of analgesic and narcotic substances available: the healing arts of the period were excellent at compounding mixtures with different effects on the body. Perhaps the drink was a bitter wine to which a measured quantity of opium had been added. The exceptional anaesthetic and sedative power of opium was well known to the Jews even in pre-Christian times. Opium is the dried form of the milky juice obtained from unripe seed-heads of one species of poppy (*Papaver somniferum*). This poppy was widespread in Palestine, so it is certainly possible that Jesus was given opium dissolved in some liquid while on the Cross.

The narcotic effect of opium is so strong that it can lead to a state of complete torpor, in which a person has no external sensation whatever. The principal alkaloid in opium (its most active constituent) is morphine, which is a powerful sedative and narcotic, and which can depress respiration. A second alkaloid in opium, papaverine, has no analgesic effect but is an excellent muscle-relaxant.

In combination, and together with other pharmaceutical substances, opiate solutions are not difficult to adjust to have any specifically required effect. Indeed, such a drug cocktail would have been ideal for the purposes of Joseph and his colleagues: not only was Jesus given the best of pain-killers, the dose was designed to make him lose consciousness in a short time and so be able to hang limply 'dead' on the Cross. The appearance of sudden death was enhanced by the fact that opium reduces and sharply slows the heartbeat, it depresses breathing to an extraordinary degree, and it renders the body completely limp. And yet, administered in the correct dosage, as known to the experienced Essene Therapeuts, it constituted no real danger to the heart – on the contrary, it was actually beneficial to it.

On the other hand, perhaps the supposed drink of vinegar instead contained the active ingredients of the sacred drink of the

Indians and Persians, Soma and Haoma (respectively). Persian cultic worship of Mithras included a Haoma sacrifice very similar to the Christian Mass (Holy Communion or Eucharist). Professor Seydel writes:

> The form of the sacrifice of Haoma was identical to the usual Persian sacrifices for the dead. Small round pieces of bread the size of a thaler coin were offered up and consumed with the Haoma drink. Haoma was originally the pressed juice of the soma plant *Asclepias acida*, with which the Vedic Aryans sprinkled the sacrificial fire. It was considered a symbol of divine life, a drink of the gods, and the drink of immortality . . .[27]

Soma, the sacred drink of India, enabled an adept to enter a death-like state for several days, and to awaken afterwards in an elated state that lasted a few more days. In this state of ecstasy, a 'higher consciousness' spoke through the adept, and he had visionary powers. In addition to *Asclepias acida*, the Soma might also have contained Indian hemp (*Cannabis indica*) – tradition has it that it featured in the drink of Zarathustra, at least. Pictures of *Asclepias acida* are found inscribed by the graves of the early Christians in the catacombs of Rome, where it is shown as a variety that bears longish fruits – a variety not to be found anywhere in Europe.

A European equivalent of *Asclepias acida* (which is a milkweed), in many respects, is the swallowwort (*Vincetoxicum hirundinaria*). Its efficacy as an antidote to poison is demonstrated by its Latin name: *vince-toxicum* is literally 'defeat the poison'. Dioscorides, the Greek physician and pharmacologist of the first century, called the plant the 'dog strangler' in his *Materia Medica*, and wrote that the leaves mixed with meat could kill dogs, wolves and foxes (*Mat. Med.* 4,80). Yet the poison could also be used as an antidote for the bites of poisonous animals (*Mat. Med.* 3,92). A botanical reference book written in 1563 (Mattioli, p.337) also eulogizes it: 'This is a splendid root against all poisons, of consummate substance and quality, which is why it is called *Vince-toxicum* in Latin – that is, conqueror of every poison. It is thus used even against the plague, and taken in wine, after which one sweats profusely.' Pronounced sweating and a dry mouth (note 'I thirst', John 19:28) are symptoms typical of poisoning. In Switzerland, swallowwort is called the 'Master-herb', and in Austria, 'Jewish herb' or 'White Cross herb'. Could there just possibly be an ancient memory of the plant's most historically important use echoed in these names?

A magical potion that has the property of putting living people into a long-lasting state resembling death is by no means unheard of, and is even comparatively common in stories and literature. The best-known example is *Romeo and Juliet*. In every case, the 'death' involved is actually a state resembling coma, in which all the life-signs, such as respiration, heartbeat and pulse, are no longer noticeable.

Had Jesus actually been close to suffocation on the Cross – and it is suffocation that virtually all the forensic experts assume was the cause of death – the loud cry before he 'died', as specifically mentioned by the three Synoptic evangelists, would have been quite imposssible. A choking, breathless person could hardly have managed to gasp out a whisper. But Jesus cried out. And John relates that, 'When Jesus therefore had received the vinegar, he said, It is finished: and he bowed his head, and gave up the ghost' (19:30). Jesus was able to say these words once he had taken the drink and felt its narcotic effect increasing. He was able to say them because he was close not to death but to a deep, induced state of stillness.

Traces on the Cloth

Now let us compare what we are told in the Gospel accounts with what we know about the impression of the body on the Turin Shroud. There are bloodstains on the Shroud. If a corpse had been buried in the linen cloth, the burial could not have been according to Jewish law because the corpse would then first have been washed down with warm water.

The peculiar position of the body is also striking. In a book repudiating the authenticity of the Turin Shroud, Joseph Blinzler argues that it is '. . . hardly conceivable that the disciples placed the hands in such an unseemly and impractical position, as seen in the image of the Turin Shroud, while interring the Messiah.'[28] Apart from the fact that no one has ever said that the disciples were in the sepulchre at the time, it should be pointed out that the position of Jesus' body precisely matches that of the skeletons buried in the cemetery of the Essene monastic settlement at Qumran near the Dead Sea. 'The position of the corpses in their graves is generally identical . . . As a rule, the body is in a supine position, the head to the south, and the hands are crossed together over the abdomen, or lie at the sides.'[29]

Jesus is supposed to have hung dead on the cross for three hours. If it happened, the consequences can be described with absolute certainty. According to all modern medical authorities, rigor mortis would have begun setting in some thirty or so minutes after death. The muscles of the body would have become completely stiff and immobile in three to six hours, depending on the temperature of the surroundings – the higher the ambient temperature, the faster the stiffening. Rigor mortis is caused by complex biochemical processes, but centres principally on a decline in levels of the metabolic energy compound ATP (adenosine triphosphate) after cessation of the heartbeat. The entire skeletal musculature becomes utterly rigid in whatever position the body has assumed in death, and only when rigor mortis relaxes and wears off – after four to seven days – can the body's posture be changed.

Once Jesus lost consciousness on the Cross, his body would have sagged. His weight, previously supported primarily by his legs as held fast by the nail through his feet, would instead have been taken by his arms as held fast by the nails through the wrists. His legs would thus have bent acutely at the knees. His head would have fallen forwards, his chin coming to rest at the top of his breastbone. And after the three or four hours that the body is said to have been left on the cross, it would have become rigid in this position. But a close look at the impression of the back of the body on the Shroud immediately reveals that the whole of Jesus' body was laid out quite flat on the cloth. The legs are straight, not bent, and the arms were evidently mobile when positioned (or they would have tended to spring apart to the posture of the Crucifixion).

A few Shroud commentators have suggested that the arms were probably bound together at the wrists. But any such cords or straps would have obscured the bleeding at the wrists, which can plainly be seen on the cloth. Monsignor Giulio Ricci, a member of the Centre for Shroud Research in Rome, has an individual solution to the problem: he assumes that the Shroud was itself tied tightly around the rigidly stiff and grotesquely bent corpse with external cords.[30] But this explanation is utter nonsense, for the impression clearly shows that the Shroud was initially spread out flat, both underneath and on top of the body. Otherwise extreme distortions in the width would be apparent (rendering the computerized scan impossible).

The fact that there was obviously no rigor mortis at the time when Jesus was taken down from the Cross is proof enough that

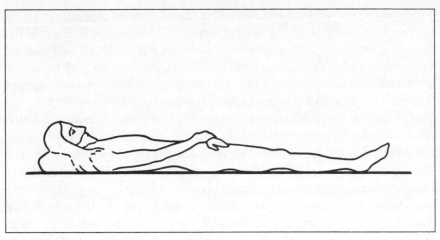

The body lay stretched out quite flat on an even surface, and was slightly cushioned (with cloths).

he was not dead. And even more cogent evidence is provided by the bloodstains visible on the Shroud.

For two separate bouts of bleeding can be clearly distinguished. Firstly, there are traces of the blood which flowed when Jesus was nailed to the Cross. Secondly, there are vestiges of the fresh blood which flowed from the body when Jesus was already lying horizontally in the cloth!

To take the bloodstains on the head first: the sharp points of the mass of thorns which was pressed mockingly on to Jesus' head would have left minute punctures, small but penetrating, in the thin skin of the head. As long as the 'crown of thorns' was on the head, the thorns sealed the tiny wounds (diameter between 1 and 2 millimetres) quite well. The small amount of blood that managed to flow out past the thorns coagulated at once and became encrusted in the hair, and this is the case in all the lesser wounds. But at the back of the head, the image on the Shroud clearly shows many blood trails of a larger size, and streaming in all directions. This blood obviously trickled on to the cloth when the body was laid on the linen only shortly after the thorns had been removed. The blood vessels in the thin skin of the head are numerous but very small, and well supplied with blood as long as the circulatory system remains intact. In a dead person, as soon as the heart stops, the blood is withdrawn from the capillary vessels just under the surface of the skin, turning the skin 'as pale as a corpse', and there is no way any more blood can emerge from such small wounds because intravascular blood clotting immediately sets in.

On the portrait of Jesus in the Shroud, a large bloodstain on the forehead is visible in the shape of a backwards 3. Such an unusual shape can only be formed if the head is slightly raised from the horizontal (some kind of pillow was most probably placed under the back of his head as he lay on his back). The slowly flowing blood then runs down to a crease in the forehead, collects a little, and as more fresh blood joins it, spills over and down to the next crease in the forehead. This forehead wound, also caused by the crown of thorns, is located on the uppermost point of the entire body (lying flat). Even if it is possible for blood to flow from large wounds on a corpse under certain conditions, it is not possible under any circumstances at the highest part of the forehead. Such bleeding is possible only if the circulatory system is fully operational!

Almost as far from the ground as the forehead are the hands, one placed over the other. Here it is particularly evident how fresh blood has run on to the cloth in addition to blood that had already dried. Three trails of blood can clearly be distinguished on the wrists, running in different directions. Simple measurement of angles provides unambiguous indications of how these blood trails originated. The left hand lies over the right and covers its nail wound, so the calculations only involve the visible wound on the left hand. When the nail was driven through, some blood ran into the furrow between the tensed muscles along the forearm and finally dropped vertically downward, under the influence of gravity. These small, vertical streamlets all run nearly parallel. From their direction we can work out the angle of the arms in relation to the crossbeam of the Cross: it was about 20°. This also makes possible the calculation of the difference in vertical height between the upright and sagging postures of the body on the Cross.

But in relation to the position of the arms there remains one item of great curiosity. Two of the major blood trails confirm the angle of the arms while Jesus was on the Cross, but the third blood trail, from the same point of origin, is distinctly visible on the Shroud at a totally different angle, and has not been mentioned in the studies of any of the better-known Shroud commentators. In fact, they have kept very quiet indeed about it – and no real wonder: the shape and direction of this third blood trail prove that it could only have been formed after the nails were removed from the wounds. The removal of the nails at the wrists made the wounds start bleeding again, and the blood spread across the hand

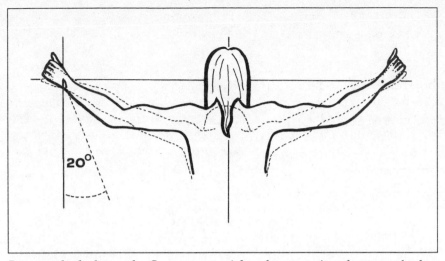

Because the body on the Cross was upright when conscious but sagged when unconscious, two markedly different positions can be mathematically defined by calculation of the angles of the blood trails on hands and arms.

as it lay flat. It is clearly visible in addition that the edges of the third blood trail are much less sharply defined than those of the two other trails, indicating that the first two blood trails had already dried and were moistened again by the aloes in the cloth, whereas the fresh blood of the third trail is surrounded by fringes of watery serum. Such serum fringes are formed by the activity of the clotting factor fibrin present in fresh blood, and appear only when blood collects on a surface that slopes shallowly and cannot flow away freely. As long as Jesus was hanging on the Cross, the blood could flow from the wounds, leaving trails of coagulated blood without any serum fringes and with clearly defined edges.

On the Shroud the right arm appears a little longer than the left. Such minor distortions in the front-view image show that the linen did not lie stiffly across the body. Because the cloth instead conformed to the curved shape of the body, the wound in the side has also left a clear imprint. On the frontal view, next to one of the patches on the burned areas, there are sharply defined trails of blood that stem from the wound in the side, and which coagulated on the Cross.

Parallel with the wound in the side, a conspicuous blood trace runs transversely across the back. The blood has an appearance quite different from the blood on the front of the body. Again there are clear edges of blood surrounded by serum fringes, a sure sign

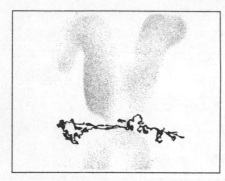

Blood collected in the lumbar arch between the mid–back and the buttocks. This blood can only have flowed after the body had been laid out horizontally.

that this too was blood that flowed while the body was lying in the cloth. The blood – and there is a considerable quantity of it – can only have flowed on to the cloth when the body was already lying horizontally. A trail of blood would otherwise lead down towards the lower abdomen. This blood certainly comes from the wound in the side. As Jesus lay in the healing cloth, the lateral incision started to bleed again. Naturally, the stream of blood did not run down the length of the body but took the shortest route under gravity to the surface the body was lying on, under the right arm, to collect across the back and in the arch of the lumbar region.

Let us look at what the experts have to say about this. If the arms of the body are raised into the position of the crucifixion, the wound in the side shifts upwards by quite a margin. The scientists at the East Midlands Forensic Laboratory consider it most unlikely, nonetheless, that a spear-thrust at the site of the side wound could have touched the heart. They see no life-threatening danger even if the point penetrated to some depth. The spear would only have pierced the membrane lining the chest cavity, causing 'blood and water' to flow out, a watery pleural fluid that had collected between the lungs and the chest wall during the violent treatment.[31]

On the matter of Jesus' wound in the side, someone once asked Dr W. Bonte, a forensic specialist and Director of the Institute for Forensic Medicine at Dusseldorf University, whether blood could flow from an open wound between the fifth and sixth ribs about 10 centimetres right of centre, from a corpse lying flat on its back, without applying mechanical pressure from outside. The wound had initially been inflicted while the body was upright, and the body was later laid on its back. To ensure a truly unbiased opinion, the expert was not told which 'criminal case' was involved. The answer given by the forensic expert is extremely informative:

1. Blood flows spontaneously from a wound in a corpse only if
    a) the wound opening is located in an area in which the blood has collected (hypostasis) as may be evident from skin discoloration (livor mortis), or
    b) the wound opening leads to a blood-filled cavity, the blood is still (at least in part) liquid, and the level of the cavity is vertically higher from the ground than the opening of the wound.

2. According to your description, however, the wound opening was situated in the right front thoracic wall, about 10 centimetres to the right of the centre line. With the corpse in a supine position, this corresponds fairly exactly to the highest point of the corpse. So neither of the above conditions is satisfied:
    a) the opening of the wound opening was not in an area of hypostasis, and
    b) blood could not have flowed out through the wound from the right thoracic cavity because it would first have to rise up against the fluid pressure. The same holds for other possible sources of bleeding (lung, lung vessels, heart chambers).

3. I therefore consider a spontaneous postmortal evacuation of blood from a wound aperture in such a location to be out of the question.

4. On the other hand, an outflowing of blood in the quantity you describe, together with the direction of flow, would be in agreement with the supposition that the person concerned was at this time still alive. It is not uncommon to find, in forensic medical practice, that blood flows from a wound opening in precisely the location described here and in the direction of flow you have described, from a victim still living, lying on the back. This is especially true if larger arterial vessels are punctured and if the blood pressure provides the necessary *vis a tergo* [force from beneath] for the blood column to rise against the hydrostatic pressure.[32]

This reply from an expert who was unaware of the delicate subject on whom he was giving his expert opinion is remarkable in many ways. It shows that an unbiased analysis of the facts leads to results quite different from those presented by people who want to

use the Shroud to prove that Jesus died. When Karl Herbst afterwards informed Professor Bonte about the real subject of his expert
opinion, and told him of some of his colleagues' arguments, his
response was clear: 'I do not wish to revise my earlier reasoning. In
my view everything suggests that the circulation had not yet
stopped. Of course I concur with Professor Bollone that an emission of blood from a stab wound in the chest can occur during the
transport of a corpse in a sort of passive way. But then one would
have to ask whether the shroud was wrapped around the body
when the transporting began. And if this were the case, no "static"
traces and imprint patterns would have been formed, which
always allow a direct topographic alignment with a supine body. I
would rather have expected numerous traces from brushing contact, arranged in a more random and irregularly scattered manner.
To my mind the pattern actually found suggests that the person
concerned was wrapped in the cloth only at the entombment, and
this most probably by first laying the body flat on the cloth and
then placing the other half of the cloth over the body. I cannot see
how a passive emission of larger quantities of blood could happen
during this operation of laying out the body.'

Severe bleeding is also evident from the wounds caused by the
nail through the feet. On the rear image it is clear that the blood
from the wound runs down to the heels, collects there and,
because fresh blood is still pumping out, flows on to the cloth to
the right.

The 17-centimetre-long trail of blood is interrupted because the
blood comes up against a fold in the cloth, before flowing further
to the right. The last part of this blood trail can be found at the
very far end of the Shroud, where one end of the sheet lay over the
other so that the fresh blood stained both places. Once more the
fact remains: blood simply cannot flow like this from a corpse that
has been dead for several hours. The heart and circulatory func-
tions were still intact, although respiration might have been greatly
reduced.

The haemorrhaging in the region of the feet shows the flow of
fresh blood very clearly. Bodily movements made while laying out
the body caused the open wounds to start bleeding again, and the
blood spread out in all directions. The dark impression of the blood
streamlets leaves no doubt that this blood reached the cloth only
after the entombment. Because the fabric was steeped in resinous
aloes at the spots where it touched the skin, the blood could not be
absorbed into the cloth but spread out across its surface.

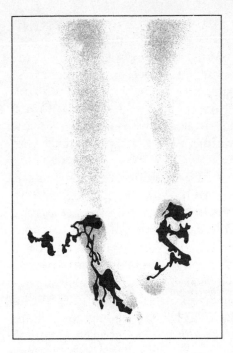

The blood traces on the feet show particularly well how the blood spread out in all directions on the surface of the Shroud after the body had been taken down from the Cross.

To establish clinical death presents doctors with difficulties even today. The use of modern drugs, for example, can induce so deep a coma that false diagnoses may easily be made. A well-known method for establishing death used to be to make a small incision in the heel or the wrist. If arterial blood flows, the circulatory system is still operating. Corpses just do not bleed!

In Jesus' case, there were a total of twenty-eight wounds that continued to bleed even after his removal from the Cross. This proves that Jesus could not possibly have been dead when his body was laid in the tomb.

The Open Rock-Tomb

From the moment that Jesus was seen to hang unconscious from the Cross, Joseph made haste to secure the release of the body as soon as was humanly possible. He exerted all his influence on Pilate to obtain an instant release. One scriptural authority even suggests that the wealthy Joseph paid a high sum in bribery to speed things up.[33] It is by no means inconceivable. Joseph was pressed for time, and any means would have seem justified to him if it would cut short the slow bureaucratic process. The men crucified with Jesus had their legs broken, but in Jesus' case the centurion just checked with his spear-thrust that he was dead. Pilate released the 'corpse', and at once Joseph and Nicodemus took Jesus from the Cross and brought him to the tomb in the rock near by.

In the seclusion of the tomb cavern, preparations for the healing of Jesus got under way on the ledge in the middle of the floor. The opium drink helped him to sleep deeply, out of pain. He was packed around with the vast quantity of medicinal herbs to make his wounds heal faster. But Joseph and Nicodemus knew they could not leave Jesus in the tomb for long. The Jews were extremely suspicious and were already expressing fears that Jesus' followers might steal the body to pretend there had been a miraculous resurrection. According to Matthew (27:62–66), they asked Pilate for someone to guard the tomb. They could not form a watch at the sepulchre themselves because it was the Sabbath. The longer time went on, the more difficult it would become to get Jesus out and away unobserved. It is not possible, at this distance in time, to tell whether a Roman guard was in fact assigned to the tomb, although Matthew (alone) does say so. It may well be, however, that it was introduced into his text to add dramatic effect to the appearance of the angel. The Jews' urgent desire to have a guard set over a corpse must have seemed bizarre to the Romans, and it is very unlikely that they complied with such a request.

So for the Sabbath, at least, the team had the time to take care of Jesus. As soon as he was able, though, he would have to be quickly moved elsewhere, to avoid further problems from the Jewish authorities.

When the women came to the tomb with the oils for anointing, on the first day of the week, they found the stone rolled aside and the tomb empty. Let us see what the Gospel accounts say. Luke writes:

> Now upon the first day of the week, very early in the morning, they came unto the sepulchre, bringing the spices which they had prepared, and certain others with them.
> And they found the stone rolled away from the sepulchre.
> And they entered in, and found not the body of the Lord Jesus.
> And it came to pass, as they were much perplexed thereabout,

behold, two men stood by them in shining garments:

And as they were afraid, and bowed down their faces to the earth, they said unto them, Why seek ye the living among the dead?

(Luke 24:1–5)

Mark tells it like this:

And when they looked, they saw that the stone was rolled away: for it was very great.

And entering into the sepulchre, they saw a young man sitting on the right side, clothed in a long white garment; and they were affrighted. And he saith unto them, Be not affrighted; Ye seek Jesus of Nazareth, which was crucified: he is risen; he is not here: behold the place where they laid him.

(Mark 16:4–6)

After his so-called 'resurrection' Jesus is said to be constantly entering through locked doors and appearing to the surprise of his followers (John 20:19–26). So why, it seems pertinent to ask, was the massive stone rolled aside from the tomb entrance, from the very place where this miraculous 'resurrection' was held to have happened? It would surely have been a more astonishing 'miracle' if the stone had had to be rolled aside to let in the women with the oils for anointing, only then for it to be discovered that Jesus had vanished from the sealed chamber. The open tomb is evidence that someone had had to act fast and move Jesus out of the tomb. Essene friends were obviously still at the tomb – Luke's men with the shining garments, Mark's young man with the white garment. The shining white robe certainly implies that they were Essenes. Jesus had probably been led out just a short while earlier. Because the festival of the Passover always coincided with the full moon, it was easy to travel in the bright moonlit night. Perhaps the Essenes who stayed behind were there to collect certain items and seal the tomb. The shocked women received clear replies from the Essenes to their questions: Jesus had risen again and was therefore no longer there. He had indeed arisen – that is, out of his drug-enhanced coma. The Luke text is even clearer: 'Why seek ye the living among the dead?' Does that not compel us to believe that Jesus was alive, that it had been possible to save him? Is this not the clear message we get from these Gospel passages?

John, who does not report the episode with the women at the sepulchre, relates in detail an event which it seems must have taken place before the women arrived (John 20:1–18). Mary Magdalene comes to the tomb early in the morning, when it is still dark, and sees the stone rolled away. Shocked, she runs to Peter and John, and wails that someone has taken the Lord out of the sepulchre. When the pair arrive at the tomb and peer in, they see only the linen cloths: there is no trace of Jesus anywhere. Mary Magdalene, who stands weeping before the tomb, asks the gardener if he had carried the body away. When the supposed gardener addresses her by name, she realizes it is Jesus.

It is remarkable that Mary Magdalene mistakes Jesus for the gardener. Is this the One resurrected in glory – a figure unrecognized by one of his closest companions and thought by her to be the gardener? What probably happened was that they had only just led Jesus out of the tomb when Mary Magdalene appeared. So as not to attract attention, they had dressed him in simple garments such as a gardener might wear. The weakened Jesus may even have been given a garden implement as a makeshift walking stick to lean on. All of these factors then led to the mix-up. In addition, gardeners have their skin tanned to a darker brown by their constant work out in the sun. The face of Jesus was swollen by the injuries, and the aloes and myrrh solution leaves a characteristic brown coloration. This was surely why Mary Magdalene did not recognize her master in the early twilight, and not because he showed himself in a 'transfigured' body as one resurrected.

The apocryphal *Gospel of Peter* describes how the guard at the tomb saw three men emerge from the tomb 'and two of them supported the other one'! Does a person resurrected in glory need such support? Certainly not – but an injured person who has to be brought to safety, and who has just come round from a coma, does.

After relating these events, the Gospels, in the passages concerning Jesus, become sparser and less reliable, because from here on they are entangled in the myth of the 'resurrection' and in a theological interpretation by which Jesus corresponds to the resurrected Christ. One thing is certain, however: Jesus was with his disciples again for a while, perhaps in Jerusalem, but mainly in Galilee.

Very few precise conclusions can be drawn about the events that took place during the period of time after Jesus' disappearance from the tomb, because the descriptions given are so confused. That there were three days said to have passed between Crucifixion and reappearance corresponds merely to a mystical period that played a role in older resurrection myths. Jesus may well have been looked after for a longer time, until he gradually took to showing himself once more to his followers. In any case, such meetings seem always to have been of short duration and in secret. He could not show himself publicly, of course, or he would instantly have been arrested again. His appearance seems to have been affected so much by his injuries at first – his face was probably very swollen for a while – that even his friends had difficulty recognizing him when they saw him.

In considering Jesus' appearances to his followers, it is essential always to bear in mind that they are recorded in writing in a way that conforms with the theology of his 'resurrection', as was developed after the event. All of Chapter 21 in the Gospel of John, which contains the appearance of Jesus by the Sea of Tiberias, is the work of an author who did not write the rest, and has simply been tacked on. The chapter seems to have been written by John the priest, and to have been included in the writings of John the favourite disciple on account of their identical names.[34]

Immediately after the Crucifixion, Jesus' disciples left to go back sadly to their former occupations. Simon Peter, Thomas, Nathanael of Cana and the sons of Zebedee resumed fishing (John 21:2). Only when Jesus told them he would meet them himself in Galilee were they fired with fresh enthusiasm (Matthew 28:10).

His encounters with his one-time travelling companions are presented as 'appearances' because Jesus is said to have entered into their midst through locked doors – and yet the physical corporeality of Jesus is emphasized at the same time. The disciples were baffled: most of them had probably not been told about the rescue operation mounted by Joseph and Nicodemus, who did not belong to their circle. The last thing the Gospels report about Jesus, shortly before his departure from Palestine,[35] is his continued endeavour to explain to the disciples once and for all that he had survived the Crucifixion and had recovered. But at first the disciples thought he must be a ghost:

> And he said unto them, Why are ye troubled? and why do thoughts arise in your hearts?
>
> Behold my hands and my feet, that it is I myself: handle me, and see; for a spirit hath not flesh and bones, as ye see me have.
>
> And when he had thus spoken, he shewed them his hands and his feet. And while they yet believed not for joy, and wondered, he said unto them, Have ye here any meat?
>
> And they gave him a piece of a broiled fish, and of an honey-comb.
>
> And he took it, and did eat before them.
>
> (Luke 24:38–43)

Jesus is keen to demonstrate to his followers that his body is quite earthly in nature, just as it had been before. He stresses his physical presence by allowing them to touch him, and by eating food, and tells them plainly that he is no ghost. To prove that his body has not been 'transformed' in any way, he also shows the marks of his wounds and even asks 'doubting Thomas' to touch the wound in his side with his hand. Later he revealed himself to the eleven as they were sitting at table, and criticized their lack of faith and their obduracy in not believing those who had seen him after his rising again (!) (Mark 16:14). That Jesus was there in person was the result of no administrative error, no trickery, no illusion; his body is as human as theirs, neither transfigured nor that of an astral projection or a ghost – this is the message he tries to get the disciples to take in.

'Resurrected' or 'Arisen'?

A comparison of the actual vocabulary in the Gospel of John and in the Synoptic Gospels affords a fairly detailed reconstruction of events. On the ledge around the central depression in the floor of the tomb cavern, a number of cloths (*othonia*) made of an undyed (*kathara*) piece of linen (*sindon*) were laid out. Over these cloths another strip of linen (*soudarion*) was spread out. A solution of the medicinal herbs aloes and myrrh was applied to the naked body of the unconscious Jesus, which was then laid on the length of linen. The end of the cloth was lifted and folded back over to cover the body. In this way the whole body was covered (*entylisso*). The quantity of the aromatic substances in the cloth (some 45 kilograms!) made the gigantic poultice-bandaging so heavy that the body was firmly and completely wrapped up (*eneileo*) as if in a hefty quilt.

If we now re-read the passage in John's Gospel that details the events surrounding the discovery of the empty tomb (John 20:1–18), bearing in mind the reconstruction as outlined so far, the full meaning automatically becomes clear.

First Mary Magdalene runs to Simon Peter and the favourite disciple of Jesus and excitedly tells them that someone has removed the body of Jesus from the tomb. What she does not say is that the body has somehow been stolen: her statement is neutral on the subject of how Jesus might have disappeared from the tomb. We are not even told why Mary Magdalene went to the tomb so early in the morning while it was still dark. John does not say that she wanted to anoint the corpse, as the Synoptic Gospels say was the case with the women they describe. When talking to Peter and John, she simply says, 'They have taken away the Lord out of the sepulchre . . .' It is as if the people she was talking to knew who 'they' were.

Based on this first sentence, a further reconstruction of events is both possible and plausible. During the night, once the medicinal packing with herbs was in hand, Joseph and Nicodemus visited some of the followers of Jesus. In particular, they approached Mary Magdalene, Simon Peter and John, who could be regarded as intimate companions. They briefly explained to the three what role they themselves had been playing, and that they were trying to save Jesus from death with the aid of Essene friends. Should their efforts be met with success, their amazed listeners could begin to hope again. But whatever happened, Jesus would have to be taken as soon as possible from the present unsafe hiding place, and brought to somewhere secure, away from the watchful eyes of the Jerusalem priesthood. To say any more might be to jeopardize everything. It was possible, after all, that one of the disciples would be arrested and, if tortured, betray their plans.

Mary Magdalene, amazed and overwhelmed at what she has heard, cannot restrain herself for long. She sets off for the tomb to see for herself how true Joseph's words were. There she finds the stone rolled away from the entrance, and runs immediately back to the two others to confirm to them that it had happened. As Joseph had said, 'they' — he and his assistants – had removed Jesus from the tomb. She was quick to add, 'and we know not where they have laid him'. If she had been talking about a grave robbery, this additional remark would have made no sense at all. The victim of a robbery obviously does not expect to know where the stolen goods have been taken. She is evidently referring to the Essenes who, after waiting as long as they could while still under cover of darkness, had taken the first steps to get Jesus away.

Now it was the turn of the two disciples to be utterly amazed, and they make for the tomb at a run. The youthful John is faster and reaches the entrance first, from where he cautiously peers inside. But the ingenuous Peter goes right on into the tomb cavern and looks around. He notices a crumpled heap of cloths and, separate from them, neatly folded, the healing cloth which Joseph had mentioned. Only at this point does John also dare to enter the tomb, and, as the report says, 'he saw, and believed'.

This most interesting passage is usually taken as the basis for the Christian doctrine of the Resurrection. The action of 'seeing and believing' in this way – an action that occupies an important place in Johannine theology – is commonly interpreted as conferring immediacy and absolute reality on the Resurrection of Jesus. At the same time, according to the Gospel writer, only the favourite disciple 'saw and believed'; Peter merely 'saw'. The next verse provides the solution: 'For as yet they knew not the scripture, that he must rise again from the dead.'

It is possible to claim that at the time the Gospel of John was being written, the doctrine of the Resurrection, as formulated by Paul (especially in chapter 15 of his first letter to the Corinthians), was already generally accepted by the early Christians. It would have been natural, therefore, that the author of the Gospel, who obtained his facts as (or from) an eyewitness, was concerned about presenting the events in a theologically correct way. So he goes on to forgive Peter for not immediately believing after seeing what he saw, because after all he was not yet aware of the biblical text in which the Resurrection had been foretold.

But we should remember that John's writing is for the most part on two different levels: one obvious and the other cryptic. In this case, then, he is not really talking about the death and resurrection, but about the rescue of Jesus. So let us briefly have a look at that scriptural passage which the disciples did not know about.

It is not easy to identify. Most scriptural authorities agree that according to Acts 2:25–28 it has to be Psalm 16:8–11. Those verses from the Psalm read:

> I have set the Lord always before me: because he is at my right hand, I shall not be moved.
>
> Therefore my heart is glad, and my glory rejoiceth: my flesh also shall rest in hope.
>
> For thou wilt not leave my soul in hell; neither wilt thou suffer thine Holy One to see corruption.
>
> Thou wilt shew me the path of life: in thy presence is fulness of joy; at thy right hand there are pleasures for evermore.

Is this the promised Resurrection, as elucidated by scriptural authority? Try as one may, it is impossible to discern any mention of resurrection here. Quite the contrary. The precondition for resurrection, as Paul stresses, is death. One can use the adjective 'resurrected' only to describe a person who has once died. It is on this basis that the Christian says in the Creed, Jesus died and then 'rose from the dead'. But the Psalm speaks rather of saving from death. Peter misinterprets it in referring to it while explaining the secret of the Pentecost as the promise of resurrection (Acts 2:25–28). Perhaps this has something to do with his not believing when he saw the linen cloths in the tomb, because he remained loyal to the mythical tradition of the Resurrection. For, taking the facts as they are, the 'seeing and believing' of the favourite disciple can only be understood as his believing what Joseph of Arimathea had told them. The favourite disciple saw that no one was buried in the grave, and the separate cloths confirmed for him the statement that Jesus was still alive. He therefore believed not in the Resurrection but in the rescue of Jesus! That is the key to this Bible passage.

It is possible that the notion of Resurrection in the Bible stems from a tradition aware of these efforts to heal Jesus. The fascinating work of the linguist and theologian Father Günther Schwarz has revealed an exciting new view of the matter. For the terms 'rise' and 'coming back to life' that are found in translations of the Bible, in the original Aramaic derive, as Dr Schwarz proves, from a verbal root meaning 'to resuscitate'![36]

Schwarz explains,

> The linguistic evidence is conclusive: not 'resurrection' but 'resuscitation' is the only meaning possible for both these Aramaic words, one of which Jesus would have used. I am referring to the synonymous words *achajuta* and *techijjuta*. Both nouns are derived from the verb *chaja* 'to live', and consequently mean – I repeat – 'resuscitation', and nothing else.[37]

This discovery is quite sensational and at once lends a meaning to the biblical texts that is in perfect agreement with our analysis so far. Even the New Testament Greek word corresponds in its root meaning neither with the original Aramaic concept nor with the meaning of 'resurrection' as established in the Christian usage: *anhistemi* means 'to wake', 'to rouse' (transitive), and 'to get up', 'to come up' (intransitive); *anastasis* means 'a rising up'. Only by the later Christian interpretation is *anhistemi* made to mean 'to raise from the dead' (transitive) and 'to rise from the dead' (intransitive), and *anastasis* 'resurrection'.[38]

In the light of what we now know, let us again consider the passages in Mark and Luke in which the women at the tomb are told about the disappearance of Jesus by the men clad in white. Mark writes, 'And he saith unto them, Be not affrighted: Ye seek Jesus of Nazareth, which was crucified: he is risen, he is not here: behold the place where they laid him' (16:6, comparable with Matthew 28:6, although there the actual events are given a somewhat dramatized setting involving an angel who performs theatrical magic, an earthquake, and petrified tomb guards). The curt query by the white-robed men in Luke, asking why they seek a living person among the dead (24:5), is as clear as can be. Jesus lives, he is rescued, he has no business with a tomb any more, the living belong among the living. He had gone ahead to Galilee, where his followers could see him again.

We have already seen how Jesus had great difficulty convincing the disciples of his presence in the flesh. The reason for this is twofold. Firstly, the majority of the disciples had not been told about the resuscitation attempt, and so were convinced they were looking at a reanimated corpse or a ghost. And secondly, the supposed death by crucifixion of Jesus marks the point at which history ends and Christian theology (the doctrine of the Resurrection) begins. Jesus' life as a human individual comes to a close at this point, and replacing it, the story of Christ – the mythically glorified Reality – commences.

Chapter Nine

AFTER THE CRUCIFIXION

Paul Meets Jesus at Damascus

After recovering from the ordeal of the Crucifixion, Jesus stayed in hiding. He could no longer teach in public, for his persecutors would soon recognize him and they would not let him escape a second time. He had to get right away from the threat posed by his enemies: 'And he led them out as far as to Bethany, and he lifted up his hands, and blessed them. And it came to pass, while he blessed them, he was parted from them, and carried up into heaven. And they worshipped him, and returned to Jerusalem with great joy' (Luke 24:50–52).

To picture the farewell scene, the best way is to reconstruct the events at the very place where they happened. From outside the city of Jerusalem the path to Bethany climbs quite steeply over the southernmost foothills of the range that includes the Mount of Olives, up to the 'Peak of the Ascension'. A person who walks over the summit and down the other side is quickly lost to sight.

But there is an eyewitness to testify that Jesus did not just disappear once and for all, and whose testimony cannot be dismissed out of hand as a fabrication: it is Paul. Although he was not personally present as a witness at the events after the Crucifixion, he did meet Jesus some time after the 'Ascension' – an encounter that was to change his whole life.

Paulus (Saulus) had been one of the most zealous and fanatical opponents of the New Covenant movement. He may even have heard rumours to the effect that Jesus, although presumed dead, was continuing his activity in hiding. 'And Saul, yet breathing out threatenings and slaughter against the disciples of the Lord, went unto the high priest, And desired of him letters to Damascus to the synagogues, that if he found any of this way, whether they were men or women, he might bring them bound unto Jerusalem' (Acts 9:1–2).

After much intensive research, the psychiatrist Wilhelm Lange-Eichbaum,[1] was able to draw up a detailed portrait of the personality of Paul in his well-known work *Genius, Madness and Fame*. In external appearance, Paul was frail, unprepossessing and shortish, but at the same time his temperament was austere, ascetic, impetuous and impulsive. The zeal he displayed in the persecution of Christians compensated for his own feelings of inadequacy.

Quite the most attractive feature of Paulinism is its notion of redemption and release from inner tensions (particularly sexual needs and the fear of death). Paul had boundless energy and a matching ego. He suffered sorely from blackouts and moods, which he blamed on demons. Recent commentators have shown that the cause of what he often described as a 'thorn in the flesh' (2 Corinthians 12:17, cf Galatians 6:17), was not epilepsy, as formerly suggested, but was probably (and tragically) his own homosexuality. The problem gave him a strong dislike of sex and sexuality altogether, a disposition that was fundamental to his development of an ascetic doctrine of marriage that has turned out to be central to the notions of women and of sexuality that have dominated Christian attitudes from then until now. Jesus, on the other hand, had an open, almost 'modern' attitude towards women. In contrast with the misogynous outlook of contemporary society, he had female disciples and taught women as well as men. Apocryphal tradition says that Mary Magdalene was especially close to him, and was one of his most intimate companions and most faithful followers. The four Gospels of the Bible also report that she was the first person to see Jesus after the Crucifixion. But Paul gives his own list of the people who saw the resurrected Christ: the list contains no mention of Mary Magdalene and includes only men.

The amazing experience that Paul underwent near Damascus was thus no mere vision (nor even a hallucination brought on by an epileptic attack, as often suggested):

> And as he journeyed, he came near Damascus: and suddenly there shined round about him a light from heaven:
>
> And he fell to the earth, and heard a voice saying unto him, Saul, Saul, why persecutest thou me?
>
> And he said, Who art thou, Lord? And the Lord said, I am Jesus whom thou persecutest: it is hard for thee to kick against the pricks.
>
> And he trembling and astonished said, Lord, what wilt thou have me to do? And the Lord said unto him, Arise, and go into the city, and it shall be told thee what thou must do.
>
> (Acts 9:3–6)

Now Damascus was in the middle of Syria, where the Jews had been hated since the uprising of the Maccabees (165 BC), and where the spiritual centre of the Essene Order also happened to be at the time. Perhaps Saul had taken part in an initiation ritual, and was 'blinded' for three days (Acts 9:8–9) by the Soma drink.

Sossianus Hierocles was an important Roman official; the governor of Phoenicia, Lebanon, Bithynia and Egypt, he was even in his day considered one of the most brutal persecutors of the early Christian communities. A sentence in his book *To the Christians* runs, 'After fleeing [!] from the Jews, Christ collected as many as nine hundred men all given to robbery.'[2] We have already noted elsewhere what kind of people such terms as 'bandits' and 'robbers' were usually applied to by Latin speakers. It is quite possible that the Essene community in Damascus had nine hundred members.

Paul was baptised and introduced to the teachings by Ananias, a follower of Jesus living in Damascus. According to Acts 9, Ananias was asked by Jesus himself to visit Saul, but he was at first very reluctant because he knew of the persecutor's record to date. Jesus dismissed this objection with the words: 'Go thy way: for he is a chosen vessel unto me, to bear my name before the Gentiles, and kings, and the children of Israel: For I will shew him how great things he must suffer for my name's sake' (Acts 9:15–16).

Henceforward Paul would be the most zealous proclaimer of the new faith. He felt the fascination of Jesus' personality, and at once recognized the wider significance of the task that the Nazarene had given him. With even greater zeal than in his persecution of Jesus and his followers, Paul took on the task of spreading his own interpretation of the new teaching. The encounter between Jesus and Paul in Damascus took place around two years after the Crucifixion. No less than 300 kilometres north of Jerusalem, Jesus must have felt relatively safe from his enemies in the care of the Essenes.

The Journey to Paradise

Provided a religious community accepted the Roman state cult, Rome tolerated the exercise of other religious practices. But the Jews had special privileges, and were exempt even from having to participate in the state cult. The first expansion of the New

Covenant took place under the protection of the Jewish exemption regulations. But when it became clear to the Romans that the followers of Jesus had little connection with Judaism, and might in addition be numbered among political agitators, the Christians (as they became known collectively) forfeited all claims to tolerance, and hostility was openly manifested instead. At first, the Christian communities were persecuted by the Roman state system at the local level only, as alleged disturbers of the peace. A state-controlled general persecution was not to start until the second half of the third century.

Immediately after the Crucifixion, the animosity of the Jews in Jerusalem forced the first Christians to expand their universal mission to address the much wider territory of the Roman Empire.

In Damascus, then, Jesus could enjoy the benefit of Essene protection. About five kilometres outside Damascus there is a place that is still called Mayuam-i-Isa, 'The place where Jesus lived'. The Persian historian Mir Kawand cites several sources which state that Jesus lived and taught here after the Crucifixion.

The followers of the 'new teaching' continued to grow in number, not least because of Jesus' own personal efforts. But rumours of Jesus' presence in Damascus – rumours that Paul had actually travelled to investigate, after all – would have become more and more substantial, and it must gradually have become too dangerous for the Nazarene to continue to reside in the Roman province of Syria.

Persian traditions tell how, while Jesus was staying in Damascus, he received a letter from the King of Nisibis in Asia Minor, in which the king asked Jesus to come to cure him of an illness. Jesus then sent his close disciple Thomas on ahead, with the message that he himself would soon follow. And shortly after, he travelled to Nisibis with his mother Mary. In *Jami-ut-Tawarik*, the Persian scholar Fakir Muhammad says that the king had already been healed by Thomas before Jesus arrived in Nisibis with his group. Imam Abu Jafar Muhammad wrote in his famous work *Tafsir-Ibn-i-Jarir at-Tabri* that Jesus' stay in Nisibis came to represent a considerable danger to the Nazarene, and that it was at the risk of his life that he appeared in public.[3]

From Nisibis, Jesus first went north-west. At any rate, the apocryphal *Acts of Thomas* relate that Jesus visited the court of the King of Andrapa, where he suddenly appeared during the festivities at the princess' wedding. Andrapolis was in Paphlagonia (modern Iskilip, in the extreme north of Anatolia), and had belonged to the

Roman province of Galatia since 7 BC. The wedding festivities at the royal court were the scene of a reunion for the apostle Thomas and his master, for they had apparently travelled there separately.

Thomas was commissioned by Jesus to go to India.

> But he did not want to go there, and said he could not travel because of weakness of the flesh. 'How can I, a Hebrew, travel and preach the truth to the people of India?' And as he reflected and spoke thus, the Saviour appeared to him in the night and spoke to him: 'Do not be afraid, Thomas. Go to India and preach the word there, for my Grace is with you.' But he would not obey, and said: 'Send me anywhere you want, but somewhere else! For I shall not go to India.'
>
> *(Acta Thomae* I)[4]

According to the *Acts of Thomas*, Jesus thereupon sold the reluctant Thomas as a slave to the Indian merchant Abban, who had been asked by King Gundafor (Gondaphares) to find him a carpenter. (Discoveries of ancient coin hoards have confirmed that the Indo-Parthian King Gundafor was indeed on the throne during the first century.) Jesus signed a contract with Abban, 'settled for a sum of three pounds of unstamped silver'. This unusual story presumably indicates that Thomas' fare to India was paid by Jesus, and that in this way Jesus was making sure that Thomas would get there.

Like the apocryphal *Gospel of Thomas*, the *Acts of Thomas* are of Syrian origin, and can be traced back in tradition to the missionary activity of Thomas himself in Edessa. Tradition furthermore has it that during the fourth century, long after the apostle had died near Madras in southern India, his remains were brought back to Edessa. The *Acts of Thomas* and the *Gospel of Thomas* are closely related. Both are esoteric works of the Gnostics written in Syrian Aramaic (Syriac), and used at the beginning of the third century by the late-Gnostic Manicheans (Mani was born in 217). A 'Gospel of Thomas' is first mentioned and quoted by Hippolytus (Ref. V 7,20) in his report on the 'Naassenes' in about AD 230.

The name of the apostle Didymus Judas Thomas means 'Judas the Twin' (Greek *didymus* and Aramaic *toma'* both mean 'twin'), and it may well indicate a particularly close relationship with Jesus. In Coptic texts, the word 'twin' seems to be replaceable by (and therefore synonymous with) the expression 'friend and companion'. The *Acts of Thomas* state that Thomas was afforded the privilege of being let into Jesus' deepest secrets. In Chapter 39, the apostle is addressed with his special title, 'Twin brother of Christ, apostle of the Highest, and initiate, sharer in the knowledge of the hidden word of Christ, thou who receivest his secret pronounce-ments'. And in another version: 'You who have had knowledge of the secret Word of the Giver of Life, and who have received the hidden Mysteries of the Son of God'.[5] Thomas is thus the keeper (the root meaning of 'Nazarene') of the secret words of Jesus revealed uniquely to him.

In the *Gospel of Thomas* (in the Coptic Gnostic texts of Nag Hammadi), there is the following passage:

> Jesus said to his disciples, 'Compare me to someone and tell Me whom I am like.' Simon Peter said to Him, 'You are like a righteous messen-ger.' Matthew said to Him, 'You are like a man who is a wise philoso-pher.' Thomas said to Him, 'Master, my mouth is wholly incapable of saying whom You are like.' Jesus said, 'I am not your master. Because you have drunk, you have become intoxicated from the bubbling spring which I have given.' And He took him and withdrew and told him three words. When Thomas returned to his companions, they asked him, 'What did Jesus say to you?' Thomas said to them, 'If I tell you one of the things which he told me, you will pick up stones and throw them at me, and a fire will come out of the stones and burn you up.'

(Logion 13)[6]

Thomas had evidently penetrated to the deeper dimensions of knowledge, and now seemed to be almost an equal of Christ.

Conversions effected by the apostles play a great role in the *Acts of Thomas*. There are many descriptions of rites of initiation that include sacramental elements. The new convert was 'sealed' by anointment with oil, and by participation in the Eucharist. Only bread was consumed at this Mass or Eucharist (or Holy Communion), for the chalice was only used to contain water. In the second part of the *Acts of Thomas*, the Indian king Misdai says that oil, water and bread were elements in the apostles' 'magic'. The initiate was called a servant or handmaid of God, was said to share in the Power of God, and was thereafter considered a mem-ber of the fold. Becoming the 'servant' or 'handmaid' 'in the power of' God explains how it came about that Thomas was 'sold as a slave' to someone called Abban (*Abba*, 'Father').

Elevation from ordinary Brother of the Essene Order to a higher Nazarene was sealed by anointment of the head with consecrated oil, and further anointing the naked initiate.

The Nazarenes must have looked very similar to one another. They were all clothed in the same white robes , and all wore their hair and beards in the same style. So it is possible that the term 'twin', when applied to Thomas, was simply an allusion to the similarity in outward appearance between the two men. Accounts of mistaken identity in the *Acts of Thomas* read like a comedy of errors, although Thomas was a good ten years younger than Jesus.

On the same wedding night, the King of Andrapa showed the apostle Thomas into the bridal chamber, so that he might convert the newly wedded couple. After Thomas had prayed with the couple, everyone else left the room.

> But after everyone had left and the doors had been closed, the bridegroom raised the curtain of the bridal chamber to call his bride. And he saw the Lord Jesus speaking with the bride, resembling Judas Thomas, who had just blessed them and left them. The groom said to Jesus: 'Did you not just leave? How did you get back in?' But the Lord replied: 'I am not Judas surnamed Thomas; I am his brother.' And the Lord sat down upon the bed, asking them to sit down on couches, and proceeded to tell them: 'Remember, my children, what my brother said to you and to whom he commended you . . .'
>
> *(Actae Thomae* 11–12)[7]

An earlier chapter (Chapter 8) describes the meeting between Thomas and a Hebrew woman who played the flute at the wedding festivities. Since the fall of the kingdom of Israel (722 BC) there had probably been Israelite communities scattered throughout the Middle East. It is likely that as he travelled ever eastwards, Jesus was always able to find a welcome among the far-flung Children of Israel, or at least with sympathizers of the Israelites. In Parthia (modern Iraq and Iran) there were major Israelite settlements, according to the Book of Esther. The Israelite communities later formed an alliance to put up strong resistance to the Emperor Trajan's invasion (around AD 115).

Many of the place-names along the old Silk Route suggest a connection with Jesus or Mary, especially as stopover stations. Near Ephesus, on the west coast of what is now Turkey, for instance, stands a 'House of Mary'. Perhaps Jesus and his mother sojourned there before continuing their journey eastwards.

A number of historical documents refer to Jesus' stay in Persia. The name and title of Jesus vary from country to country, and are constantly adapted from language to language, according to local conditions and traditions. In places where Jesus stayed for a longer period, local names are more likely to have been preserved over the years. After all, it seems that more than sixteen years elapsed after Jesus' Crucifixion before he arrived in Kashmir with his entourage.

In Parthia, Jesus was evidently known by the name Yuz Asaf. The meaning of the name is given in the *Farhang-i-Asafia*, an ancient work recounting the history of Persia, which relates that Jesus (*Hazrat Issa*[8]) healed some lepers, who were thereafter called *Asaf* – 'the purified' – having been cured of their complaint. *Yuz* means 'leader', so Yuz Asaf can be taken to mean 'leader of the healed', a common epithet for Jesus, and probably alluding to Jesus' mission to cleanse 'impure spirits', and lead all back to the true Faith. Jesus would probably be able to move with greater safety and evade his persecutors more easily under this new name – after all, the Persian priests were not likely to have forgotten his earlier visit to their land.

According to the traditions, the prophet entered the land from the west. His words and teachings in content no different from those of Jesus Christ, he is also said to have resided in Mashag, where he visited the grave of Shem the son of Noah (*Jami-ut-Tawarik*, Vol. II). Various manuscripts have been preserved which tell how Yuz Asaf preached all over Persia (modern Iran), and converted a large number of people. Details of his teaching (such as Agha Mustafai's *Ahwali Ahaliau-i-Paras*) confirm again and again that Yuz Asaf and Jesus were one and the same man.

The official poet at the court of Akbar, the Moghul Emperor of India, called Jesus *Ai Ki Nam-i-to Yus o Kristo*, or 'Thou, whose name is Yuz or Christ'. Although the Greek title *Christos* has assumed various derivative forms that have become established in various languages of the West, in the East it is the name Yuz Asaf that has been preserved down the centuries.

Place-names which apparently commemorate the presence and activity of Jesus are also to be found in modern Afghanistan and Pakistan. For example, there are two plains that bear the name of the prophet Yuz Asaf in eastern Afghanistan, near the towns of Ghazni and Jalalabad, to which tradition says Jesus once went.

Then there is the presence of Jesus and Thomas in Taxila (now in Pakistan) at the court of King Gundafor during the twenty-sixth year of his reign (AD 47), as recorded in the *Acts of Thomas*. Thomas is asked by the king to build a magnificent palace, but the apostle instead distributes the money meant to pay for it among the needy. Thomas thanks Jesus for this opportunity to render service:

> 'I thank thee, O Lord, in every way that I can, you who died for a short while [!] that I might live eternally in You; and for your selling me, in order to liberate many others through me.' And he never ceased to

teach and give relief to the troubled, saying, 'The Lord gives this to you, and ensures that everyone receives nourishment. For he is the nourisher of orphans and the provider for widows, and offers the gift of tranquillity and peace to all who are troubled.'

(*Actae Thomae* 19)[9]

Eventually, the king himself was converted, to mark the event receiving a 'palace in heaven'! Thomas initiated Gundafor and his brother Gad, 'sealed' them by baptism with water, by anointing with oil, and by celebrating the Eucharist, and so brought them as sheep into the fold of the Lord. 'For we have heard said that the God that you worship recognizes his sheep by his seal.' At the conclusion of the initiation rite, Jesus himself appeared, and said, 'Peace be with you, Brothers' (*Actae Thomae* 27)[10]

The text continues, 'And [Thomas] . . . took bread, oil, vegetables and salt, blessed them, and gave them to the assembly. He himself continued his fast, however, for the Day of the Lord was dawning.'

Jesus apparently did not reside continuously at the court of the king, although he returned there regularly. At any rate, the following night he again visited Thomas, who was expecting him, and told him:

> Thomas, rise early, bless everyone, and after prayer and worship, go along the path east for two miles, and there I shall show you my glory. Through the work that you are about to begin, many will come to seek refuge in me, and you will triumph over the world and the power of the enemy.
>
> (*Actae Thomae* 29)[11]

At the place described by Jesus, the apostle found a young boy who seemed to be dead. He brought him back to life, in the presence of a number of spectators. The youth, who is described as 'comely', told Thomas that he had seen Jesus: 'For I saw that man, as he stood next to you, and I heard what he said to you: "I have many miracles to perform through you, and there are great works that I shall accomplish through you . . . "'[12]

The next clue to the road taken by Jesus on the way east is located in a small town called Mari, 70 kilometres east of Taxila. In this idyllically situated mountain resort (formerly spelled Murree on English maps) on the border with Kashmir, a grave has been maintained and honoured from as far back as anyone can remember, and is known as Mai Mari da Asthan, the 'Final Resting-Place of Mother Mary'.

When Jesus reached this area with his group, his mother would have been over seventy years old, and no doubt tired after the long journey. Because there is no evidence of a tomb of Mary anywhere else, it is quite conceivable that Mary was buried here. Jesus would certainly not have gone on without her otherwise, leaving her behind unprotected and at the mercy of his enemies. Like many graves in the Kashmir region, this tomb is aligned in an east-west orientation, whereas in areas of Islamic culture the graves are always oriented north-south. The tomb of Mary is located on Pindi Point, a mountain outside the small town, and is revered by the Islamic population as the tomb of the mother of Jesus. (By Muslims, Jesus, or Issa, is revered as one of the greatest prophets.) Today the site belongs to a military exclusion zone becaue of its proximity to the ceasefire line.

The area around Mari was Hindu at the time of Christ. But the Hindus normally cremate their dead and scatter the ashes; only monks (*sadhus*) and saints are interred. Because the grave dates from pre-Islamic (therefore Hindu) times, the person buried there must have been regarded as a saint.

When the Islamic hordes pressed through to northern India in the eighth century and part of the native population was converted, the conquerors destroyed many of the places of worship of the 'infidels'. The shrine of Mary's tomb, however, was left unharmed, presumably because the Muslims were able to recognize from the special position of the grave that it was a shrine of one of the 'Peoples of the Book' – the Christians or the Jews – whom they respected (Plate 39).

In 1898, the British army built a watchtower right next to the monument, but this did not deter the many pilgrims from visiting the sacred shrine. Then in 1917, the order went out from one Captain Richardson to raze the tomb to the ground in order to keep the pilgrims away from the military zone. Loud cries of protest from the population prompted local officials to intervene, and destruction of the shrine was halted before it could be completed. The struggle over the Tomb of Mary is all on record in the archives of the local administration, filed under the date 30 July 1917. The tomb was restored in 1950, soon after which the watchtower was removed. Today the tomb is 'decorated' with the mast of a television transmitter.

An asphalt road now runs from Mari, through wooded mountain scenery, to Srinagar, the capital of Kashmir, 170 kilometres away. About 40 kilometres south of Srinagar, between the villages

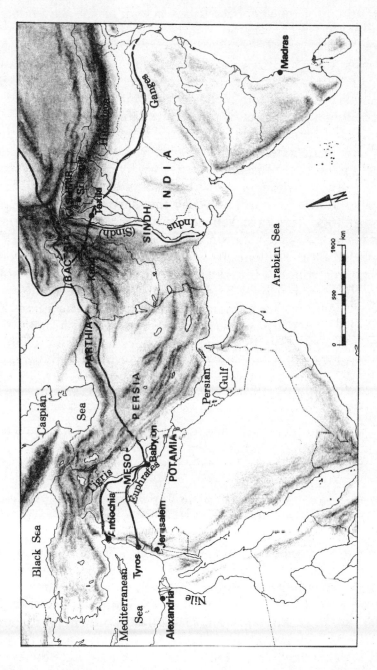

The Route Jesus took to India.

of Naugam and Nilmag, in a broad open valley, lies the Yus-Marg, the 'Meadow of Jesus', where Jesus preached – or so it is stated in the tradition of the shepherd tribes known as the Bani-Israel, the 'Children of Israel', who are said to have settled in the area from 722 BC.

The *Acts of Thomas* go on to tell how the apostle Thomas lived for a while as a missionary at the court of the Indian King Misdai in southern India, where he again won many followers and converted a great number of people. Eventually he fell into disfavour, however, and met the fate of a martyr. When Marco Polo returned to Europe in 1295 from his twenty-five-year stay in the Far East, he brought news of the masses of Christians living on the east coast of southern India, who worshipped the tomb of the apostle Thomas, and who used a red earth tinted by the martyr's blood to perform faith healings. The great Venetian traveller also found Christians on the Malabar coast on the west side of southern India (now Kerala), who called themselves 'Thomas Christians'. Their form of Christianity 'could be traced back a long way', Marco Polo noted.

But there are much earlier documents which bear witness to the presence of Christians in India.[13] Tertullian lists India among those lands 'ruled' by Christianity. Ephraem Syrus (or Ephraim of Syria, about AD 306–373) tells of the missionary activity of Thomas in India, and Anorbius (around AD 305) also counts India among the Christian countries. And one of the dignitaries attending the Council of Nicea bore the title Bishop of all Persia and Greater India.

The tomb of the apostle Thomas is revered by Christians to this day in the southern Indian town of Mylapore near Madras, even though his bones are said to have been taken from there to Edessa long since, at the beginning of the fourth century.

In the year 1900, a short article appeared in an English journal which attracted the attention of the entire theological world. The report announced that among the ruins of the Indian city of Fatehpur Sikri (not far from Agra, some 175 kilometres south of Delhi), a saying of Jesus that was completely unknown in the Christian West had been found engraved on a wall. Fatehpur Sikri was for a brief period the capital of the Moghul Empire in India under the Great Moghul Akbar (1542–1605), only to be abandoned a few years after it was built. The Great Moghul made a triumphal entry into the city in May 1601, and to commemorate the event he had the aforesaid inscription carved on the southern main gate (Buland Darwaza) of the grand mosque. Almost twenty years earlier, in 1582, Akbar had proclaimed a rational monotheism (Din-i-Ilahi) in an attempt to combine the many religions of India. He had made a thorough study of Hinduism, Parseeism and Jainism, and he learned all he could about the Christian Gospels from Portuguese Jesuits who lived at his court. His plan was to unite India, which at the time was split into religious factions, with a single religion to be based on the essential tenets of all the teachings. Akbar must have selected this particular saying of Jesus because it seemed to him to be the best possible formulation of his ideas, or he would hardly have given the quotation such precedence.

The words are inscribed on the left side of the enormous archway, as one leaves the precincts of the mosque via the main gate, along with a reference to the occasion it commemorated and the date:

> Jesus (peace be with him) said: 'The world is a bridge. Pass over it – but do not settle down on it!'

In another place, above the archway of the north wing of the mosque (Liwan), the same saying is found in a modified form, 'Jesus (peace be with him) said: "The world is an over-proud house. Take this as a warning, and do not build on it!"'

The Portugese missionaries could not possibly have told Akbar of this *agraphon* (Greek 'unwritten': the technical term for a saying of Jesus not contained in the Gospels) for the saying is not to be found in any Christian text. Nor is it included in the very extensive *Life of Jesus* that the Jesuit Jerome Xavier wrote for Akbar. So it is quite possible that the agraphon really does derive from the early Thomas Christians. The initial words of the sayings, an introductory phrase that is always the same, is also found in the later Islamic accounts of Jesus, which has led most Orientalists to infer that the saying came to India via Islam. But this need not be the case, for there is conspicuous agreement between these sayings and the far earlier sayings of Jesus in the apocryphal *Gospel of Thomas*, both in form and in content. The *Gospel of Thomas* is now accessible in its entirety thanks to the sensational finds at Nag Hammadi in 1945. The 'Gospel' is not a coherent narrative like the biblical Gospels, but a collection of 114 sayings of Jesus (Logia), in an arbitrary order. Most of the Logia are introduced with the same formula, 'Jesus said . . .'.

The *Gospel of Thomas* opens by saying what it is: 'These are the secret words that Jesus spoke while he was alive, and that Didymus Judas Thomas wrote down. And he [Jesus] said,

"Whoever comes to understand these sayings will not taste death."'[14]

Even if it were not possible to prove that the apostle Thomas visited India, there is considerable evidence of missionary activity throughout India long before the Muhammadan conquest. Pantainos of Alexandria is said to have stumbled on Matthew's Gospel in Aramaic while on his missionary travels in India in about AD 180.

The *Chronicle of Seert* (I section 8, para 5) relates that Bishop David of Basra (a contemporary of Metropolitan Papa who died in AD 316) went to India and preached there with great success.

In about the year 335 (as reported later by Philostorgios, before AD 433), the Emperor Constantine sent Bishop Theophilus to India to reform the liturgy and ritual worship of the Church there.

At the end of the fourth century, Symeon of Mesopotamia mentions the martyrdom of Indian 'barbarians' for their Christian faith.

In about AD 490, Bishop Ma'an of Persia sent his writings to India (according to the *Chronicle of Seert*, II section 9).

And finally, Cosmas Indicopleustes has left us a record of a journey to India that he undertook in around AD 525, giving precise geographical details. He found Christians on the island of Sri Lanka, and on the Indian west coast, 'in Male, where the pepper grows [that is, Malabar], and in the place called Kalliana [Kalyan, near Bombay]', and he states that Kalliana was the seat of a bishop who had been to Persia.[15]

Although it is evident that Jesus was known in India long before the arrival of Islam, statements about him in the Koran are revealing. The Koran says that Jesus did not die on the Cross, but survived the attempted execution and then lived in a 'happy valley'.

The 'True' Jesus in Islam

Issa, the name commonly used for Jesus in Islam, derives from the Syriac *Yeshu*. The reason that the accounts of the prophet Issa in the Koran are so extensive is probably to correct the 'distorted and twisted image in the writings of his followers'. Jesus is thought of as the last great prophet before Muhammad. He is even said to have prophesied the coming of the 'greatest of all prophets':

31 'The Good Shepherd.' Jesus as an Apollo-like youth. By the third century, the authentic portrait of Jesus as on the Mandylion had still not yet become widely known.

32 The ruins of the royal palace in Nisibis, now Nusaybin. The border between Syria and Turkey runs right through the site of the excavations.

33 *The agraphon engraved on a wall of the palace of King Akbar in Fatehpur Sikri near Agra.*

34 *The ruins of the royal palace in Andrapa, now Iskilip in Turkey.*

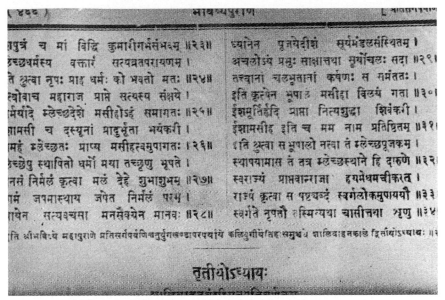

णपुत्रं च मां विद्धि कुमारीगर्भसंभवम् ॥२३॥
र्च्छधर्मस्य वक्तारं सत्यव्रतपरायणम् ।
ते श्रुत्वा नृप: प्राह धर्म: को भवतो मत: ॥२४॥
र्वोवाच महाराज प्राप्ते सत्यस्य संक्षये ।
र्मर्यादे म्लेच्छदेशे मसीहोऽहं समागत: ॥२५॥
णामसी च दस्यूनां प्रादुर्भूता भयंकरी ।
महं म्लेच्छत: प्राप्य मसीहत्वमुपागत: ।२६॥
र्च्छेषु स्थापितो धर्मो मया तच्छृणु भूपते ।
नसं निर्मलं कृत्वा मलं देहे शुभाशुभम् ॥२७॥
र्मं जप्रमास्थाय जपेत निर्मलं परम् ।
णायेन सत्यवचसा मनसैक्येन मानव: ॥२८॥

ध्यानेन पूतयेद्रीशं सूर्यमंडलसंस्थितम् ।
अचलोऽयं प्रभु: साक्षात्तथा सूर्योचल: सदा ॥२९॥
तत्त्वानां चलभूतानां कर्षण: स नमंतत: ।
इति कृत्वेन भूपाऽ मसीहा विलयं गता ॥३०॥
ईशमूर्तिर्हृदि प्राप्ता नित्यशुद्धा शिवंकरी ।
ईशामसीह इति च मम नाम प्रतिष्ठितम् ॥३१॥
इति श्रुत्वा स भूपालो नत्वा तं म्लेच्छपूजकम् ।
स्थापयामास तं तत्र म्लेच्छस्थाने हि दारुणे ॥३२॥
स्वराज्यं प्राप्तवान्राजा ह्यमेधमचीकरत् ।
राज्यं कृत्वा स पञ्चब्दं स्वर्गलोकमुपाययौ ॥३३॥
स्वर्गेते नृपतौ तस्मिन्यया चासीत्तथा श्रृणु ॥३४॥

त्ति श्रीभविष्ये महापुराणे प्रतिसर्गपर्वणिचतुर्युगखण्डापरपर्चणि ये कलियुगीयेतिहासे समुच्चये शालिवाहनकाले द्वितीयोऽध्याय: ॥

<h2 style="text-align:center">तृतीयोऽध्याय:</h2>

35 *A passage from the Bhavishyat Maha-Purana (as shown in a recent edition),
in which the residence of Jesus in Kashmir is mentioned.*

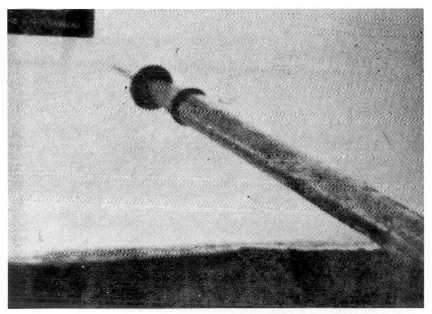

36 *The so-called 'Staff of Jesus'.*

37 *The inscription on the 'Throne of Solomon' above the city of Srinagar.*

38 *A page from the historical writings of Mullah Nadiri (1413).*

39 *A seal from Haran.*

40 *The tomb of Mary, the mother of Jesus, in Mari, Pakistan.*

41 *In this plaster cast of the 'footprints', the scars left by the Crucifixion are easily recognizable as crescent–shaped swellings above the toes.*

42 *In the middle of Srinagar's old town stands the building known as Roza Bal, which is constructed over the burial place of Yuz Asaf, who was, the evidence strongly suggests, none other than Jesus.*

43 *The stylized footprints within the tomb building, lit by candles.*

44 *Within the tomb building stands a wooden shrine.*

45 *The tombstone is covered by a thick cloth.*

46 *The tombstone is a kind of cenotaph or memorial, acting as marker to the actual sarcophagus, which is located in a crypt beneath.*

I have yet many things to say unto you, but ye cannot bear them now. Howbeit when he, the Spirit of truth, is come, he will guide you into all truth: for he shall not speak of himself; but whatsoever he shall hear, that shall he speak: and he will shew you things to come.

He shall glorify me: for he shall receive of mine, and shall shew it unto you.

(John 16:12–14)

Muhammad considered himself to be the promised 'Spirit of truth', and therefore felt that he was called upon to re-interpret the teaching of Jesus, and to rehabilitate the man after his supposed shameful death on the Cross. After being relieved of the humiliation of death by crucifixion, Jesus was welcomed into the Islamic fold as the one preparing the way for Muhammad. At the same time, 'The Messiah, the son of Mary, was a Messenger; other Messengers [like him] had gone before' (Koran 5,76).

About Jesus' mission, the Koran says: 'And verily, to Moses We [that is, God] gave the Book and we sent other Messengers in his footsteps, and we gave Jesus, the son of Mary, visible signs, and strengthened him with the Spirit of Holiness' (Koran 2,88).

The Koran clearly rejects the assertion of Christian theology that Jesus is man and God:

People of the Book, do not transgress the bounds of your religion. Speak nothing but the truth about Allah. Truly the Messiah, Jesus the son of Mary, was only a Messenger of God and [a fulfilment of] his Word which he sent down to Mary, and a gift of Grace from him. So believe in God and his Messengers, and do not say: [there are] 'Three'. Forbear, and it shall be better for you. Truly, God is one God alone. It is far from his holiness that he should have a son!

(Koran 4,172)

And in another place,

. . . They imitate the infidels of old. God confound them! How they are led astray! They worship their rabbis and their monks as gods besides God, and the Messiah the son of Mary. And yet they were ordered to serve the one God only. There is no God but him. Exalted be He above those whom they deify beside Him!

(Koran 9,30–31)

The Koran clearly states that Jesus did not die on the Cross, and that the Jews were deceived:

They denied the truth, and uttered a monstrous falsehood against Mary. They declared, 'We have put to death the Messiah Jesus the son of Mary, the Messenger of God.' They did not kill him, nor did they crucify him, but he was made to appear [as one crucified] to them. Those that disagreed about him were in doubt about his death; what they knew about it was sheer conjecture. . . . In reality, God lifted him up to His presence; He is mighty and wise.

(Koran 4,156–157)

The Arabic word for 'crucify' here clearly denotes 'put to death by crucifixion'. But this passage shows that in the Koran a crucifixion without the death of the one crucified is not out of the question. What is more, at the time the Koran was written the Jews themselves seem to have been in doubt about whether Jesus really died on the Cross.

The Koran also does not neglect to provide an answer to the question of where Jesus went after the Crucifixion: 'We made the son of Mary and his mother a sign to mankind and gave them a shelter on a peaceful hillside watered by a fresh spring' (Koran 23,51). How well this description of the place of refuge applies to Kashmir is absolutely astonishing. In another translation, the place in the mountains is even called 'a green valley'.

According to Mirza Ghulam Ahmad (founder of the Islamic Ahmadiya reform movement, born in Qadian, Punjab, in 1835) the Koran confirms the truth that Jesus was saved from death on the Cross, and so from an accursed death that would have been unworthy of him.

One or two passages of the Gospels seem also to confirm Jesus' survival of the Crucifixion. Jesus made a statement comparing himself to Jonah, who had survived being ingested into the belly of a whale and had then reappeared. If Jesus had been lying dead in his sepulchre, there would be no parallels to be drawn between the two. 'For as Jonas was three days and three nights in the whale's belly; so shall the Son of man be three days and three nights in the heart of the earth' (Matthew 12:40).

For the Ahmadiya sect (still a popular form of Islam today), Jesus' overcoming of the torment of crucifixion is a fulfilment of prophecies in the Old Testament. Isaiah's 'righteous servant', for example, 'was cut off out of the land of the living: for the transgression of my people was he stricken. . . . Yet it pleased the Lord to bruise him; he hath put him to grief: when thou shalt make his soul an offering for sin, . . . he shall prolong his days, and the pleasure of the Lord shall prosper in his hand' (Isaiah 53:8, 10). 'Cut off out of the land of the living' and some other references to what might be taken for death notwithstanding, the Book of the prophet Isaiah nowhere says that the promised servant of the Lord actually dies.

Even the prophecies of Psalm 34 say nothing about a death of the future Messiah: 'Many are the afflictions of the righteous: but the Lord delivereth him out of them all' (Psalms 34:19). So God can hardly have planned for Jesus to die the shameful death of crucifixion. From the traditional viewpoint of the Arab, a man is only accursed if he turns away from God in his heart, 'becomes black', has no love for God, is robbed of God's mercy for all time, and is void of all knowledge of God; if he, like Satan, is full of the poison of deceit, and is no longer reached by a single ray of the light of love; and if he rejects all relations with God, and is full of resentment, hate and enmity towards God, so that God becomes his enemy and turns from him in disgust! Mirza Ghulam believed that Christians could not ever have been made fully aware of the horror and shame attached to the description 'accursed on the wood', or they would never have made death on the Cross such a feature of their worship of the virtuous Jesus.

Some modern specialists in Eastern philosophies are of the opinion that the truth about Jesus and his teaching has, in some ways, actually been better preserved in Islam than in Christianity. Arabia, they say, became Christian at the time. The Christian Muhammad attempted through his message to protect the original teaching of Jesus against the proliferating distortions, but his message too was distorted after his death just as the teaching of Jesus had been earlier.[16]

Jesus in Kashmir

If Jesus really did live in Kashmir for a considerable length of time – if, in other words, tradition is right in averring that he eventually died in Srinagar when he was over 80 years old – then it should be possible to find some evidence in ancient Indian literature of how he spent the last thirty to forty years of his life.

The trouble is, writers in India in those ancient days refused to allow foreign influences to impinge upon their own culture, even in referring to historical events. One example of this is the complete absence of contemporarily written records or descriptions even of Alexander the Great's imposing military incursion into India. Specialists in Indian history are agreed that there was no systematic written history in India before the spread of Islam.[17]

The ancient narratives of the Hindus are called the Puranas (Sanskrit, *purana* 'old'). From the fifth or fourth century BC until the seventeenth century AD they have been constantly extended by the addition of further 'stories'.[18] The entire collection currently runs to eighteen volumes, all written in Sanskrit, the old sacred language of India. The ninth volume, called the *Bhavishyat Maha-Purana* and written between the third and the seventh centuries AD, contains a supplement that describes how Jesus came to India. The description is so clear that there can be no doubt about who its subject is.

The Purana reports that Israelites came to live in India, and then, in verses 17–32, describes Jesus' appearance on the scene:

> Shalivahana, the grandson of Vikramajit, came to power. He vanquished the attacking hordes of Chinese, Parthians, Scythians and Bactrians. He drew a border between the Aryans and the Mleccha (the non-Hindus), and ordered the latter to withdraw to the other side of the Indus. One day, Shalivahana, the lord of the Shakas, came to a snowy mountain. There, in the Land of the Huna, the powerful king saw a handsome man seated on the mountain. He had a white body, and he wore white garments.
>
> The king asked the holy man, 'Who are you?'
>
> The other replied: 'Know that I am Ishaputra [Sanskrit, 'Son of God'], born of a virgin, proclaimer of the teachings of the barbarians [*Mleccha*], which bear the truth.'
>
> The king then asked him, 'What teachings do you mean?'
>
> The other replied, 'At the end of the Satya Yuga,[19] the Golden Age, I appeared as Masiha [the Messiah] in the depraved land of the unbelievers. The goddess Ishamasi also appeared before the barbarians [*Dasyu*] in a terrible form. I was brought before her in the manner of the unbelievers and attained the Masiha-tva [Messiah-hood]. Hear, O king: I brought the religion unto the unbelievers. After the purification of the spirit and the cleansing of the impure body, and after seeking refuge in the prayers of the *Naigama*, man will come to worship the Eternal. Through truth, meditation and recollection of spirit, man will find his way to Isha [Sanskrit, 'God'], who dwells in the centre of Light, who remains as constant as the sun, and who dissolves all transient things for ever. Thus was Ishamasi destroyed, and the Form of Isha was revealed in the heart, ever pure and bestowing happiness; and I was called Isha-Masiha.'
>
> After the king heard these words, he bowed before the teacher of the barbarians and sent him on his way to their terrible land.[20]

The 'teacher of the unbelievers' refers to himself as Isha-Masiha.

The Sanskrit word *Isha* means 'Lord' and is used for 'God'. *Masiha* corresponds to the word 'Messiah'. Thus *Isha-Masiha* means 'the Lord, the Messiah'. Elsewhere the white-robed man calls himself Isha-putra, 'Son of God', and says that he was born of a virgin (Sanskrit *kumari*). Because there is no comparable legend to be found before this in Indian literature, the person described has to be Jesus. The 'goddess Ishamasi' appears to be a general expression for everything evil and wicked: the name is not found anywhere else in the literature. The word *Naigama* is evidently the name of some holy scripture(s), but there are no references to it/them anywhere else either. Some translators assume that it refers to the Vedas.

According to Professor Hassnain, King Shalivahana ruled in the Kushan period from AD 49 to 50. Other commentators put the start of the Shaka or Shalivahana era at AD 78.

The only 'snowy mountains' in India are in the Himalayan ranges. Scholars have not yet been able to locate the 'land of the Huna' precisely, but it must be a region of the western Himalaya, somewhere between the foothills in the Punjab and Kailash mountain in western Tibet near the Indian border; this vast area also includes Ladakh.

Further evidence that Jesus visited the Himalayan area is provided by a grave mentioned by the painter Nicholas Roerich in *The Heart of Asia*, published in 1930. The grave lies to the north of Ladakh in neighbouring East Turkestan, now the Chinese province of Sinkiang (Xinjiang), nearly 10 kilometres from the town of Kashgar, and is said to be that of a certain Mary who was among Jesus' following. The apocryphal *Gospel of Philip* mentions three women who did not leave Jesus' side after the Crucifixion. All three were called Mary: his mother, her sister (the wife of Cleopas, perhaps?), and Mary Magdalene 'who was called his companion'. The notion that this grave near Kashgar is of (one or other) Mary could very well thus be based on fact.

During the latter years of his life in India, Jesus would not have remained at the same place but would have moved from place to place as an itinerant minister for as long as his health permitted. There are, however, many indications that he always came back to Kashmir.

About 60 kilometres south-east of Srinagar and only 12 kilometres from Bijbihara (the place of the 'Stone of Moses') is Aish-Muqam, a cave extending some twelve metres into the mountainside, at the entrance to which a magnificent shrine has been erected. The sacred building contains the reliquary of Zainuddin Wali, an Islamic saint, who lived in the cave during the rule of Sultan Zainul Abidin Badshah (1408–61).

The most prized possession of this saint was a staff that had been given to him by Sheikh Noor Din Wali. The staff is still there, considered to be a most valuable relic, and is closely watched over by the tomb attendants, who always keep it covered with a green cloth. When the faithful of the region perceive themselves to be under threat from some emergency, especially an epidemic, they make a pilgrimage to Aish-Muqam confident of being helped by the miraculous power of the staff. The dark brown staff is over 2.3 metres long, and 25 millimetres thick; it is made of olive wood, and is known either as the 'Rod of Moses' or as the 'Rod of Jesus'. Those who reverence this relic believe that that the traveller's staff first belonged to Moses, who used it when he made his way to Kashmir, and was later used by Jesus as a symbol of his Mosaic heritage. The staff was formerly kept in the Khangahi Muhalla quarter of Srinagar, before it found a worthy site in Aish-Muqam.

The name *Aish-Muqam* is said to refer to Jesus. *Aish* is said to derive from Isha or Issa, and *muqam* means 'place of rest (or repose)'. This rather suggests that the isolated cave might once have served as a place where Jesus could withdraw for a while to devote himself to quiet meditation. There is, of course, no longer anything to prove the truth of such traditions.

But there is evidence for the presence of Jesus in Kashmir that is much more solid than mere oral traditions: testimonies in stone which have survived the vicissitudes of the centuries, more or less intact, as archaeological treasures. One such lapidary piece of testimony to the presence of Jesus in Kashmir is an inscription on the Takht-i-Suleiman, the 'Throne of Solomon', the history of which is recounted by Mullah Nadiri, a historian who lived during the rule of Sultan Zainul Abidin. In his *History of Kashmir* (*Tarikh-i-Kashmir*), written in 1413, he reports that the Temple of Solomon (which was already a thousand years old at the dawn of the Christian era) was restored by a Persian architect, by royal command, during the reign of Gopadatta, son of Rajah Akh. The Hindus noticed that the Persian was a 'barbarian' who followed a foreign religion. During the renovation work, four sayings in Old Persian were inscribed at the side of the steps leading up to the grand entrance:

Maimar een satoon raj bihishti zargar, sal panjah wa chahar.
'The constuctor of these columns is the most humble Bihishti Zargar, in the year fifty and four.'

Een satoon bardast khwaja rukun bin murjan.
'Khwaja Rukun, son of Murjan, had these columns built.'

Dar een wagat yuz asaf dawa-i-paighambar-imikunad. Sal panjah wa chahar.
'At this time, Yuz Asaf announced his prophetic mission. In the year fifty and four.'

Aishan yuzu paighambar-i-bani israil ast.
'He is Jesus, prophet of the sons of Israel.'

Mullah Nadiri continues:

At the time of Gopadatta's reign, Yuz Asaf came from the Holy Land up into this valley, and announced that he was a prophet. He epitomised the peak of piety and of virtue, and proclaimed that he was himself his own message, that he lived in God day and night, and that he had made God accessible to the people of Kashmir. He called the people unto him, and the people of the valley believed in him. When the Hindus came to Gopadatta in indignation, pressing him to deal with the man, he turned them away.

I have also read in a Hindu book that this prophet is really Hazrat Issa,[21] the Spirit of God (God's peace and good will be on him), and he adopted the name Yuz Asaf. True knowledge is with God. He spent his life in this valley.

After his passing, his body was laid to rest in Mohalla Anzimarah. It is also said that the light of prophecy emanates from the tomb of this prophet. King Gopadatta ruled 60 years and two months, before passing away. After him, his son Gikaran mounted the throne and ruled for the span of 58 years.[22]

King Gopadatta ruled in Kashmir from the year 53 onwards. The year given in the text as year 54 of Rajah Gopodatta's reign was AD 107 by modern reckoning. The Rajah's rule thus fell within the reign of the great King Kanishka of the Kushan dynasty. The text does not indicate whether Jesus was still alive at the time.

No fewer than twenty-one references in ancient texts have been found so far to bear witness to Jesus' stay in Kashmir. Geographical testimony is provided by the names of many towns and places in Kashmir, for instance:

Aish-Muqam	Yus-Marg
Arya-Issa	Yusnag
Issa-Brari	Yusu
Issa-eil	Yuzu-dha
Issah-kush	Yuzu-dhara
Issa-mati	Yuzu-gam
Issa-Ta	Yuzu-hatpura
I-yes-Issa	Yuzu-kun
I-yes-th-Issa-vara	Yuzu-maidan
Kal-Issa	Yuzu-para
Ram-Issa	Yuzu-raja
Yus-mangala	Yuzu-varman

At the time when Jesus lived in Kashmir, the 'Happy Valley' was the centre of a great religious, cultural, intellectual and political revival. The kingdom of Kashmir was the centre of the enormous Indo-Scythian empire, and was ruled by the great King Kanishka I (AD 78–103) of the Kushan dynasty. An excellent statesman, and a kindly and wise ruler, Kanishka attempted to unite the motley mixture of races in his country through a policy of toleration and generosity. The combined harmony of Indian and Greek philosophy reached a peak in the culture of Gandhara. The academic centre of this meeting of cultures was the ancient University of Taxila, which was already famed far and wide.

In Buddhism Kanishka saw the perfect matrix for the realization of his ideas, and sought advice and instruction among the Buddhist monks. He was dismayed, however, to find that the Buddha's teaching had fragmented into so many schools and sects. Following the advice of the philosopher Parshwa, Kanishka summoned the Council of Haran (Harwan in Kashmir) with the aim of restoring unity to the fragmented religious community by a process of scrutinizing and formalizing the Buddhist texts. After more than three hundred years, another Buddhist Council took place – the Fourth – attended by 1500 scholars and monks. This Council helped to establish the new Mahayana as a popular religion. The priests of the Hinayana were reluctant to lose their privileges, and attempted a final stand in opposition to the Council, but they were unable to hold sway. Instead, the Mahayana was finally confirmed as an independent religion, opening a way to salvation for all people.

The present version of the *Lalitavistara* – the Buddhist text which shows the greatest similarities to the New Testament – also dates from the Council of Haran.

Haran's location, just 12 kilometres from Srinagar, permits the speculation that Jesus himself might have been present at this important meeting; he may even have played an important part in it.

Kanishka was so impressed with the results of the Council that he converted to Buddhism himself, and he turned the administration of his kingdom over to the community of Buddhist monks, whose spiritual leader was the great Nagarjuna, the most influential philosopher of Mahayana Buddhism.

One more clue to the residence of Jesus in ancient Kashmir is provided by the text of the *Rajah Tarangini*, a history of Kashmir written in Sanskrit verses by Pandit Kalhana in the twelfth century. It counts as one of the earliest genuinely historical records in the literature of India. The *Rajah Tarangini* contains a great number of legends and stories passed down by oral tradition from ancient times. Many of these narratives were richly embellished, however, over the course of time, making it difficult now to recognize the historical facts. The work relates the story of a holy man named Isana, who performed miracles very similar to those of Jesus. Isana is said in addition to have saved the influential statesman Vazir from death on the cross, and to have brought him back to life. Afterwards Vazir became the ruler of Kashmir, and governed for forty-seven years. According to Kalhana, Isana was the last reformer in Kashmir, and lived and worked in the first century AD. It seems likely that the god-man Isana was none other than Issa-Jesus.

The Tomb of Jesus in Srinagar

During the Middle Ages, the story of Barlaam and Josaphat was a literary theme familiar to every educated person. There was a great variety of translations and versions of the story throughout Europe and the Near East, but the original has been attributed to St John of Damascus (John Damascene), a distinguished Arab Christian who lived in Jerusalem in around 700. The story – also known in some countries as 'The Prince and the Dervish' – may be quickly summarized.

Abaner, a powerful king of India, is told by an astrologer that his handsome and virtuous son Josaphat (or Joasaph) will convert

from Islam to Christianity. In order to avert fulfilment of the
prophecy, the king has a magnificent palace built for the prince to
grow up in, completely isolated from the outside world. Despite
these measures taken by his father, Josaphat happens one day to
see a blind man. On another occasion he encounters an aged man.
And finally he sees a lifeless body. Because the young man has
only ever otherwise seen young and beautiful people surrounding
him in the palace, the encounters are completely new experiences
for him, and open his eyes to the realities of human life. In the end,
the prince meets the ascetic Barlaam, who converts him to
Christianity. Although the King tries to dissuade his son from joining the new faith, and even offers him half his kingdom, Josaphat
renounces all worldly riches, withdraws into solitude, and passes
the rest of his life as a devout hermit.

This charming and touching tale is full of such profound truth
that Barlaam and Joasaph were canonized as martyrs by the
Roman Catholic Church in 1583, and given a feastday in the litur-
gical calendar. Under 27 November the rubric reads: 'In India, by
the borders of Persia, Saints Barlaam and Joasaph. Their marvellous works were described by St John of Damascus.' Not for
another century did it apparently occur to anyone that the
story is simply a variant on the legend of Prince Siddhartha's
royal upbringing, which led him to renounce his family and
property and set out in search of Enlightenment. The name
Josafat/Josaphat/Joasaph sounds so Jewish that no one ever
doubted its Jewish origin. But in fact the the name can be traced
back without difficulty to an utterly different source. John
Damascene's Greek Joasaph is an attempt at the Arabic Judasaf,
itself a borrowing from Kashmiri Yusasaph. But the Kashmiri and
Arabic forms are spelling mistakes: the letters J and B are nearly
identical in Syriac, Arabic and Persian, and Judasaf corresponds in
fact to an original Budasaf – a word that is quite recognizable as
Bodhisattva, an 'Enlightenment being', a Buddha in the making.

The exotic-sounding name Barlaam can also be traced back
across the bridge of languages to its actual origin. In Arabic,
Balauhar means the same as the Sanskrit word *Bhagvan*, 'the
Exalted One', thus 'God'. The linquistic origins of Judasaf-Budasaf
now make it clear that the Islamic prophet Yuz Asaf was really a
Bodhisattva.

A Bodhisattva is characterized by all-encompassing, boundless
compassion. He takes on the suffering of all beings, and leads
them to liberation. His one aim is to save all beings from the mis-

ery of ignorance, even if this means he has to take on the guilt himself. Jesus also uncompromisingly followed this ideal, accepting the responsibility for all the sins of the world, and even finally allowing himself to be nailed to the Cross as a 'sacrificial lamb'. All the characteristics of a Bodhisattva are also to be found in Jesus.

The embodiment of limitless compassion in Buddhism is Avalokiteshvara, whose name derives from *Ishvara* ('Lord ruler') and *ava-lokita* ('[he] who looks down in compassion [on the world]'). Avalokiteshvara possesses great and miraculous powers which enable him to surmount all difficulties and dangers. From the beginning of the second century, Avalokiteshvara has often been portrayed in the visual arts with marks on the surfaces of his hands and feet symbolizing the Buddhist Wheel of Doctrine. Many Western commentators have recognized the stigmata of Jesus in these wheel signs, and have seen them as proof that Avalokiteshvara and Jesus are one and the same.

When the important Fourth Council of Kashmir was held in Haran near Srinagar under the auspices of Kanishka the Great, Jesus – if he was still alive – must have been more than eighty years old. We have suggested that he might even have had some part in this event, which was to have such great significance for the Buddhist world, as a highly revered saint – a suggestion for which admittedly there is no proof, although the known facts allow scope for such speculation. At any rate, the reforms introduced by the Council were in complete accord with the teachings of Jesus.

Fatima, the daughter of Muhammad, noted a saying of the Prophet to the effect that Jesus lived to the advanced age of 120 years.[23] There is, it is true, no archaeological evidence for this claim, but such an advanced age does not seem to be uncommon among the saints given to an ascetic way of life, who keep the physical body under the complete control of the spirit. There are many reports of Tibetan holy men who have attained ages of 130, 150, or even more.

The historian Sheikh Al-Sa'id-us-Sâdiq, who lived until AD 962 in Khurasan (Iran), tells of the two journeys of Jesus to India, and of the ending of his life as Yuz Asaf in Kashmir in his famous work *Ikmâl-ud-Dîn*. This book was republished in Iran in 1883, and later translated into German by the famous expert on the East Max Müller. The book contains a parable of Yuz Asaf that is found in almost identical form in the New Testament:

People, hear my words: a farmer goes to sow his fields. Then the birds come and eat the seed. Other seed falls on the path. And behold, some falls on the rock where there is no earth, and withers away. Some falls under the thorns and cannot grow. The seed that falls on the good earth, however, sprouts and brings forth fruit. The sower is the sage and the seeds are his words of wisdom. The seeds that are eaten by the birds are like people who do not understand the words. The seeds that fall on to the rock are the words of wisdom that go in one ear and come out the other. The seeds that land under the thorns are those who actually hear and see, but do not act accordingly. But the seeds that land on the good earth are like those who hear the words of wisdom and act accordingly.[24]

An Arabic version of the story of Barlaam and Josaphat, *The Book of Balauhar and Budasaf* (pp.285–286), published in Bombay, tells how Yuz Asaf died:

And he reached Kashmir, which was the farthest region in which he ministered, and there his life came to a close. He left the world and bequeathed his inheritance to a certain disciple called Ababid who had served him; everything he did was perfect. And he admonished him and said to him, 'I have found a worthy shrine and decorated it and brought in lamps for the dying. I have gathered together the flock with the true face, which had been scattered and for whom I was sent. And now I shall draw breath in my ascent from the world, freeing my soul from my body. Heed the commands that were given to you, and do not stray from the path of truth but keep firmly to it with gratitude – and may Ababid be the leader.' He then bid Ababid to level off the place for him; then he stretched his legs out and lay down; and, turning his head to the north and his face to the east, he passed away.[25]

The tomb of the prophet Yuz Asaf is today located in the middle of Srinagar's old town, Anzimar, in the Khanyar quarter. The building later constructed around the tomb is called Rozabal or Rauza Bal. *Rauza* is a term used to denote the tomb of a celebrated personality: someone noble, wealthy or saintly. The building is rectangular in plan, and a small porch has been added to it. Above the entrance to the actual burial chamber is carved an inscription which declares that Yuz Asaf entered the valley of Kashmir many centuries ago, and that his life was dedicated to manifesting the truth. There are two different tombstones in the floor of the innermost burial chamber, surrounded by wooden railings to which strong beams have been added, covered over with a heavy cloth. The larger tombstone is that of Yuz Asaf, the smaller that of the Islamic saint Syed Nasîr-ud-Dîn, who was buried here as recently as in the fifteenth century.[26]

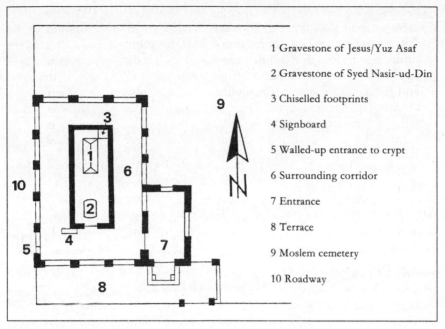

1 Gravestone of Jesus/Yuz Asaf

2 Gravestone of Syed Nasir-ud-Din

3 Chiselled footprints

4 Signboard

5 Walled-up entrance to crypt

6 Surrounding corridor

7 Entrance

8 Terrace

9 Moslem cemetery

10 Roadway

Plan of the Tomb of Jesus

Both tombstones are aligned north-south, following Islamic custom. As is also usual for Islamic tombs in India, these tombstones are just markers: the actual graves are located in a crypt below the floor of the building. A tiny opening allows a visitor to look down into the burial chamber below. The sarcophagus containing the earthly remains of Yuz Asaf is aligned east-west, in accordance with Jewish custom! This is clear proof that Yuz Asaf could not have been an Islamic saint. And among the Hindus and Buddhists, only ascetics (*sadhus*) and saints are buried (corpses are normally cremated). So here lies a person who was revered as a saint even before the arrival of Islam, when Kashmir was Mahayana Buddhist and Tantric Hindu. The etymology of the name Yuz Asaf has shown that it can have derived from *Bodhisattva*. This means that a person lies buried here who was revered in pre-Islamic times as a future Buddha, who according to legend came from the West, and whose grave is aligned in an east-west orientation, like the graves of the Jews. All this does not prove that it is the body of Jesus the Nazarene that rests in the ground here. Yet the many factors that indicate a close connection between Mahayana Buddhism and the origins of Christianity, the literary and historical evidence that Jesus survived the Crucifixion, and the equally substantial references to Jesus' spending the last years or decades of his life in India, especially in Kashmir, would all together appear to justify the assumption that the body of Jesus does indeed lie buried in Rozabal.

It has always been a practice of worshippers to place candles around the tombstones. When the centuries-old layers of wax were removed some time ago, a sensational discovery was made: a pair of footprints was carved into the stone – a widespread tradition in Asia at the shrines of saints – and beside them lay a crucifix and a rosary. The footprints were meant to indicate the identity of the deceased, rather like a fingerprint.[27] As with the swastikas on Buddha's footprints, Yuz Asaf's footprints feature a unique and unmistakable mark of identification. The sculptor of the relief has very clearly shown the scars of the Crucifixion wounds. The position of the wounds even shows that the left foot had been nailed over the right, a fact that is confirmed by the bloodstains on the Turin Shroud. Because crucifixion was unknown as a form of death penalty in India, it is not only possible that the body of Jesus lies buried here, it is very likely indeed!

Many ancient literary works in Kashmir testify to the fact that Yuz Asaf and Jesus are the same person. One old manuscript describes the shrine as the grave of Issa Rooh-Allah ('Jesus, the Spirit of God', the Holy Spirit).[28] Thousands of the faithful make pilgrimages to this tomb – not just Muslims, but Hindus, Buddhists and Christians as well. The true importance of this modest shrine has been preserved in the memory of the descendants of the ancient Israelites to this day: they call the shrine 'the tomb of Hazrat Issa Sahib', the tomb of the Lord Jesus.

Age-old documents state that a protective building had already been constructed over the crypt by AD 112. Since that time, the tomb has been tended by the same family, with the office of tomb attendant being passed down in an unbroken line from father to son. In 1766, the keepers of the tomb were issued with a charter officially confirming the importance of the sacred site. In the formal decree issued by the Grand Mufti (or 'Teacher of Islamic religious law') Rahman Mir are the words: 'Here lies Yuz Asaf, who rebuilt the Temple of Solomon at the time of King Gopadatta, and who came as a prophet to Kashmir. He ministered to the people, declared his unity with God, and was a lawgiver to the people. Since then his tomb has been honoured by kings, state officials, high dignitaries and the common folk.'

I visited Srinagar in 1984 as a member of a delegation of specialists and journalists, and our team was formally received by the Governor of the state of Jammu and Kashmir, Dr Farooq Abdullah. On that occasion I told Dr Abdullah that I would be very interested and gratified if the sarcophagus could be opened and examined. Some time previously, I had transferred a considerable sum of money – totalling many thousands of deutschmarks, the generous donation of a lady reader of the first edition of this book – to the administrators of the tomb, and the renovation work it financed was under way at that very moment, so I judged it a good opportunity to suggest opening up the grave. Governor Abdullah at once made all the necessary arrangements for the unsealing and inspection of the tomb chamber, and even assured us of police protection should any physical attack be made by irate fundamentalists.

On the evening before the projected tomb opening, an outbreak of shooting in the old town of Srinagar resulted in the loss of seven lives. The chief of police thereupon urged us not to proceed with the operation, fearing a further escalation of the disturbances, and saying that he could no longer vouch for our safety.

During the 1960s, the unexplained disappearance of a hair of the Prophet Muhammad's beard that had been kept in the Hazratbal mosque in Srinagar, regarded as the most sacred Islamic relic in the country, led to a public uprising in Kashmir which lasted for weeks. The people of the valley considered the central government in Delhi responsible: the joining of Kashmir with the Indian Union in 1948 has never been accepted by large sections of the (predominantly Islamic) population, and this has made the 'Happy Valley' a chronic trouble spot.

In the face of such potentially explosive religious sensitivities, we were unfortunately obliged to postpone the operation we had planned to some later date.

And up to the time of writing (May 1993), it has still not been possible to have the sarcophagus opened and studied. Since the summer of 1989 a situation tantamount to civil war has developed in Kashmir due to the activities of various guerrilla groups. All tourist travel in the valley has ground to a halt. The old town area of Srinagar, in which the tomb is located, is the central lair of the underground fighters who, for the most part, lie hidden while the Indian army scours every street corner and alleyway. Regretfully, I must therefore strongly discourage any visits to the tomb until the situation in Kashmir improves. There seems to be little prospect of that at the moment. In any case, in view of the fact that the site of the tomb is right next to the River Jhelum and must have been flooded many times over the past two thousand years, not too much should be hoped for from the opening of the sarcophagus.

Jesus or Paul?

Many faithful Christians may object that with the arguments I adduce in this book I am robbing Christianity of an essential element, an element that alone can give hope and solace: redemption from sin (which causes the suffering in the world) by the vicarious sacrificial death of Jesus Christ, for all those who acknowledge his teaching. But it is precisely this form of the doctrine of salvation in traditional Christianity that rests almost exclusively on the work of Paul, and was never taught by Jesus. Paul taught that the whole function of Jesus centres on his sacrificial death, that through the shedding of his blood he has absolved the faithful of their sins and released them from chaos and the domination of Satan. In fact, Paul does not relay a single syllable of the direct teaching of Jesus in his epistles, nor does he tell a single one of his parables. Instead, he builds up a philosophy of his own on the basis of his own personal understanding (or misunderstanding) of Jesus' teaching.

Paul insists that on account of the sin of Adam all people are subject to the wrath of God from the start (see Ephesians 2:3), and are lost without exception (Romans 5:18; 1 Corinthians 15:18), for all are subject to sin (Romans 3:9; Galatians 3:22; Colossians 2:14). God has given his judgement of condemnation against all people (Romans 5:16).

Out of the Good News brought by Jesus, Paul has made news that is dark and threatening, from the menace of which only he could show the way out. And this way out was the salvation of humanity through the sacrificial death of Christ: 'Therefore as by the offence of one, judgement came upon all men to condemnation; even so by the righteousness of one the free gift came upon all men unto justification of life' (Romans 5:18). And in the letter to the Colossians he describes Jesus as 'Blotting out the handwriting of ordinances that was against us, which was contrary to us, and took it out of the way, nailing it to his cross' (Colossians 2:14).

But the terrible thing about the doctrine of salvation according to Paul is his attitude that the individual can contribute nothing towards his salvation in his miserable life: not through any good works of his own, not through any change of lifestyle however much for the better, can the individual justify his being saved, reconciled with God (cf Romans 3:24, 9:16; 1 Corinthians 1:29; Galatians 2:16).

For according to Paul it is exclusively the grace of God which brings us to salvation: 'For by grace are ye saved through faith; and that not of yourselves; it is the gift of God. Not of works, lest any man should boast' (Ephesians 2:8–9).

According to Paul a person may be saved merely by the single act of baptism, becoming a child of God and a completely new being. Every claim to cooperating in salvation by one's own effort is, by this teaching, to be regarded as a belittling of the sacrifice of Jesus, as an attempt to save oneself that cannot but fail. Conversely, every person, however good and exemplary a life he may have led, must in this schema be considered lost if he fails to accept the sacrifice on the Cross for himself personally as his complete salvation. Such ideas are totally alien to Jesus.

Most Christians are of the opinion that the greatness, the uniqueness, of Christianity stands and falls with this teaching. Yet it proves to be a fiction, far removed from the ideas of Jesus. Not even a hint of this so-called Christian doctrine of salvation is to be found in the Sermon on the Mount – the quintessence of Jesus' message – or in the Lord's Prayer (the Our Father), or in the traditional parables told by Jesus!

Jesus was not concerned with constructing a philosophy that might be based on his life and on his message that might free people from the sufferings of earthly existence – he actually lived what he taught. Toleration at all times, care for the welfare and benefit of others (human and animal), giving and sharing, selflessness in helping others to carry the burden of their suffering, a universal and unconditional love for all – this is the way of perfection that Jesus demonstrated in his life.

APPENDIX

Chronological Table

The Middle East

BC

c.1750	Abraham leaves Haran with his tribe
c.1730	Hebrew tribes travel to Egypt, led by Joseph
c.1550	Rule of Hyksos ends: start of oppression
c.1250	Moses; the Exodus from Egypt
c.1200	Settlement in Palestine
965-926	King Solomon
after 926	Partition into the northern kingdom of Israel and the southern kingdom of Judah
c.870	The prophet Elijah
722	Sargon II of Assyria conquers Israel; the ten tribes of Israel disappear for ever.
c.590	Possible reference by prophet Ezekiel to the Temple in Kashmir
587	End of the kingdom of Judah
	Babylonian Exile (lasting about 50 years)
7	Birth of Jesus
4	Death of Herod the Great

AD

6	Archelaus is deposed; 12-year-old Jesus in Temple
6-c.30	First journey of Jesus to India
c.30	Return from India, and entry into Jerusalem
31	John the Baptist executed
33	Crucifixion of Jesus
c.35	Paul meets Jesus in Damascus and is converted
c.36	Jesus with the king of Andrapa
post-36	Jesus in Edessa and with the king of Nisibis

India

BC

c.2500	Indus Culture (Harappa)
c.1300	Compilation of Vedas
6th century	The 'Lost Tribes of Israel' settle in northern India
563-483	Gautama Siddhartha Sakyamuni, (the) Buddha
5th century	First writing of Buddhist sutras
c.250	The Indian Emperor Ashoka sends Buddhist missionaries as far as Marseilles (Roquepertuse)
1st century	Mahayana Buddhism moulded by the idea of the Saviour (Bodhisattva)

AD

before 50	Jesus stays in the university town of Taxila (Punjab); appears at the court of the Indo-Parthian ruler, Gundafor
c.50	Jesus at the court of the local king Gopananda (Gopadatta), ruled about 49-109
post-50	Jesus travels as a itinerant preacher under the name Yuz Asaf in Kashmir and neighbouring regions
post-70	Jesus meets the local king Shalivahana
78	Inscription on the Temple of Solomon in Srinagar
c.78-103	Reign of King Kanishka
c.80	Fourth Buddhist Council at Haran (Harwan) in Kashmir
post-80	The body of Jesus entombed in Srinagar

The 'Nazarenes'

Over the past decade I have received letters from hundreds of readers expressing gratitude for their new perspectives on faith, as opened to them by my book *Jesus Lived in India*. Many felt that only now, with the new information they had in front of them, could they grasp the true significance of the historical Jesus. Among them were ex-priests who had turned in disappointment from the Church or even from religion altogether, and had pursued other professions in the resolve never again to get embroiled in matters of faith. Such people wrote to me saying that after reading my book they had found a new way of reaching the original teachings of Jesus. Some told me about the dramatic circumstances of a serious crisis of faith, from which they were rescued by reading it. Others wanted to know if there was a community they could join which was striving to put the teachings described in the book into practice and to live them.

In view of the overwhelming number of readers favourably inclined to the idea, I have now decided to set up a foundation that has the specific aim of studying the genuine, original teachings of the Nazarene with the aid of experts in various fields, under the auspices of a newly established institute, and of publishing the knowledge thereby gained in an appropriate form.

This should make it possible to start up small groups of 'Nazarenes' in many different places and in many different forms, all of whom will strive to practise once more the original and unadulterated teaching of the Nazarene Jesus, and to spread it by their own example.

These groups could then be supported by a main centre offering spiritual inspiration, information, and material assistance in addition. The principles of the foundation have already been drawn up, and the active support of a businessman in Munich has been secured.

Readers who are interested in these ideas and would like to offer their support are invited to contact me.

Society of THE NAZARENES
c/o Holger Kersten
Post box 961
79 009 FREIBURG
Germany

NOTES

Chapter 1: The Unknown Life of Jesus

1. A second road to Ladakh has recently (1990) been opened for foreigners, leading over the Rohtang Pass from the mountain town of Manali in the state of Himachal Pradesh.
2. Nikolas Notovitch, *The Unknown Life of Jesus Christ*, translated from the French edition of 1894, revised, and with an added preface by Notovitch, London, 1895.
3. Issa is the Muslim Arabic name for Jesus.
4. Persian *panj* 'five', *ab* 'water'; literally therefore 'five waters'.
5. Jainism, a very old Indian monastic religion, closely related to Buddhism, but more ascetic. It was established in its present form by Mahavira, a contemporary of Buddha.
6. Pali, a north Indian dialect of the centuries after Buddha's death, used for the scriptural canon of southern Theravada (Hinayana) Buddhism.
7. Biographical information is given in the *Dictionnaire National des Contemporains*, Vol.3, p.274, Paris, 1901.
8. E. V. Bogdanovitch, *L'Alliance franco-russe*.
9. Bibliothèque Nationale, Paris, Fol.R.226.
10. See Public Record Office, Kew, FO 371/113 No.29196.
11. Bibliografija Periodicheskikh Izdaniy Rossiy (1901–1906). Leningrad, 1958.
12. N. C. Chaudhuri, *Scholar Extraordinary*, London, 1974; p.325.
13. Year 10, p.211, Berlin, 1895.
14. *The Hindustan Times*, New Delhi, 11 July 1988.
15. N. Roerich, *Altai-Himalaya, A Travel Diary*, New York, 1929; p.89.
16. H. Merrick, *In the World's Attick*, London, 1931; p.215.
17. Bibliothèque Nationale, Paris, Fol.M.715.
18. Inventory number 88.177.
19. In the *Dictionnaire National des Contemporains*, Vol. 3, p. 274, Paris, 1901, it is recorded that Notovitch was accepted into the Légion d'Honneur with the grade of *Officier de l'Instruction publique* in the year 1889 *pour avoir donné au musée du Trocadero de précieuses collections d'objets rapportés de l'Inde et de la Perse*.
20. Moravian Church, also called the Herrnhüter community.

Chapter 2: Who Was Jesus?

1. Tacitus, *Annals* 15:44.
2. Pliny the Younger, *Letters*, 10:96f.
3. Suetonius, *Vitae Caesarum*; Nero (16); Claudius (25:4).
4. Flavius Josephus, *The Antiquities of the Jews* XX,9:1; XVIII,3:3.
5. 1:47.
6. Arthur Drews, *Die Christusmythe*, Jena, 2nd edition 1911; p.3.
7. Translated from the German edition by Wilhelm Reeb, Leipzig, 1923.
8. Clement of Alexandria, *Stromateis* 7; 89:2f.
9. Origen, *Contra Celsum* 3:12.
10. G. Bornkamm, *Jesus of Nazareth*, Stuttgart, 9th edition 1971.
11. Quoted from *Der Spiegel* No. 14, 1966.
12. J. Jeremias, 1951.
13. Quoted from *Der Spiegel* No. 14, 1966.
14. W. Nestle, *Krisis des Christentums*, 1947; p.89.
15. F. Overbeck, *Christentum und Kultur*, published posthumously, 1919.
16. Quoted from H. Ackermann, *Entstellung und Klärung der Botschaft Jesu*, 1961.
17. A. Deissmann, *Paulus*, Tübingen, 2nd edition 1925.
18. E. Grimm, *Die Ethik Jesu*, 1917.
19. A. Schweitzer, *Geschichte der Leben-Jesu-Forschung*, Tübingen, 2nd edition 1913; p.512.
20. Quoted from *Der Spiegel* No. 14, 1966.
21. *Der Stern* No. 16, 1973.
22. Dardic: a group of ancient Indo–European languages spoken in western Himalaya, Karakorum and the Hindu Kush. The best attested are Kashmiri and Shina.
23. Anagarika Govinda, *The Way of the White Clouds*.

Chapter 3: Moses and the Children of God

1. J. Juergens, *Der biblische Moses*, Munich, 1928.
2. Prof. Flinders Petrie, *Researches in Sinai*, 1906.
3. Cf Exodus 19:11, 24:17, 33:9; Deuteronomy 4:11, 4:24, 4:33, 4:36, 5:4, 5:5, 5:23, 9:3, 32:22.
4. W. F. Irland, *Die Memoiren David Rizzios*, Leipzig, 1852.
5. Dummelow, *Commentary on the Holy Bible*, p.115.
6. Dr Mateer, *The Land of Charity*, quoted in H. P. Blavatsky, *Isis Unveiled*, Vol. II.
7. Cf F. Max Müller, *Indien* in Weber, *Indische Skizzen*, Berlin, 1857.
8. F. Bernier, *Travels in the Moghul Empire*, London, 1891; p.432.
9. G. Konzelmann, *Aufbruch der Hebräer*, Munich, 1976; p.37ff.
10. A sound-change in Old Persian transformed *Sindh* into *Hind*, and this word soon came to denote the entire subcontinent and its inhabitants

(*Hindu*). In later times the h was also dropped, leaving Ind-, which then became *India*.

11. Cf Joshua 24:2–3.
12. Cf Leviticus 11; Deuteronomy 14.
13. The Revd Dr Joseph Wolff, *Narrative of a Mission to Bokhara in the Years 1843–1845*, Vol. I, pp.13–20, London, 1845.
14. Wolff, as above, p.58.
15. London, 1840, p.166.
16. Dr J. Bryce and Dr K. Johnson, *A Comprehensive Description of Geography*, London and Glasgow, 1880; p.25.
17. G. Moore, *The Lost Tribes*, London, 1861.
18. K. Jettmar, *Felsbilder im Karakorum*, in *Spektrum der Wissenschaft*, December 1983; p.22–32.

Chapter 4: The Childhood of Jesus

1. G. Kroll, *Auf den Spuren Jesu*, Leipzig, 1964; p.63ff.
2. P. Schnabel, *Der jungste Keilschrifttext*, in *Zeitschrift für Assyrologie*, NF 2(36); p.66ff.
3. Origen, *Gen. Hom.* XIV, 3.
4. Translated in quotation from Hennecke-Schneemelcher, *Neutestamentliche Apokryphen*, Vol. I, Tübingen, 4th edition 1968; p.98.
5. The teaching of reincarnation is based on the principle that each soul goes through a process of evolution lasting many lifetimes, and is consequently reborn in a human or other body again and again, in order to accumulate further experience and finally achieve the divine state.
6. The Dalai Lama, *My Country and My People*.
7. Heinrich Harrer, *Seven Years in Tibet*.
8. Vicki Mackenzie, *Reincarnation: The Boy Lama*, London, 1988.
9. E. J. Eitel, *A Handbook of Chinese Buddhism*, Tokyo, 1904.

Chapter 5: Eastern Wisdom in the West

1. Cf Le Coq, *Ostturkistan: Waldschmidt, Zentralasien*, Lüders, *Die literarischen Funde*.
2. From H.-J. Klimkeit, *Gottes- und Selbsterfahrung in der gnostisch–buddhistischen Religionsbegegnung Zentralasiens*, in *Zeitschrift für Religions- und Geistesgeschichte*, Vol. 35, 1983, p.236–247.
3. Although a pre-Christian date of compilation for the texts has been accepted for many years, several researchers have recently suggested that parts of the texts were written around the time of Jesus' birth or shortly afterwards, and refer to Jesus directly. Cf M. Baigent and R. Leigh, *The Private Jesus: The Dead Sea Scrolls and the Truth about Early Christianity*, Munich, 1991.

4. In art this inscription is usually shown as the abbreviation for the Latin words *Iesus, Nazarenus, Rex Iudaeorum*, or INRI.
5. The Arabs called the early Christians *Nasrani* or *Nasara*.
6. John M. Robertson, *Die Evangelienmythen*, Jena, 1910; p.51ff.
7. *The Antiquities of the Jews* XVIII, 5:2.
8. Quoted from J. Klausner, *Jesus von Nazareth*, 1952; p.144.
9. Abbreviated form: 1QIs.
10. Abbreviated form: 1QIIs.
11. Abbreviated form: 1Qp Hab.
12. Abbreviated form: 1QS.
13. Abbreviated form: 1QSa.
14. Abbreviated form: 1QH.
15. *The Jewish War* II, 8:3.
16. From Albert Schweitzer, *Geschichte der Leben-Jesu-Forschung*.
17. *The Jewish War* II, 8:7.
18. The Jewish year has twelve months that alternate between 29 and 30 days each, totalling 50 weeks of seven days. To adjust to fit the actual solar year a thirteenth month, the second Adar or Veadar, has to be inserted seven times in every nineteen–year period. The 'emergent year' in relation to Jewish chronology is the 'Day of Creation' corresponding in the Gregorian calendar to 20 September 3760 BC.
19. A. Hilgenfeld, *Zeitschrift für wissenschaftliche Theologie* (1860–1862); Bauer, *Essener*, in Pauly-Wissowa, *Suppl. bd.* IV, S p.426ff.
20. Cf Emile Burnouf, *Le Bouddhisme en Occident*, in *Revue des Deux Mondes*, 1888.
21. Origen, *Contra Celsum* 6:27.
22. Nag Hammadi Codex II 3, 121:15–19.
23. According to Edmunds, *Buddhist and Christian Gospels*, there are 112.
24. C. G. Montefiore, *The Synoptic Gospels*, 2nd edition 1927.
25. Cf Genesis 17:1ff.
26. Cf Exodus 12:43ff; Ezekiel 44:9.
27. Hennecke-Schneemelcher, *Neutestamentliche Apokryphen*, Vol. II; p.210.
28. The Syrian Arabic form is *Alavites*, the Turkish *Alevites*, while in areas in which Farsi (Persian) is spoken, the general term is *Ali–Ilahi* ('Ali-deifier').
29. The Nusairis themselves derive their name from that of one of their leaders during the 8th century, Ibn Nusair, a derivation regarded as highly dubious by academics because it was probably formulated in order to exonerate the Nusairis from a charge of heresy. Cf R. Dussaud, *Histoire et religion des Nosairis*, Paris, 1900; I. Goldziher, *Archiv für Religionswissenschaft*, 4/1901; H.-J. Schoeps, *Theologie und Geschichte des Urchristentums*; G. Lüling, *Die Wiederentdeckung des Propheten Muhammad*, Erlangen, 1981.

30. The Alawite groups of Anatolia (Kizilbas, Tahtaci, Yürükas, and the spiritual élite of the Bektashi dervishes), who live mostly as mountain farmers, keepers of cattle and nomads, represent around 15 to 30 per cent of the entire Turkish population.
31. This does not apply to the Syrian Nusairis, whose religious traditions are the privilege of men only.
32. E. Müller, *Kulturhistorische Studien zur Genese pseudo-islamischer Sektengebilde in Vorderasien*, Wiesbaden, 1967.
33. A. J. Dierl, *Geschichte und Lehre des anatolische Alevismus–Bektashismus*, Frankfurt, 1985.
34. A. J. Dierl, as above, p.125f.
35. Further literature on this topic includes: J. K. Birge, *The Bektashi Order of Dervishes*, Hartford, 1937; E. Gross, *Das Vilajetname des Hadji Bektash*, Leipzig, 1927; A. Haas, *Die Bektashi*, Berlin, 1987; G. Jacob, *Die Bektashije...* in *Abhdlg. d. königl. bayer. Akademie d. Wissensch.* I.Kl.XXIV,Bd.III, Munich, 1909; *Beiträge zur Kenntnis des Derwisch–Ordens der Bektaschije*, Berlin, 1908; *Das Fortleben von antiken Mysterien und Altchristlichem im Islam*, in *Der Islam*, 1911, p.232ff; H. Kirchmaier, *über die Yezidi*, in *Der Islam*, 34, 1959; E. Kohn, *Vorislamisches in einigen vorderasiatischen Sekten und Derwischorden*, in *Ethnologische Studien*, 1931, p.295ff; Henri Lammens, *L'Islam*, Beirut, 1941; R. Strothmann, *Morgenländische Geneimsekten in der abendländischen Forschung*, Berlin, 1953; *Der Islam: Sekten*, in *Hdb. d. Rel. wissensch.*, Berlin, 1948.

Chapter 6: The Secret of Jesus

1. Gallup Poll on European Values, London, 1983; G. Gallup jr, *Encounters with Immortality*, 1983.
2. According to L. von Schröder (*Pythagoras und die Inder*, Leipzig, 1884), Pythagoras was 'the bringer of Indian traditions to Greece'. But leaving aside the question of whether Pythagoras really visited India in person, cultural contacts between Greece and the India of Buddha's day are uncontested.
3. Friedrich Weinreb, *Das Buch Jonah*, Zurich, 1970; p.90ff.
4. The *Antiquities of the Jews* XVIII, 1:3.
5. *The Jewish War* II, 8:14.
6. For example: Philo of Alexandria (around 25 BC to AD 50) in his work *On Dreaming* (I, 139); Justin Martyr (about 100–165) in his *Dialogue with Tryphon the Jew* (LXXXVIII, 5); Tatian (2nd century) in his *Speech to the Greeks* (VII, 5–6); Synesius of Cyrene (around 370–413) in *About Dreams* (140 B); and Augustine (354–430) in *On the Greatness of the Soul* (XX, 34) and in *Confessions* (I, 6,9)

7. Eusebius, *Historia Ecclesiastica* V, 9; E. Benz, *Indische Einflüsse auf die frühchristliche Theologie,* Wiesbaden, 1951.
8. Cf E. Pagels, *Versuchung durch Erkenntnis. Die gnostischen Evangelien.*
9. H de Lubac, *Textes Alexandrins et Bouddhiques, RechScRel* 27, 1937.
10. Clement of Alexandria, *Stromateis* I, 15.
11. Clement of Alexandria, *Admonition* I, 6.
12. Clement of Alexandria, *Stromateis* IV, 160:3.
13. E. Seeberg, *Ammonios Sakas,* in *Zeitschrift für Kirchengeschichte,* Bd. LX, 1941; E. Benz, *Indische Einflüsse auf die frühchristliche Theologie,* as above; Cope, quoted in Karl Hoheisel, *Das frühe Christentum und die Seelenwanderung,* in *Jahrbuch für Antike und Christentum,* 1984–1985.
14. Origen, *De Principiis.*
15. Origen, *Contra Celsum.*
16. Gregory of Nyssa, *The Catechetical Oration* VIII, 9.
17. M. Pryse, *Reincarnation in the New Testament,* Ansata, 1980.
18. Bhagvan Dass, *Krishna and the Theory of Avatars.*
19. Sri Yukteswar, *The Holy Science* (Self-Realization Fellowship, Los Angeles).
20. F. Hitching, *Die letzten Rätsel unserer Welt,* Frankfurt, 1982; p.118ff.

Chapter 7: The Shroud – A Legacy of Jesus

1. Flavius Josephus, *The Antiquities of the Jews* XVIII, 1:1,6.
2. According to more recent linguistic research by the philologist the Revd Dr Günther Schwarz, however, this is an error of translation. The Aramaic word for 'sword', *zeyana,* is distinguished only by a tiny hook mark from *ziyyuna,* '(spiritual) nourishment', a meaning that would give the quotation a completely different sense.
3. Epiphanius, *Her.* 30.
4. W. Marxsen, *Die Auferstehung Jesu,* Gütersloh, 1960.
5. Cf Kersten and Gruber, *The Jesus Conspiracy: The Truth About the Resurrection,* Element Books, 1994. The following sections on the subject of the Turin Shroud are largely based on this work. Because the results of Dr Gruber's historical investigation represent the most up-to-date stage of Shroud research and significantly support my own argument, some fundamental passages are quoted and/or paraphrased here. The same is true of passages in Chapter Eight.
6. Ian Wilson, *The Turin Shroud,* London, 1978.
7. Jerome, *De Viris Illustribus* II.
8. Eusebius, *Historia Ecclesiastica* I, 13; II, 6–8.
9. The pilgrim Aetheria of Aquitaine visited Edessa in 383 on her return from the Holy Land, and brought from there a copy of the letter to the West. Cf J. F. Gamurrini (ed.), *S Hilarii Tractatus et Hymni et S*

Silviae Aquitanae Perigrinatio ad loca sancta. . . ex cod. Arretino depromps, Biblioteca dell'Academia Storico-Giuridica, Vol. IV, Rome, 1887; H. Pétré, *Peregrinatio Aetheriae, Sources Chrétiennes*, 21, Paris, 1948.

10. W. Cureton, *Ancient Syriac Documents Relative to the Earliest Establishment of Christianity in Edessa and the Neighbouring Countries*, London, 1864; G. Philips (ed.), *The Doctrine of Addai the Apostle*, London, 1876.

11. *Narratio* (PG 113), English translation printed in Wilson, *The Turin Shroud*, as above.

12. E. von Dobschütz, *Christusbilder*, Leipzig, 1899; p.182.

13. Evagrius, *Historia Ecclesiastica*, Migne, PG, LXXX, VI/2, Sp. 2748–49.

14. W. Bulst, *Das Grabtuch von Turin*, Karlsruhe, 1978; p.111.

15. P. Vignon, *Le Saint Suaire de Turin devant la science, l'archologie, l'histoire, l'iconographie, la logique*, Paris, 1938; E. A. Wuenschel, *Self-Portrait of Christ: The Holy Shroud of Turin*, New York, 1954; Wilson, *The Turin Shroud*, as above. Paul Maloney further reduces the Vignon list from twenty features to just nine that even the most sceptical of observers would have to accept. P. Maloney, *The Shroud of Turin: Traits and Peculiarities of Image and Cloth Preserved in Historical Sources*: talk given at the International Symposium 'La Sindone e le Icone', Bologna, May 1989.

16. Quoted in M. Green, *Enshrouded in Silence, Ampleforth Journal 74*, 1969; p.319–345.

17. Ordericus Vitalis, *Historia Ecclesiastica*, TLIII,IX,8.

18. Gervase of Tilbury, *Otia Imperialia*, III.

19. Quoted from Wilson, *The Turin Shroud*, as above.

20. In Rome, Genoa and Paris, Mandylions were on display at this time, but were all hand–painted copies; none of them claimed to be the original. The so-called 'Towel of Veronica' is a copy of this type; its name can be traced to the description *vera icon* ('true image') used of the Mandylion.

21. E. Hezck, *Genua und seine Marine im Zeitalter der Kreuzzüge*, Innsbruck, 1886; p.66.

22. *Epist. Innoc.*, Migne, PL 215, Sp. 433f.

23. Charny is the same name as Charnay; at that time the French language had not yet developed a standardized orthography.

24. For further details of the exciting history of the cloth, see Kersten and Gruber, *The Jesus Conspiracy*, as above.

25. H. Thurston, *The Holy Shroud...*, in *The Month*, 101, 1903; p.19.

26. J. Reban, *Christus wurde lebendig begraben*, Zurich, 1982.

27. W. Bulst, *Das Grabtuch von Turin*, Karlsruhe, 1978; p.123.

28. Kersten and Gruber, *The Jesus Conspiracy*, as above.

Chapter 8: 'Death' and 'Resurrection'

1. C. H. Dodd, *Historical Tradition in the Fourth Gospel*, Cambridge, 1963; p.423; S. G. F. Brandon, *Jesus and the Zealots*, Manchester, 1967; p.16.
2. H. Lincoln, M. Baigent and R. Leigh, *The Holy Grail and its Legacy*.
3. G. Ghiberti, *La Sepoltura di Gesù*, Rome, 1982; p.43.
4. P. Barbet, *Die Passion Jesu Christi in der Sicht eines Chirurgen*, Karlsruhe, 1953; W. Bulst and J. Pfeiffer, *Das Turiner Grabtuch und das Christus bild*, Frankfurt, 1987, p.87f; N. Currer-Briggs, *The Holy Grail and the Shroud of Christ*, Maulden, 1984; p.16.
5. P. G. Bagatti and J. T. Milik, *Gli scavi del 'Dominus flevit', La necropoli del periodo Romano*, Jerusalem, 1958.
6. The only correct design of a tomb structure is described in the Mishnah, in *Baba Bathra* 6,8.
7. P. Savio, *Ricerche storiche sulla Santa Sindone*, Turin, 1957; p.33ff.
8. G. Zaninotto, *GV* 20, 1–8, *Giovanni testimone oculare della risurrezione di Gesù?*, *Sindon*, 1, 1989; p.148. A passage in the *Acta Philippi* (143) is of special interest on this point, 'Philip asked to be buried in papyrus leaves, and that no linen cloth was laid on him, so as avoid being treated in the same way as Christ, who was wrapped in a Sindon' (*en sindoni eneilethe*).
9. The embalming of Jacob and Joseph (Genesis 50:2–3,26) are exceptions, representing the ancient Egyptian custom.
10. E. Haenchen, *Das Johannes-Evangelium: Ein Kommentar*, Tübingen, 1980; p.556.
11. Shabbat 23:5.
12. A. Dessy, *La sepoltura dei crocifissi*, Sindon, 1, 1989: p.42.
13. L. Boulos, *Medicinal Plants of North Africa*, Algonac, 1983, p.128; J. A. Duke, *Medicinal Plants of the Bible*, New York, 1983, p.19; H. N. Moldenke and A. N. Moldenke, *Plants of the Bible*, New York, 1952; p.35. Cf further G. W. Reynolds, *The Aloes of South Africa*, Johannesburg, 1950; p.394ff.
14. F. N. Hepper, *The Identity and Origin of Classical Bitter Aloes*, Palestine Exploration Quarterly, 120, 1988; p.146–148.
15. D. Grindlay and T. Reynolds, *The Aloe Vera Phenomenon: A review of the properties and modern uses of the leaf parenchyma gel*, Journal of Ethnopharmacology, 16, 1986; p.117–151.
16. Moldenke and Moldenke, *Plants of the Bible*, as above.
17. A. W. Anderson, *Plants of the Bible*, New York, 1957.
18. A. Feuillet, *The Identification and the Disposition of the Funerary Linens of Jesus' Burial According to the Fourth Gospel*, SSI, 4, 1982, p.18; Zaninotto, *Sindon* as above, p.160. Blinzler was the first to point this out: J. Blinzler, *Das Turiner Grablinnen und die Wissenschaft*, Ettal, 1952.

In Matthew and Luke the verb *eneileo* suggesting the 'weight' of the packing is moderated by using the verb *entylisso*, which means merely 'wrapped in'.

19. H. Mödder, *Die Todesursache bei der Kreuzigung*, in *Stimmen der Zeit*, 144, 1948, p.50–59; F. T. Zugibe, *Death by Crucifixion, Canadian Society of Forensic Science Journal*, 17, 1984.

20. 'The Son of Man came eating and drinking, and they say, Behold a man gluttonous, and a winebibber . . .' (Matthew 11:19).

21. Flavius Josephus, *Vita* IV, 75.

22. Petrus de Natalibus, *Catalogus Sanctorum*, Lyon, 1508. Petrus de Natalibus bases his statements on John of Damascus.

23. B. Bagatti and E. Testa, *Il Golgota e la Croce*, Jerusalem, 1978; p.24. The apocryphal Gospel of Peter calls the place where the tomb was excavated 'Joseph's Garden'.

24. Flavius Josephus, *The Jewish War* IV, 5:2.

25. At least one scriptural authority also finds it extremely odd that Joseph had his own tomb constructed right next to a place of execution: Haenchen, *Das Johannes–Evangelium*, as above; p.564.

26. But John was possibly making a reference to Christ as the symbol of the true Paschal Lamb. Hyssop served an important function in the ritual commemorating the first Passover (Exodus 12:22). In Mark, the corresponding passage says the sponge of vinegar was stuck on a reed (*kalamos*). Did John intentionally use hussopos ('*hyssop*') as a replacement for *kalamos*?

27. R. Seydel, Das Evangelium von Jesus, Leipzig, 1882; p.273.

28. J. Blinzler, *Das Turiner Grablinnen und die Wissenschaft*, as above, p.31.

29. H. Bardtke, *Die handschriftenfunde am Toten Meer*, Berlin, 1958; p.42.

30. G. Ricci, *Kreuzweg nach dem Leichentuch von Turin*, Rome, 1971; p.68ff.

31. R. Hoare, *The Testimony of the Shroud*, London, 1978; p.53.

32. Letter of 6 March 1990.

33. J. S. Kennard, *The Burial of Jesus*, *JBL* 74, 1955; p.238.

34. Cf R. Thiel, *Jesus Christus und die Wissenschaft*, Berlin, 1938; p.100f.

35. At the so-called 'Ascension', Jesus evidently withdrew from the area in which he had been working, and possibly travelled as far as India.

36. G. Schwarz, *'Anhistemi' und 'anastasis' in den Evangelien*, in *Biblische Notizen, Beiträge zur exegetischen Diskussion*, 10, 1979; p 35–40.

37. G. Schwarz, *Tod, Auferstehung, Gericht und ewiges Leben nach den ersten drei Evangelien, Via Mundi*, 55, 1988.

38. Cf G. Schwarz, *Wenn die Worte nicht stimmen: Dreissig entstellte Evangelientexte wiederhergestellt*, Munich, 1990; p.56ff. Because the tradition has obviously confused 'resuscitation' with the theological concept of 'resurrection', it is not possible to pinpoint the exact meaning in the biblical texts.

Chapter 9: After the Crucifixion

1. W. Lange-Eichbaum, *Genie, Irrsinn und Ruhm*, Munich, 6th edition 1967; p.496ff.
2. Lactantius, *Institutiones* 5:3.
3. Vol. 3, p.197ff.
4. Hennecke-Schneemelcher, *Neutestamentliche Apokryphen*, as above, Vol. II, p.299ff.
5. Cf *Neutestamentliche Apokryphen*, Vol. I, p.199ff.
6. *Neutestamentliche Apokryphen*, Vol. I, p.206ff.
7. *Neutestamentliche Apokryphen*, Vol. II, p.303.
8. Arabic for 'Revered Jesus'.
9. *Neutestamentliche Apokryphen*, Vol. II, p.316.
10. *Neutestamentliche Apokryphen*, Vol. II, p.319.
11. *Neutestamentliche Apokryphen*, Vol. II, p.320.
12. *Neutestamentliche Apokryphen*, Vol. II, p.322.
13. J. Jeremias, essay in *Nachrichten aus der Akad. d. Wiss. Göttingen, I. Phil.-Hist. Kl.*, 1953; p.95ff.
14. Hennecke-Schneemelcher, *Neutestamentliche Apokryphen*, Vol. I, p.199ff.
15. Cf J. Jeremias, *Nachrichten* as above, p.99f.
16. G. Lüling, *über den Ur-Quran*, Erlangen, 1977; *Die Wiederentdeckung des Propheten Muhammad*, Erlangen, 1981.
17. Cf H. Glasenapp, *Die Literaturen Indiens*, Stuttgart, 1961; p.129–135.
18. From H. R. Hoffmann, *Kalacakra Studies* I, in *Central Asiatic Journal*, Vol. 13, 1969, p.52–73; Vol. 15, 1972, p.298–301.
19. First and best of the four ages (*yuga*).
20. Quoted in translation from A. Hohenberger, *Das Bhavishyapurana*, in *Münchener Indologische Studien* 5, Wiesbaden, 1967; p.17f.
21. Arabic for 'Revered Jesus'.
22. *Tarikh-i-Kashmir*, p.69
23. Source: *Kans-ul-Ammal*, Vol. II, p.34.
24. *Ikmâl-ud-Dîn*, p. 327; cf Matthew 13:1–23; Mark 4:1–20; Luke 8:4–15.
25. Quoted from D. W. Lang, *The Wisdom of Balahar*, New York, 1957, p.37.
26. In recent years the tomb has been renovated and altered a number of times. This has probably led to modification also of the surrounding structures in some way, but because Kashmir has been out of bounds since 1989 (due to continuing unrest and guerrilla activity), there is no reliable information about the present condition of the tomb. A portion of the grille was sold to a visitor in 1989, and is now in my possession.
27. According to Aziz Kashmiri, editor of the journal *Roshni* published in Srinagar, the footprints were discovered in 1958 by a Mrs Ketkar, the daughter of Lord Kitchener's adjutant.
28. Quoted from M. Yasin, *Mysteries of Kashmir*, Srinagar, 1972.

BIBLIOGRAPHY

Abbot, S., *The Fourfold Gospels*, Cambridge 1917.

Abdul Hag Vidyarthi, M., *Rohi Islam*, Lahore 1966.

Abdul Qadir bin Qazi-ul Qazzat Wasil Ali Khan, *Hashmat-i-Kashmir*, MS. No. 42, Asiatic Society of Bengal, Calcutta.

Ackermann, H., *Entstellung und Klärung der Botschaft Jesu*, Göttingen 1961.

Albright, W. F., *The Archeology of Palestine*, London 1951.

Allegro, J. M., *The Dead Sea Scrolls and the Christian Myth*, Newton Abbey 1979.

- -, The Treasure of the Copper Scroll. The opening and decipherment of the most mysterious of the Dead Sea Scrolls. A unique inventory of buried treasure, London 1960.

Allen, Bernard M., *The Story behind the Gospels*, Methuen, London 1919.

Anderson, A. W., *Plants of the Bible*, New York 1957.

Ansault, Abate, *La Croix avant Jésus-Christ*, Paris 1894.

Anselme, P., *Histoire de la Maison royale de France*, Paris 1730.

Aron, R., *Jesus of Nazareth: The Hidden Years*, (tr.) 1962.

Assemani, J. S., *Bibliotheca Orientalis Clementino-Vaticana*, Rome 1719.

Augstein, R., *Jesus Menschensohn*, Hamburg 1974.

Augustine, *De moribis ecclesiae catholicae*, I,34, Migne, PL 32.

At-Tabri, Iman Abu Ja'far Muhammad, *Tafsir Ibn-i-Jarir-at-Tabri*, Cairo.

Bagatti, B. and Testa, E., *Il Golgota e la Croce*, Jerusalem 1978.

Baigent, M. and Leigh, R., *The Private Jesus*.

Barber, M., 'The Templars and the Turin Shroud', *Shroud Spectrum International*, 1983.

Darbet, P., *Die Passion Jesu Christi in der Sicht des Chirurgen*, Karlsruhe 1953.

Bardtke, H., *Die Handschriftenfunde am Toten Meer*, Berlin 1952.

- -, *Die Handschriftenfunde am Toten Meer: Die Sekte von Qumran*, Berlin 1958.

- -, *Die Handschriftenfunde in der Wüste Juda*, Berlin 1962.

Barth, F., *Die Hauptprobleme des Lebens Jesu*, Gütersloh 1918.

Barth, M., *Israel und die Kirche im Brief an die Epheser* (= Theologische Existenz heute, N.F., No. 75), Munich 1959.

- -, Jesus, *Paulus und die Juden*, Zurich 1967.

Barthel, M., *Was wirklich in der Bibel steht*, Düsseldorf 1980.

Bartscht, G., *Von den drei Beträgern*, Berlin 1960.

Basharat, Ahmad, *The Birth of Jesus*, Lahore 1929.

Bauer, F. C., *Kritische Untersuchungen über die Kanonischen Evangelien*, Tübingen 1847.

Bauer, M., *Anfänge der Christenheit. Von Jesus von Nazareth zur frühchristlichen Kirche*, Berlin 3rd edition 1960.

Bauer, W., *Rechtgläubigkeit und Ketzerei im ältesten Christentum. Beiträge zur Historischen Theologie 10*, 1934.

Baus, K., *Von der Urgemeinde zur frühchristlichen Grosskirche*, Freiburg 3rd edition 1973.

Bell, Major A. W., *Tribes of Afghanistan*, London 1897.

Bellew, H. W., *The New Afghan Question*, or *Are the Afghans Israelites?*, Simla 1880.

- -, *The Races of Afghanistan*, Calcutta n.d.

Ben-Chorin, *Bruder Jesus, der Nazarener in jüd.* Sicht, Munich 1967.

Bengalee, Sufi Matiur Rahman, *The Tomb of Jesus*, Chicago 1946.

Bergh von Eysinga, G. A. van den, *Indische Einflüsse auf evangelische Erzählungen*, Göttingen 1904.

Berna, K., *Jesus ist nicht am Kreuz gestorben*, Stuttgart 1957.

- -, John Reban's Facts: *Christus wurde lebendig begraben*, Zurich 1982.

Bernier, F., *Travels in the Moghul Empire*, London 1891.

Bertelli, C., *Storia e vicende dell'Immagine edessena*, Paragon, 217, 1968.

Betz, O., *Offenbarung und Schriftforschung der Qumran-Texte*, Tübingen 1960.

Bhavishya Maha-Purana, see Sutta, Pandit.

Blank, J., 'Der Christus des Glaubens und der historische Jesus', in *Der Mann aus Galiläa*, ed. E. Lessing, Freiburg 1977.

- -, *Paulus und Jesus*: Eine theologische Grundlegung, Munich 1968.

Blavatsky, H. P., *Isis Unveiled*, Vols. I & II.

- -, *Die indische Geheimlehre*, Leipzig 1899.

Blinzler, J., *Das Turiner Grablinnen und die Wissenschaft*, Ettal 1952.

- -, *Der Prozess Jesu. Das jüdische und das römische Gerichtsverfahren gegen Jesus Christus auf Grund der ältesten Zeugnisse dargestellt und beurteilt*, Regensburg 2nd edition 1955.

Bock, E., *Kindheit und Jugend Jesus*, Stuttgart 1940.

Bomann, Th., *Die Jesusüberlieferung im Lichte der neueren Volkskunde*, 1967–69.

Bonnet-Eymard, B., *Le Soudárion Johannique negatif de la gloire divine*, Bologna 1983.

- -, *Les témoignages historiques surabondent. La Contre-Réforme Catholique au XXe Siècle*, Numéro Spécial 271, February–March 1991.

Bornkamm, G., *Die Bibel. Das Neue Testament. Eine Einführung in seine Schriften im Rahmen der Geschichte des Urchristentums*, Stuttgart/Berlin 1971.

- -, *Das Ende des Gesetzes*, Paulus-Studien, Munich 1952.

- -, *Geschichte und Glaube, I & II*, Munich 1969–1971.

- -, *Jesus von Nazareth*, Stuttgart 3rd edition 1968.

Bowman, S. G. E., Ambers, J. S. and Leese, M. N., 'Re-evaluation of British Museum radiocarbon dates issued between 1980 and 1984', *Radiocarbon*, 32, 1990.

Braun, H., *Qumran und das Neue Testament, I & II*, Tübingen 1966.

- -, *Spätjüdischer-häretischer und frühchristlicher Radikalismus. Jesus von Nazareth und die essenische Qumran-Sekte*, 1969.

Bréhier, L., *L'église et l'orient au moyen age: Les Croisades*. Paris 1928.

Brown, R.E., *The Gospel According to John*, The Anchor Bible, London 1978.

Bruhl, Revd J. H., *The Lost Ten Tribes, Where are They?*, London 1893.

Bryce, J. and Johnson K., *A Comprehensive Description of Geography*, London 1880.

Bulst,W., *Das Grabtuch von Turin. Zugang zum historischen Jesus?* Der neue Stand der Forschung, Karlsruhe 1978.

- -, 'New problems and arguments about the pollen grains', *Shroud Spectrum International*, 27, 1988.

- -, Betrug am Turiner Grabtuch. *Der manipulierte Carbontest*, Frankfurt 1990.

- – and Pfeiffer, H., *Das Turiner Grabtuch und das Christusbild, Vol. I*, Frankfurt 1987; Vol. II 1991.

Bultmann, R., *Geschichte der synoptischen Tradition*, Göttingen 1957.

- -, *Das Evangelium des Johannes*, übers. u. erklärt, Göttingen 1950.

- -, *Die Theologie des Neuen Testamentes*, Tübingen 1977.

- -, *Exegetica. Aufsätze zur Erforschung des Neuen Testaments*, selected, introduced and ed. by Erich Dinkler, Tübingen 1967.

- -, *Jesus Christus und die Mythologie*, Tübingen 1958.

- -, *Das Urchristentum im Rahmen der antiken Religionen*, Zurich 1949.

Burdach, K., *Der Gral*, Darmstadt 1974.

Burrows, M., *The Dead Sea Scrolls*, with translations by the author, London 1956.

- -, *More Light on the Dead Sea Scrolls* and new interpretations with translations of important recent discoveries, London 1958.

Campenhausen, H. von, *Der Ablauf der Osterereignisse und das leere Grab*, Heidelberg 1958.

- -, *Aus der Frühzeit des Christentums*, Studien zur Kirchengeschichte des ersten und zweiten Jahrhunderts, Tübingen 1963.

- -, *Die Entstehung der Christlichen Bibel* (Beiträge zur Historischen Theologie, No. 39), Tübingen 1968.

Carmichael, J., *The Death of Jesus*, London 1963.

- -, *Steh auf und rufe Seinen Namen. Paulus, Erwecker der Christen und Prophet der Heiden*, Munich 1980.

Chadurah, Khwaja Haidar Malik, *Waquiat-i-Kashmir* or *Tarikh-i-Kashmir*, Lahore.

Chandra Kak, Ram, *Ancient Monuments of Kashmir*, New Delhi 1971.

Chevalier, U., *Le Saint Suaire de Turin est-il l'original ou une copie?*, Chieri 1899.

Cohn, H., *The Trial and Death of Jesus*, London 2nd edition 1972.

Cole, Major H. H., *Illustrations of Ancient Buildings in Kashmir*, London 1869.

Crispino, D, 'The Charny Genealogy', *Shroud Spectrum International*, 37, 1990.

Currer-Briggs, N., *The Holy Grail and the Shroud of Christ*, Maulden 1984.

D'Arcis, P., 'Memorandum an Clemens VII', in Thurston, H., 'The Holy Shroud and the Verdict of History', *The Month*, 101, 1903.

Damian of the Cross, 'The tomb of Christ from archaeological sources', *Shroud Spectrum International*, 17, 1985.

Danielov, Jean, *Qumran und der Ursprung des Christentums*, Mainz 1959.

Dautzenberg, Gerhard, *Der Jesus-Report und die neutestamentliche Forschung*, Müller, Würzburg 1970.

Deissmann, A., *Paulus*, Tübingen 1911.

Deschner, K., *Abermals krähte der Hahn*, Reinbek 1978.

Dibelius, M., *Die Formgeschichte des Evangeliums*, Tübingen 1919.

- -, *Botschaft und Geschichte. Gesammelte Aufsätze, I & II*, Tübingen 1953–56.

Dietz, M., *Die Zeugnisse heidnische Schriftsteller des zweiten Jahrhunderts über Christus*, Sigmaringen 1874.

Divyanand, Swami: *Jesus überlebte die Kreuzigung*, Herrischried 1987.
Dobschütz, E. V., *Christusbilder*. Untersuchungen zur christlichen Legende, Leipzig 1899.
Docker, M. A., *If Jesus Did Not Die on the Cross*: A Study in Evidence, London 1920.
Doughty, Marion, *Through the Kashmir Valley*, London 1902.
Drews, A., *Die Christusmythe*, Jena 1910.
Drower, E. S., *The Mandaeans of Iraq and Iran*. Their cults, customs, magic legends and folklore, Leiden 1962.
- -, *The Secret Adam*. A study of Nasoraean Gnosis, Oxford 1960.
- -, *Water into Wine*. A study of Ritual Idiom in the Middle East, London 1965.
Dubarle, A. M., *Histoire ancienne du Linceul de Turin jusqu'au XIIIe siècle*. Paris 1985.
- -, *La date des premières brûlures observées sur le Linceul de Turin*. Lecture at the International Symposium La Sindone e le Icone, Bologna, May 1989.
Duke, J. A., *Medicinal Plants of the Bible*, New York 1983.
Dummelow, Revd J. R., *Commentary on the Holy Bible*, London 1917.
Dutt, Jagdish Chandra, *The Kings of Kashmir*, Calcutta 1879.

Eckert, W. P., et al., *Antijudaismus im Neuen Testament? Exegetische und systematische Beiträge*, Munich 1967.
Edmunds, A. J., *Buddhist and Christian Gospels*, Philadelphia 1908–1909.
- -, *Gospel Parallels from Pali Texts*, Chicago 1900–1901.
Eifel, E. J., *Three Lectures on Buddhism*, London 1873.
- -, *Handbook of Chinese Buddhism*, Tokyo 1904.
Eliot, Sir H. N., *History of India as Told by its Own Historians*, 8 vols, Calcutta 1849.
Enrie, G., *La Santa Sindone rivelata della fotografia*, Turin 1933.
Epstein, L. M., *Sex Laws and Customs in Judaism*, New York 1948.

Faber-Kaiser, A., *Jesus Died in Kashmir*, London 1978.
Farquhar, Dr J. N., *The Apostle Thomas in South India*, Manchester 1927.
Ferrari, K., *Der Stern der Weisen*, Vienna 1977.
Ferrier, J. E., *History of the Afghans*, London 1858.
Feuillet, A., 'The identification and the disposition of the funeral linens of Jesus' burial according to the Fourth Gospel', *Shroud Spectrum International*, 4, 1982.
Fiebig, P., *Die Umwelt des NT*, Göttingen 1926.
Filas, F. L., *The dating of the Shroud of Turin from coins of Pontius Pilate*, Youngtown 1982.
Finkel, A., *The Pharisees and the Teacher of Nazareth*. A study of their background, their halachic and midrashi teachings. The similarities and differences, London 1964.
Flusser, D. 'The Last Supper and the Essene', in *Immanuel*, Jerusalem 1973.
- -, 'Jesus und die Synagoge', in *Der Mann aus Galiläa*, ed. E. Lessing, Freiburg 1977.
- -, *Jesus* – in Selbstzeugnissen und Bildern dargestellt, Hamburg 1978.
Frei, M., 'Identificazione e classificazione dei nuovi pollini della Sindone', in *La Sindone, Scienza e Fede*, Bologna 1983.
- -, 'Nine years of palinological studies on the Shroud', *Shroud Spectrum International*, 3, 1982.

George de Nantes, 'Le trois substitutions du docteur Tite', *La Contre-Réforme Catholique au XXe Siècle*, Numéro Spécial 271, February–March 1991.

Ghulam Ahmad, Hazrat Mirza, *Jesus in India*, Rabwah, Pakistan, 1962.

- -, *Masih Hindustan mein*, Qadian, Pakistan 1908.

Gilbert, R. and Gilbert M. M., 'Ultraviolet-visible reflectance and fluorescence spectra of the Shroud of Turin', *Applied Optics*, 19, 1980.

Gillabert, E., *Paroles de Jésus et Pensée Orientale*, Montélimar 1974.

Glasenapp, H. von, *Die nichtchristlichen Religionen*, Frankfurt 1957.

Goddard, D., *Was Jesus Influenced by Buddhism?* Thetford, Vermont 1927.

Goeckel, H., *Die Messias-Legitimation Jesu. Er überlebte Golgatha*, Mainz 1982.

Goldstein, M., *Jesus in the Jewish Tradition*, New York 1959.

Govinda, A., *The Way of the White Clouds*, London 1966

Grabar, A., *Christian Iconography, A Study of its Origins*, Princeton 1980.

Graetz, H., *Geschichte der Juden von den ältesten Zeiten bis auf die Gegenwart. Aus den Quellen neubearbeitet, III & IV*, Leipzig 1888 ff.

Grant, M., *Jesus*, London 1977.

- -, *Jesus*, Bergisch Gladbach 1979.

- -, *The Jews in the Roman World*, London 1973.

- -, *Saint Paul*, London 1976.

- -, *Paulus, Apostel der Völker*, Bergisch Gladbach 1978.

Graves, R., and Podro, J., *The Nazarene Gospel Restored*, London 1953.

Grimm, E., *Die Ethik Jesu*, Leipzig 1917.

Grönbold, G., *Jesus in Indien*, Munich 1985.

Haig, Sir T. W., *The Kingdom of Kashmir*, Cambridge 1928.

Harnack, A. von, *Das Wesen des Christentums*, Munich 1964.

- -, *Die Mission und die Ausbreitung des Christentums in den ersten drei Jahrhunderten*, Leipzig 4th edition 1924.

Harrer, H., *Seven Years in Tibet*, Frankfurt 1966.

Hart, G. V., Kvas, I., Soots, M. and Badaway, G., 'Blood group testing of ancient material', *Masca Journal*, 1, 1980.

Headland, A. C., *The Miracles of the New Testament*, Longmans Green, London 1914.

Heiler, F., *Christlicher Glaube und indisches Geistesleben*, Munich 1926.

Heller, J. H. and Adler, A. D., 'A chemical investigation of the Shroud of Turin', *Canadian Forensic Society Scientific Journal*, 14, 1981.

- -, 'Blood on the Shroud of Turin', *Applied Optics* 19,1980.

Hennecke, E. and Schneemelcher, W., *Neutestamentliche Apokryphen, I & II*, Tübingen 3rd edition 1959/4th edition 1968.

Herford, R. T., *Christianity in Talmud and Midrash*, London 1903.

Hitching, F., *The World Atlas of Mysteries*, London, 1978.

Hoare, R., *The Testimony of the Shroud*, London 1978.

Holl, A., *Jesus in schlechter Gesellschaft*, Stuttgart 1971.

Hollis, C. and Brownrigg, R., *Heilige Stätten im Heiligen Land*, Hamburg 1969.

Hugh, Revd J., *A History of Christians in India from the Commencement to the Christian Era*, London 1839.

Instinsky, H. U., *Das Jahr der Geburt Jesus*, Munich 1957.
Irland, W. F., *Die Memoiren David Rizzios*, Leipzig 1852.

Jacolliot, L., *Le spiritisme dans le monde*, New York 1966.
James, E. O., *Myth and Ritual in the Ancient Near East: An Archaeological and Documentary Study*, London 1958.
Jeremias, J., *Unbekannte Jesusworte*, Zurich 1948.
- -, *Studien zur neutestamentlichen Theologie und Zeitgeschichte*, Göttingen 1966.
- -, *Jerusalem zur Zeit Jesu*, Göttingen 1958.
- -, *Die Gleichnisse Jesus*, Göttingen 1970.
- -, *Jerusalem und seine große Zeit...z .Z.* Christi, Würzburg 1977.
John, Sir William, 'Journey to Kashmir', in *Asiatic Researches*, Calcutta 1895.
Juergens, J., *Der biblische Moses als Pulver- und Dynamitfabrikant*, Munich 1928.
Jung, E., *Die Herkunft Jesu*, Munich 1920.

Kähler, Martin, *Der sogenannte historische Jesus und der geschichliche, biblische Christus*, Munich 1969.
Kak, R. B. Pandit Ram Chand, *Ancient Monuments of Kashmir,*London 1933.
Kamal-ud-Din, Al-Haj Hazrat Khwaja, *A Running Commentary on the Holy Qur'an*, Surrey 1932.
- -, *Islam and Christianity*, Surrey 1921.
- -, *The Sources of Christianity*, Surrey 1922.
Kappstein, T., *Buddha und Christus*, Berlin 1906.
Käsemann, E., *Exegetische Versuche und Besinnung*, Göttingen 1964.
- -, *Jesu letzter Wille nach Johannes XVII*, Tübingen 1967.
Kaul, Pandit Anand, *The Geography of Jammu and Kashmir*, Calcutta 1913.
Kaul, Pandit Ghawasha, *A Short History of Kashmir*, Srinagar 1929.
Kautzsch, E., *Die Apokryphen und Pseudoepigraphen des Alten Testaments, I & II*, Tübingen 1900.
Kehimkar, H. S., *Bani Israel of India*, Tel Aviv 1937.
Keller, W., *Und wurden zerstreut unter alle Völker. Die nachbiblische Geschichte des jüdischen Volkes*, Munich 1966.
Kenyon, Sir Frederick, *Our Bible and the Ancient Manuscripts, being a History of the Texts and Translations*, London 1939.
Kersten, H., *Jesus Lived in India*, Shaftesbury 1986.
- and Gruber, E., *The Jesus Conspiracy*, Shaftesbury 1994.
Khaniyari, Mufti Ghulam Mohammed Nabi, *Wajeez-ut-Tawarikh*, Srinagar.
Kissener, H. (ed.), *Der Essäerbrief*, Munich 1968.
Klatt, N., *Lebte Jesus in Indien?* Göttingen 1988.
Klausner, J., *Jesus von Nazareth*, Berlin 1930.
Klijn, A. F. J., *The Acts of Thomas*, Leiden 1962.
Konzelmann, G., *Aufbruch der Hebräer*, Munich 1976.
Kosmala, H., *Hebräer, Essener, Christen*, Leiden 1959.
Kroll, G., *Auf den Spuren Jesu*, Leipzig 1974.
Kühner, H., 'Die Katharer', in Schultz, H.-J. (ed.), *Die Wahrheit der Ketzer*, Stuttgart, Berlin 1968.
Küng, H., *Christ Sein*, Munich 1974.

La Santa Sindone. Ricerche e studi della commissione di esperti nominata dall'Arcivescovo di Torino, Car. Michele Pellegrino, nel 1969. Appendix to Rivista diocesana Torinese, Turin 1976.

'La traque des faussaires', *La Contre-Réforme Catholique au XXe Siècle*, Numéro Spécial 271, February–March 1991.

Lang, D. W., *The Wisdom of Balahar*, New York 1957.

Lange, J.: *Das Erscheinen des Auferstandenen*. Würzburg 1973.

Lange-Eichbaum, W. and Kurth, W., *Genie, Irrsinn und Ruhm*, Munich 1967.

Lawrence, Sir Walter, *The Valley of Kashmir*, London 1895.

Lehmann, J., *Jesus-Report, Protokoll einer Verfälschung*, Düsseldorf 1970.

- -, *Die Jesus GmbH*, Düsseldorf 1972.

- -, *Buddha*, Munich 1980.

Levi, *The Aquarian Gospel of Jesus Christ*, London 1964.

Lewis, Spender, H., *The Mystical Life of Jesus*, California 1929.

Loewenthal, Revd I., *Some Persian Inscriptions Found in Kashmir*, Calcutta 1895.

Lloyd Davies, M. and Lloyd Davies, T. A., 'Resurrection or Resuscitation?' *Journal of the Royal College of Physicians of London*, 25, 1991.

Lohse, E., *Die Texte aus Qumran*, Kosel 1964.

Lord, Revd J. H., *The Jews in India and the Far East*, Bombay 1907.

Maier, J., *Die Texte vom Toten Meer, I & II*, Munich 1960.

- -, *Jesus von Nazareth in der talmudischen überlieferung*, Darmstadt 1978.

Maloney, P.,*The Shroud of Turin; Traits and Peculiarities of Image and Cloth Preserved in Historical Sources*, lecture at the International Symposium La Sindone e le Icone, Bologna, May 1989.

Marxsen, W., *Einleitung in das NT*, Munich 1964.

- -, *Die Auferstehung Jesu als historisches und theologisches Problem*, Munich 1965.

McCrone, W., 'Light microscopical study of the Turin Shroud I–III', *The Microscope*, 28, 1980; 29, 1981.

Mensching, G., *Leben und Legende der grossen Religionsstifter*, Darmstadt 1955.

- -, *Buddha and Christus*, Stuttgart 1978.

Merrick, Lady Henrietta S., *In the World's Attick*, London 1931.

Messina, R. and Orecchia, C., 'La scritta in caratteri ebraici sulla fronte dell'uomo della Sindone: Nuove ipotesi e problematiche', *Sindon*, 1, 1989.

Mir Khwand, Rauzat-us-Safa, *Arbuthnot*, London 1891.

Mödder, H., 'Die Todesursache bei der Kreuzigung', *Stimmen der Zeit*, 144, 1948.

Moore, G., *The Lost Tribes*, London 1861.

Mozundar, A. K., *Hindu History* (3000 BC to 1200 AD), Dacca 1917.

Mumtaz Ahmad Faruqui, Al-Haj, *The Crumbling of the Cross*, Lahore 1973.

Murphy, H., *Sai Baba*.

Naber, Hans see Berna, Kurt

Narain, A. K., *The Indo-Greeks*, Oxford 1962.

Nazir Ahmad, Al-Haj Khwaja, *Jesus in Heaven on Earth*, Lahore 1973.

Nestle, Wilhelm, *Krisis des Christentums*, Stuttgart 1947.

Noelinger, Henry S., *Moses und Agypten*, Heidelberg 1957.

Notovitch, N., *La Vie inconnue de Jésus-Christ* 1894.

- -, *The Unknown Life of Jesus Christ*, tr. from French by Violet Crispe, London 1895, with added Note to the Publishers by Notovitch.

Nyawang, Lobsang Yishey Tenzing Gyatso (XIV Dalai Lama), *My Land and My People*, New York 1962.

O'Rahilly, A., 'The Burial of Christ', *Irish Ecclesiastical Record*, 59, 1941.
Overbeck, F., *Christentum und Kultur*, Basel 1919.

Pagels, E., *The Gnostic Gospels*, London 1979.
Pannenberg, W., *Grundzüge der Christologie*, Munich 1964.
Pesch., R., *Jesu ureigene Taten?* Freiburg 1970.
Potter, C. F., *The Lost Years of Jesus Revealed*, Greenwich, Conn. 1958.
Prause, G., *Herodes der Grosse, König der Juden*, Hamburg 1977.
Pryse, J. M., *Reinkarnation im NT*, Interlaken 1980.

Raes, G.: *Rapport d'analyse du tissu, in La Santa Sindone*, 1976.
Rahn, O., *Kreuzzug gegen den Gral*, Stuttgart 1974.
Ramsay, Sir William, *Was Christ Born in Bethlehem?*, London 1905.
Rangacharya, V., *History of Pre-Musulman India*, Madras 1937.
Rapson, Prof. E. l. J., *Ancient India*, Cambridge University Press, Cambridge 1911.
Rau, Wilhelm, Indiens Beitrag zur Kultur, Wiesbaden 1975.
Ray, H. C., *The Dynastic History of Northern India*, 2 vols, Calcutta 1931.
Ray, Dr Sunil Chandra, *Early History and Culture of Kashmir*, New Delhi 1969.
Reilson, Col. W., 'History of Afghanistan', *J. Ryland's Library Bulletin*, 1927.
Ricci, G., *Kreuzweg nach dem Leichentuch von Turin*, Rome 1971.
Riggi di Numana, G., Rapporto Sindone (1978/1987), Milan 1988.
- -, *Prélèvement sur le Linceul effectué le 21 avril 1988*, lecture at the Symposium Scientifique International de Paris sur le Linceul de Turin, September 1989.
Rihbani, A., *Morgenländische Sitten im Leben Jesu*, Basel 1962.
Ristow, H. and Matthiae, K., *Der geschichtliche Jesus und der kerygmatische Christus*, Berlin 1961.
Robertson, J. M., *Die Evangelienmythen*, Jena 1910.
Rockhill, W. W., *The Life of Buddha*, London.
Rodgers, Robert William, *A History of Ancient India*, London 1929.
Rose, Sir G. H., *The Afghans: The Ten Tribes and the Kings of the East*, London 1852.
Runciman, S., *Geschichte der Kreuzzüge*, Munich 1968.

Scavone, D. C.: 'The Shroud of Turin in Constantinople: The Documentary Evidence', *Sindon* 1, 1989.
Schelkle, K. H., *Die Gemeinde von Qumran und die Kirche des NT, Die Welt der Bibel*, Düsseldorf 1960.
- -, *Die Passion Jesu in der Verkündigung des NT*, Heidelberg 1949.
Scheuermann, O., *Das Tuch*, Regensburg 1982.
Schoeps, H. J., *Aus frühchristlicher Zeit, religionsgeschichtliche Untersuchungen*, Tübingen 1950.
Schrage, W., *Das Verhältnis des Thomas-Evangeliums zur synoptischen Tradition und zu den koptischen Evangelien-übersetzungen. Zugleich ein Beitrag zur gnostischen Synoptikerdeutung*, Berlin 1964.
Schröder, H., *Jesus und das Geld*, Karlsruhe 1979.

Schubert, K., *Die Gemeinde vom Toten Meer*, Munich 1958.

- -, *Der historische Jesus und der Christus unseres Glaubens*, Vienna and Freiburg 1962.

- -, *Vom Messias zum Christus*, Vienna and Freiburg 1964.

- -, *Jesus im Lichte der Religionsgeschichte des Judentums*, Vienna 1973.

Schulz, P., *Ist Gott eine mathematische Formel?* Reinbek bei Hamburg 1977.

- -, *Weltliche Predigten*, Reinbek bei Hamburg 1978.

Schuré, E., *The Great Initiates*, 1927.

Schwalbe, L. A. and Rogers, R. N., 'Physics and Chemistry of the Shroud of Turin: A summary of the 1978 investigation', *Analytica Chimica Acta*, 135, 1982.

Schwarz, G.: '*Anhistemi* and *Anastasis* in den Evangelien', Biblische Notizen, *Beiträge zur exegetischen Diskussion*, 10, 1979.

- -, 'Tod, Auferstehung, Gericht und ewiges Leben nach den ersten drei Evangelien', *Via Mundi*, 55, 1988.

- -, *Wenn die Worte nicht stimmen: Dreissig entstellte Evangelientexte wiederhergestellt*, Munich 1990.

Schweitzer, A., *Geschichte der Leben-Jesu-Forschung*, Tübingen 1951.

Schweizer, E., *Jesus Christus im vielfaltigen Zeugnis des Neuen Testaments*, Munich and Hamburg 1968.

Seydel, R., *Das Evangelium von Jesus in seinem Verhältnis zu Buddha-Sage und Buddha-Lehre*, Leipzig 1882.

Shams, J. D., *Where did Jesus Die?*, London 1945.

Smith, R. G., *Early Relations between India and Iran*, London 1937.

Smith, V. A., *The Early History of India*, Oxford 1904.

Sox, D. H.: *The Shroud Unmasked*, London 1988.

Speicher, G., *Doch sie können ihn nicht töten*, Düsseldorf 1966.

Sri Yukteswar, *The Holy Science*, Los Angeles 1949.

Stauffer, Ethelbert, *Jesus, Gestalt und Geschichte*, Berne 1957.

Strack, H. L. and Billerbeck, P., *Kommentar zum NT aus Talmud und Midrasch*, I–V, Munich 1956.

Strauss, D. F., *Das Leben Jesu, kritisch bearbeitet*, Tübingen 1835.

Stroud, William, *On the Physical Cause of Death of Christ*, Hamilton and Adams, London 1905.

Sutta, Pandit, *Bhavishya Mahapurana* (MS in State Library, Srinagar), Bombay 1917.

Tamburelli, G. and Oliveri, F., *Un nuovo processamento dell'immagine Sindonica*. Papers of the 3rd National Congress of Sindonology, Trani, 13–14 October 1984.

Testore, F., *Le Saint Suaire: Examen et prélèvements effectués le 21 avril 1988*, lecture at the Symposium Scientifique International de Paris sur le Linceul de Turin, September 1989.

Thiel, R., *Jesus Christus und die Wissenschaft*, Berlin 1938.

Thomas, P., *Epics, Myths and Legends of India*, 13th edition Bombay 1973.

Thurston, H., 'The Holy Shroud and the Verdict of History', *The Month*, 101, 1903.

Tribbe, F. C., *Portrait of Jesus?*, New York 1983.

Tyrer, J., 'Looking at the Turin Shroud as a Textile', *Textile Horizons*, December 1981.

Vial, G., 'Le Linceul de Turin: étude technique', *CIETA Bulletin*, 67, 1989.
Vielhauer, P., *Geschichte der urchristliche Literatur. Einleitung in das NT, die Apokryphen und die Apostolischen Väter*, Berlin 1975.
Vigne, G. T., *A Personal Account of a Journey to Chuzin*, Kabul. London 1840.
Vignon, P., *Le Linceul du Christ: étude scientifique*, Paris 1902.
- -, 'Sur la formation d'images negatives par l'action de certaine vapeurs', *Comptes rendus hebdomadaires de séances de l'Académie des Sciences*, 134, 1902.
Vögtle, A., *Exegetische Erwägungen über das Wissen und Selbsbewußtsein Jesu*, Freiburg im Breisgau 1964.

Waddell, L. A., *Lhasa and its Mysteries*, New Delhi 1975.
Walsh, J., *Das Linnen*, Frankfurt 1965.
Warechaner, J., *The Historical Life of Christ*, London 1927.
Watzinger C., *Denkmäler Palästinas, Eine Einführung in die Archäologie des Heiligen Landes. I. Von den Anfängen bis zum Ende der israelitischen Königzeit. II. Von der Herrschaft der Assyrer bis zur arabischen Eroberung*, Berlin 1911.
Weidinger, E., *Die Apokryphen: Verborgene Bücher der Bibel*, Augsburg 1990.
Weinreb, F., *Das Buch Jonah*, Zurich 1970.
Wheeler, M., *Alt-Indiaen*, Köln 1959.
Wildengren, G., *Die Religionen Irans*, Stuttgart 1965.
Wilcox, R. K., *Das Turiner Grabtuch*, Düsseldorf 1978.
Williams, Sir Monier, *Buddhism*, New York 1889.
Wilson, H. H., *History of Kashmir, in Asiatic Researches*, Calcutta 1841.
Wilson, Ian, *The Turin Shroud*, London 1978.
Wilson, W. R., *The Execution of Jesus*, New York 1970.
Wolff, J., *Narrative of a Mission to Bokhara*, London 1845.
Wright, D., *Studies in Islam and Christianity*, Woking, Surrey 1943.
Wuenshel, Edward, *Self Portrait of Christ*, New York 1954.

Yadin, Y., Bar Kochba, Hamburg 1971.
- -, *Masada. Der letzte Kampf um die Festung des Herodes*, Hamburg 1972.
Yasin, Mohammed, *Mysteries of Kashmir*, Srinagar 1972.
Younghusband, Sir F., *Kashmir*, London 1909.

Zahrnt, H., *Es begann mit Jesus von Nazareth, Zur Frage des historischen Jesus*, Stuttgart 1960.
Zaninotto, G., GV 20, 1–8. 'Giovanni testimone oculare della risurrezione di Gesù?', *Sindon*, 1, 1989.
- -, *L'Immagine acheropita del ss. Salvatore nel Sancto Sanctorum di Roma*, lecture at the International Symposium La Sindone e le Icone, Bologna, May 1989.
Zimmermann, H., *Jesus Christus: Geschichte und Verkündigung*, Stuttgart 1973.
Zimmern, H., *Zum Streit um die 'Christus Mythe'*, Berlin 1910.
Zöckler, Otto (ed.), *Die Apokryphen des Alten Testaments*, Munich 1891.
Zugibe, F. T., *Death by Crucifixion, Canadian Society of Forensic Science Journal*, 17, 1984.
- -, *The Cross and the Shroud: A Medical Inquiry into the Crucifixion*, New York 1988.

INDEX OF PERSONS

INDEX OF PLACES